Marianne Kac-Vergne is Associate Professor at the Université de Picardie Jules Verne in Amiens, France, where she teaches courses in American cultural history at graduate and undergraduate levels. Her research focuses on gender and genre in American cinema, and she has published and presented on masculinity and femininity in science fiction, romantic comedy and western films.

'A must-read about gender politics in popular culture, this is a revealing and original historical study about constructed male identities in the flourishing genre of science fiction. Marianne Kac-Vergne eloquently coins key developments in the depiction of (hyper)masculinity in Hollywood blockbusters and traces the 1980s heroes with bulging muscles and *hard bodies* to the twenty-first century sci fi species equipped with clever minds and a heart. The only staple: women stay on the sidelines while hegemonic masculinity rules. In the current political climate Kac-Vergne teaches us invaluable new insights to engage with the ideas of race and gender in mainstream film'.
Karen A. Ritzenhoff, Professor, Department of Communication, Central Connecticut State University

'Marianne Kac-Vergne's *Masculinity in Contemporary Science Fiction Cinema: Cyborgs, Troopers and Other Men of the Future* is a brilliant analysis of contemporary science fiction cinema. It will appeal to academics and students in film studies, gender studies, and cultural studies alike: its smart contextualisations, subtle commentary of intertexts and astute close readings, combined with strong intersectional analyses of the masculinity in these well-known films will prompt re-viewing in another light. Broader audiences will find this is a highly enjoyable read, with a dose of wit and wry humour. This is truly a must-read for anyone who watches, studies, or indeed, makes science fiction films today.'
Monica Michlin, Professor of Contemporary American Studies, Université Paul Valéry Montpellier

Library of Gender and Popular Culture

From *Mad Men* to gaming culture, performance art to steam-punk fashion, the presentation and representation of gender continues to saturate popular media. This new series seeks to explore the intersection of gender and popular culture, engaging with a variety of texts – drawn primarily from Art, Fashion, TV, Cinema, Cultural Studies and Media Studies – as a way of considering various models for understanding the complementary relationship between 'gender identities' and 'popular culture'. By considering race, ethnicity, class, and sexual identities across a range of cultural forms, each book in the series will adopt a critical stance towards issues surrounding the development of gender identities and popular and mass cultural 'products'.

For further information or enquiries, please contact the library series editors:

Claire Nally: claire.nally@northumbria.ac.uk
Angela Smith: angela.smith@sunderland.ac.uk

Advisory Board:

Dr Kate Ames, Central Queensland University, Australia

Prof Leslie Heywood, Binghampton University, USA

Dr Michael Higgins, Strathclyde University, UK

Prof Åsa Kroon, Örebro University, Sweden

Dr Niall Richardson, Sussex University, UK

Dr Jacki Willson, Central St Martins, University of Arts London, UK

Published and forthcoming titles:

Ageing Femininity on Screen: The Older Woman in Contemporary Cinema
Niall Richardson
All-American TV Crime Drama: Feminism and Identity Politics in Law and Order: Special Victims Unit
Sujata Moorti and Lisa Cuklanz
Beyoncé: Celebrity Feminism in the Age of Social Media
Kirsty Fairclough-Isaacs
Film Bodies: Queer Feminist Encounters with Gender and Sexuality in Cinema
Katharina Lindner
Framing the Single Mother: Gender, Politics and Family Values in Contemporary Popular Cinema
Louise Fitzgerald
Gay Pornography: Representations of Sexuality and Masculinity
John Mercer
Gender and Austerity in Popular Culture: Femininity, Masculinity and Recession in Film and Television
Helen Davies and Claire O'Callaghan (Eds)
The Gendered Motorcycle: Representations in Society, Media and Popular Culture
Esperanza Miyake
Gendering History on Screen: Women Filmmakers and Historical Films
Julia Erhart
Girls Like This, Boys Like That: The Reproduction of Gender in Contemporary Youth Cultures
Victoria Cann
Love Wars: Television Romantic Comedy
Mary Irwin
Masculinity in Contemporary Science Fiction Cinema: Cyborgs, Troopers and Other Men of the Future
Marianne Kac-Vergne
Paradoxical Pleasures: Female Submission in Popular and Erotic Fiction
Anna Watz
Positive Images: Gay Men and HIV/AIDS in the Culture of 'Post-Crisis'
Dion Kagan
Queer Horror Film and Television: Sexuality and Masculinity at the Margins
Darren Elliott-Smith
Queer Sexualities in Early Film: Cinema and Male-Male Intimacy
Shane Brown
Shaping Gym Cultures: Body, Image and Social Media
Nicholas Chare
Steampunk: Gender and the Neo-Victorian
Claire Nally
Television Comedy and Femininity: Queering Gender
Rosie White
Television, Technology and Gender: New Platforms and New Audiences
Sarah Arnold
Tweenhood: Femininity and Celebrity in Tween Popular Culture
Melanie Kennedy

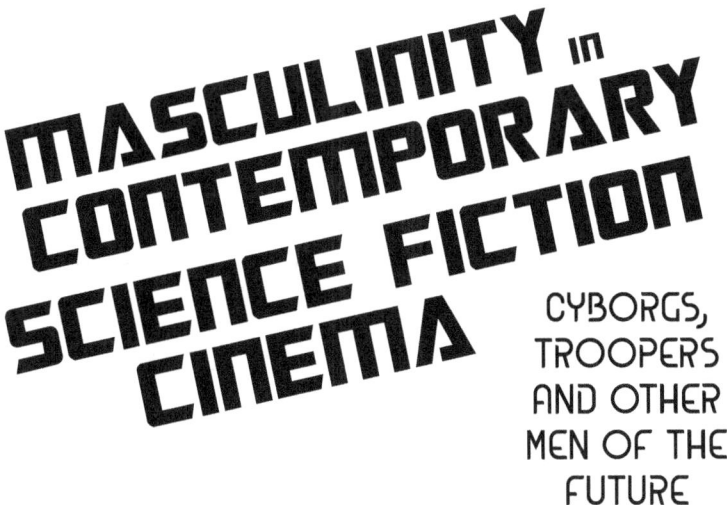

MASCULINITY in CONTEMPORARY SCIENCE FICTION CINEMA

CYBORGS, TROOPERS AND OTHER MEN OF THE FUTURE

MARIANNE KAC-VERGNE

BLOOMSBURY ACADEMIC
LONDON • NEW YORK • OXFORD • NEW DELHI • SYDNEY

BLOOMSBURY ACADEMIC
Bloomsbury Publishing Plc
50 Bedford Square, London, WC1B 3DP, UK
1385 Broadway, New York, NY 10018, USA
29 Earlsfort Terrace, Dublin 2, Ireland

BLOOMSBURY, BLOOMSBURY ACADEMIC and the Diana logo
are trademarks of Bloomsbury Publishing Plc

First published in Great Britain by I.B. Tauris 2018
This paperback edition published by Bloomsbury Academic 2022

Copyright © Marianne Kac-Vergne 2018

The right of Marianne Kac-Vergne to be identified as the author of this work has been asserted by the author in accordance with the Copyright, Designs and Patents Act 1988.

For legal purposes the Acknowledgements on p. x constitute
an extension of this copyright page.

All rights reserved. No part of this publication may be reproduced or transmitted in any form or by any means, electronic or mechanical, including photocopying, recording, or any information storage or retrieval system, without prior permission in writing from the publishers.

Bloomsbury Publishing Plc does not have any control over, or responsibility for, any third-party websites referred to or in this book. All internet addresses given in this book were correct at the time of going to press. The author and publisher regret any inconvenience caused if addresses have changed or sites have ceased to exist, but can accept no responsibility for any such changes.

A catalogue record for this book is available from the British Library.

A catalog record for this book is available from the Library of Congress.

ISBN: HB: 978-1-7807-6748-2
PB: 978-1-3502-5837-2
ePDF: 978-1-7867-3315-3
ePUB: 978-1-7867-2315-4

Series: Library of Gender and Popular Culture

To find out more about our authors and books visit
www.bloomsbury.com and sign up for our newsletters.

Contents

	List of Illustrations	viii
	Series Editors' Foreword	ix
	Acknowledgements	x
	Introduction	1
1	**Vulnerable Hypermasculinity**	9
	Reclaiming Hegemony Through Hypermasculinity	12
	Vulnerability as a Path to Victimhood	23
	Questioning Hypermasculinity	33
2	**Dystopia and Class War**	43
	Dystopian Societies	46
	Worlds Devoid of Humanity	57
	Defusing Class Warfare	67
3	**Sidelining Women**	83
	Women as Sidekicks	85
	The Fleeting Rise of Action Heroines	94
	Back to the Sidelines	108
4	**'White Folks Ain't Planning for Us to be Here'**	121
	Demons with a Purpose	124
	Integrated Members of Multiracial Teams	134
	Will Smith, Lone Black Hero	143
5	**Redefining Masculinity in Times of 'Crisis'**	157
	Away from Hypermasculinity	159
	The Turn to Fatherhood	174
	Afterword: The Gender Politics of Science Fiction Blockbusters	193
	Notes	196
	Bibliography	224
	Filmography	236
	Index	241

List of Illustrations

All studio and production details for film stills can be found in the Filmography.

1.1	Doug wakes up in *Total Recall*	13
1.2	Low-angle shots of the naked Goldblum and Schwarzenegger in *The Fly* and *The Terminator*	15
1.3	Robocop's suffering in *RoboCop 2*	30
1.4	Hegemonic masculinity is imposed on Robocop	34
1.5	Reverse shot of Lewis looking at Robocop's fractured head	35
2.1	The President's humiliation in *Escape from New York*	50
2.2	Deckard's first appearance in *Blade Runner*	56
2.3	The toilet scene in *RoboCop*	65
2.4	Benny in *Total Recall*	75
3.1	Veronica's head between Luc's legs in *Universal Soldier*	92
3.2	The castrating Terminatrix in *Terminator 3*	110
3.3	Leo leads the way in *Planet of the Apes*	116
4.1	Low-angle shot of Simon Phoenix in *Demolition Man*	126
4.2	The possibilities of whiteness in *The Matrix*	140
4.3	Whiteness as death in *I, Robot*	145
4.4	Neville fishing on the steps of the Sackler wing in *I Am Legend*	151
5.1	Johnny sprawled in bed in *Johnny Mnemonic*	160
5.2	Max holds a gun to Lenny's head in *Strange Days*	166
5.3	The Terminator hugs Sarah in *Terminator Genisys*	180
5.4	Ray isolated by the broken window in *War of the Worlds*	185

Series Editors' Foreword

Many of the books in this Library show how popular culture texts offer a space to explore issues of gender and sexuality in new and innovative ways. In terms of such texts, science fiction films hold a special place in the hearts and minds of audiences irrespective of gender. However, as Marianne Kac-Vergne shows here, these incredibly popular films are primarily conventional and conservative in their representations of gender, despite the argument that science fiction texts would seem to provide an opportunity to confront a set of normative values in terms of gender. Kac-Vergne here uses a historical approach to explore these texts, starting with the 1980s in the wake of *Star Wars*, which reignited science fiction texts as blockbusters. Since science fiction can be seen as a space of emotional expression at odds with the hegemonic model of masculinity, one of the questions raised by this book is whether Hollywood science fiction can offer an alternative vision of masculinity, if not a different future for gender relations.

As books in this Library show, popular culture provides a rich source of texts and contexts in which to explore gender. The Hollywood sci-fi blockbuster is just one of these, yet is largely a space where conventional models of gender relations are off-set against the destabilising fantasy setting in order to make them more acceptable to audiences.

—Angela Smith and Claire Nally

Acknowledgements

I am very grateful to I.B.Tauris for giving this book a chance. Many thanks to Lisa Goodrum for giving me support as well as deadlines and to Pat FitzGerald for her fine copyediting. Some of the arguments in Chapters 1 and 2 were developed in my thesis and I wish to thank my advisor, Gilles Menegaldo, for his input and encouragement, as well as the members of my jury, Raphaëlle Moine, Francis Bordat, Georges-Claude Guilbert and Divina Frau-Meigs, for their valuable remarks. This research project would not have been possible without the financial support provided by my university, the University of Picardie Jules Verne, and especially that of my research group, CORPUS. Many thanks to my wonderful colleagues Céline Mansanti, Aurélie Thiria-Meulemans, Frédérique Spill and Camille Fort for their continued interest and to Trevor Harris for his enthusiastic commitment to the project.

I have been very lucky to be surrounded by a group of energetic and encouraging film scholars gathered in SERCIA (Société d'Etudes et de Recherches sur le Cinéma Anglophone). The SERCIA conferences have been very helpful to test my ideas and receive meaningful feedback. Thanks also to Jean-François Baillon, Hélène Charlery, Anne Crémieux, Gwénaëlle Le Gras, Cristelle Maury, Anne-Marie Paquet-Deyris and Geneviève Sellier for inviting me to present my research. Special thanks to my dear friends Julie Assouly and Céline Murillo for hearing my arguments out and resolving some of the issues they presented. Finally, I wish to dedicate this book to my friend and mentor David Roche, who supported the project from the start and proofread the entire manuscript, providing extremely useful, if sometimes challenging, advice.

Thanks to Pierrot and Nancy, to my dad for pushing me to finish and especially to my mom, who discovered a new interest in science fiction film and Hollywood blockbusters.

Introduction

'Man Has Made His Match … Now It's His Problem'

The tagline for the original release of *Blade Runner* (Ridley Scott, 1982) is indicative of the conflation between man and mankind that is so common in the science fiction genre. This idea is widely present in the film industry as well as among the genre's scholars: J.P. Telotte talks about science fiction film as an 'inquiry into our very humanity',[1] while Geoff King and Tanya Krzywinska write that 'science fiction often draws upon concerns about the definition of the human'.[2] On a specific film like *Blade Runner*, both Scott Bukatman and Forest Pyle, for instance, analyse the film in terms of humanity and the human.[3] However, by using the possessive determiner 'his' twice, the tagline makes it explicit that 'Man' refers in fact to a *male* human being. The realisation that 'Man', 'mankind', 'men', and by extension 'humanity' and 'the human' almost systematically refer to males was the starting point of this book. My goal is therefore not to provide a definition of the genre, which can be found in the excellent books mentioned above,[4] but to analyse what science fiction has to say about men and masculinity, a topic that has been little examined so far in science fiction scholarship.[5]

Masculinity in Contemporary Science Fiction Cinema

Theorised as a genre of 'cognitive estrangement' by Darko Suvin, science fiction offers, according to Fredric Jameson, 'the estrangement and renewal of our own reading present'.[6] Suvin argues that science fiction literature 'confront[s] a set normative system ... with a point of view or look implying a new set of norms' – leading to estrangement – while

> see[ing] the norms of any age, including emphatically its own, as unique, changeable, and therefore subject to a cognitive view. It does not ask about the Man or the World, but which Man? In which kind of world? and why such a man in such a kind of world?[7]

Suvin thus sees science fiction as a 'fundamentally subversive genre'[8] tending towards dynamic transformation. Even though the equation Man = humanity remains in Suvin's work, the possibilities of 'cognitive estrangement' offered by science fiction in terms of gender have been taken up by feminist science fiction authors such as Margaret Atwood and Ursula Le Guin. The renewal and estrangement of gender norms and the gender order, however, have not been at the core of many Hollywood sci-fi productions.

Nevertheless, in terms of gender representations, all science fiction films confront 'a set normative system', that is, gender norms and models, with a new future world. The set normative system analysed here is hegemonic masculinity, a concept developed since the 1980s by R.W. Connell, Tim Carrigan, John Lee, Michael Messner and others at first as a response to sex role theory, which attributed fixed and unchangeable characteristics to both sexes without recognising the domination of one sex over the other. For instance, in 1969, Patricia Sexton defined masculinity in the following terms:

> What does it mean to be masculine? It means, *obviously*, holding male values and following male behaviour norms ... Male norms stress values such as courage, inner direction, certain forms of aggression, autonomy, mastery, technological skill, group solidarity, adventure, and a considerable amount of toughness in mind and body.[9]

While sex role theory moved away from seeing masculinity as a biological essence, recognising the influence of society in shaping the masculine role,

Introduction

the use of the word 'sex' and the definition of values that all men 'obviously' hold nevertheless contributed to essentialising and naturalising masculinity as a given set of behaviours. Drawing on R.W. Connell's influential work, the men's studies of the 1990s sought to emphasise the constructedness of masculinity, its historicity and the wide range of masculinities embedded in hierarchical power relations. Connell and Messerschmidt thus define the concept of hegemonic masculinity as 'the currently most honored way of being a man, requir[ing] all other men to position themselves in relation to it, and ideologically legitimat[ing] the global subordination of women to men'.[10]

Following Connell and Messerschmidt, hegemonic masculinity will first and foremost be analysed in its relationship to women, as a model that seeks to distinguish itself from femininity and maintain its power in unequal gender relations. Secondly, hegemonic masculinity must be viewed as a dominant model among many other subordinated masculinities in a hierarchy of masculinities where, in the Western world, white heterosexual middle-class masculinity dominates gay, working-class and ethnic masculinities. However, hegemonic masculinity is open to challenge: as defined by Gramsci, hegemony is different from domination in that it results from a process of persuasion (in which the media play a large part). Dominic Strinati insists on the idea of consent: 'hegemony is a contested and shifting set of ideas by means of which dominant groups strive to secure the consent of subordinate groups to their leadership'.[11] Yet that consent is never fully secure, so that the hegemonic model can be contested, for instance through queer readings of hypermasculine cyborgs,[12] or working-class challenges to elite masculinities represented as feminised, which will be at the heart of Chapter 2. Hegemonic masculinity is fundamentally unstable and constantly renegotiated, which is clear when focusing on its intersection with class and race. If middle-class men dominate others economically, working-class masculinity widely contributes to defining what is 'a real man' in cultural terms, notably through its emphasis on physical labour. In terms of race, as Demetriou argues, hegemonic masculinity appropriates from other masculinities whatever appears to be pragmatically useful for continued domination,[13] so that white masculinity often borrows from black masculinity its 'cool pose' gained from an experience of oppression in order to find a path to resistance, as we shall see in Chapters 4 and 5. Therefore, this book will study masculinity by considering other markers of identity like class, race and age, while staying focused on its relation with femininity, in an intersectional and relational approach.

Hegemonic masculinity is a cultural model that is historically and geographically specific and thus subject to change. It is a model, not a reality, and this ideal is constituted largely through media representations, which react to societal changes but also contribute to transforming gender norms and behaviours. I fully agree with David Buchbinder's argument that

> representations of men not only often reproduce dominant notions of masculinity … but also re-produce these notions … The 'dominant masculine' is re-produced as both a reflection of a particular social reality and as a model on which men in the culture may pattern themselves.[14]

Cinematic representations of hegemonic masculinity therefore need to be analysed within specific historical contexts. As Suvin and Connell underline, both science fiction and hegemonic masculinity are changeable, offering different sets of norms for different times. Consequently, this book combines a contextual approach with textual analysis to see how representations of masculinity have changed within the equally evolving genre of science fiction, 're-producing' different science fictional models of masculinity over the past 35 years.

I start with science fiction films of the 1980s, when the genre became extremely successful at the box office and production boomed after the success of the *Star Wars* trilogy. Referencing 'classics' of the 1950s and 1970s as well as cult independent productions, I have focused nevertheless mainly on contemporary Hollywood 'blockbusters', that is to say films that drew large numbers of viewers and thus had a wide impact on the population, its values and behaviours. Following Suvin's framework, I have been principally interested in films that are 'perceived as not impossible within the cognitive norms of the author's epoch' and therefore differ from 'other "fantastic" genres, that is ensembles of fictional tales without empirical validation'.[15] Suvin excludes fantasy and 'space opera', dismissing it emphatically as 'science fiction committing creative suicide'.[16] While I do

Introduction

not share Suvin's contempt for such forms, I do find that 'hard' science fiction that draws on some form of historical present offers more relevant insight into the gender norms and models of its time. The necessarily limited scope of a monograph has thus led me to leave out fantasy science fiction like the *Star Wars* series and superhero films, which have additionally already been the focus of edited collections focusing on gender.[17]

My argument is that Hollywood science fiction film generally supports hegemonic masculinity by presenting man, especially the white man, as Man, universalising and naturalising one identity as representative of humanity as a whole. As many have noted, white, heterosexual masculinity benefits from being 'unmarked',[18] deriving its power from its invisibility, which, Connell and Messerschmidt argue, 'remove[s] a dominant form of masculinity from the possibility of censure',[19] so that it 'makes the normative into the normal'.[20] According to Michael Kimmel, hegemonic masculinity becomes 'universally generalizable' with men being the universal citizens.[21] Consequently, white men 'function as the human norm', as Richard Dyer underlines: 'there is no more powerful position than that of being "just" human. The claim to power is the claim to speak for the commonality of humanity'.[22] A form of cognitive estrangement guides my analysis: my aim is to deuniversalise white men and uncover the specific and changeable sets of norms embodied by male science fiction heroes, in order to answer Suvin's aforementioned questions: 'which Man? In which kind of world? and why such a man in such a kind of world?' Hegemonic masculinity is not monolithic, nor is Hollywood science fiction film, so that this book analyses the different models of masculinity presented by different strands of science fiction, their evolution in time but also the cracks and challenges to hegemony that can be found in the genre. The hegemonic position of white men in Hollywood science fiction has indeed been challenged in recent years by historically subordinated masculinities, notably with the rise of African-American heroes, and, to a lesser extent, by women, in a few female-led productions. Science fiction also questions hegemonic masculinity from within, bringing to light its limits, its failures and its internal contradictions: how to reconcile, for instance, the emotional sensitivity that separates humanity from the machines, with the toughness and emotional restraint that traditionally characterise masculinity, especially hypermasculinity? Since science fiction can be seen as a space of emotional expression at odds with the hegemonic model of masculinity, one of the questions raised by this book is whether Hollywood science fiction can offer an alternative vision of masculinity, if not a different future for gender relations.

One of the internal contradictions highlighted by Hollywood science fiction lies at the heart of Chapter 1, which focuses on hypermasculine science fiction films of the 1980s. While those films bear the hallmarks of hypermasculinity, like the display of muscles and the insistence on the male heroes' invulnerability, they also emphasise the heroes' vulnerability and their status as victims, underlining the limits of a hypermasculine ideal that can be nefarious both for men and for women. Hypermasculinity can in fact be seen as a way to express a traditional labouring masculinity that has been discarded by the middle and upper classes. This working-class challenge to hegemonic masculinity is the focus of Chapter 2, which examines class conflicts in dystopias of the 1980s, or how the genre of science fiction works to soothe the anxieties of a certain segment of the audience, young working-class males who were left behind by the technological changes of the 1980s. The contradiction here lies in the contrast between the films' overt technophobia and their reliance on mechanised masculinity and special effects. Chapter 3 presents masculinity from a female point of view, examining the role of female characters in defining the contours of hegemonic masculinity. Heeding Connell and Messerschmidt's call to take women into account when talking about masculinity,[23] this chapter adopts a relational approach, showing how female characters are used to humanise the heroes through their compassionate gaze. With the exception of a few female heroes like Ripley in the *Alien* series, Sarah Connor in *Terminator 2* to some extent, and Lt Melanie Ballard in *Ghosts of Mars*,[24] women are used as *supporting* characters in both meanings of the word, and most often sidelined by the narrative once they have validated their male partners' masculinity. Science fiction narratives continue to place hegemonic masculinity front and centre, although Hollywood films have gradually incorporated black characters, including them in multiracial teams and, more and more often, casting them as heroes. Chapter 4 analyses the rise to prominence of black male heroes from the early 1990s to the 2000s to show

Introduction

how black masculinity calls into question the equation white man = Man. However, science fiction films with black heroes, especially those starring Will Smith, fail to fully challenge hegemonic masculinity as they continue to rely on male hegemony and the institutions of patriarchy to make black men the representatives of humanity. Finally, Chapter 5 looks at the evolution of white hegemonic masculinity from the mid-1990s until today, showing how hard science fiction has moved away from a hypermasculine model emphasising physical toughness and emotional restraint to stress emotional and intellectual intelligence as well as cooperation with others, notably women. Have these changes succeeded in challenging the basic equation of science fiction that is man = Man?

1

Vulnerable Hypermasculinity

American society in the 1980s witnessed an important shift in the representations and significance of masculinity in both politics and Hollywood. Indeed, the emergence and popularity of extremely masculine heroes embodied by the likes of Arnold Schwarzenegger can be traced back to a wider political drive, starting in the late 1970s, to bring back traditional values based on a patriarchal system where hegemonic masculinity had pride of place. Ronald Reagan's election in 1980 coalesced interest groups with different objectives but at least one common goal: shoring up hegemonic masculinity, that is to say restoring the power of white men at the expense of minority groups. White blue-collar workers, disgruntled by Democratic policies of affirmative action or what they saw as 'reverse discrimination', turned to Reagan, while former southern Democrats also joined the Republican Party in reaction to the Democratic Party's support of the Civil Rights Movement. Furthermore, Reagan was elected thanks to a powerful new force, the Religious Right, comprised of organisations like Moral Majority and Concerned Women for America (CWA), both founded in 1979, which, Susan Faludi argues,[1] strongly contributed to a 'backlash' against women's liberation and feminism. Jerry Falwell, the founder of Moral Majority, maintained that the Bible commanded women to submit to their husbands, while CWA vigorously opposed the Equal Rights Amendment and abortion rights, advocating 'pro-family' values and the return of the patriarchal family.[2] Finally, Reagan appealed to Republican hawks because his staunch anti-communism contrasted with what they saw as Carter's weakness on the international front. Carter was accused of being 'soft', connoting femininity, while Reagan appeared tough and 'hard',[3] favouring military action over diplomacy, promoting military rearmament and calling for American world hegemony.

Reagan's election and leadership were thus built on the celebration of hegemonic masculinity. His aggressive foreign policy confirmed his virility as well as the nation's, leaving the spectre of Vietnam far behind and heralding a future where a confident America would be invulnerable and omnipotent through, for instance, the Strategic Defense Initiative, Reagan's project of building a space-based nuclear shield to protect the United States. As John Orman remarks when defining Reagan as the 'quintessential macho president',[4] Reagan himself embodied a virile masculinity, photographed chopping wood or breaking horses,[5] and threatening the Soviet Union as an 'Evil Empire' that must be destroyed. This was reinforced when Reagan miraculously survived an assassination attempt on 30 March 1981, to which he reacted with courage and equanimity, joking to his wife that '[he] forgot to duck'. The attempt on his life and Reagan's response resulted in the highest popularity ratings for a president in polling history.[6] After the Watergate scandal and the 'malaise' of the Carter era, the 1980s saw the return of a strong presidency, which had a significant impact on the representations of masculinity. Based largely on film heroes and plots, Reagan's constructed masculinity, in turn, had a strong influence on the filmic representations of his time, as audiences yearned for narratives of heroism and strength both on the political scene and at the cinema. These narratives were embodied by what Susan Jeffords calls 'hard bodies' that 'enveloped strength, labor, determination and courage' and were, 'as Reagan's own, male and white', as well as staunchly heterosexual,[7] in opposition to the feminised or racialised 'soft bodies' linked to 'what Reagan's public relations workers characterised as the "weakened" years of the Carter administration'.[8]

Vulnerable Hypermasculinity

Hollywood responded to, and participated in, this drive to reassert the central and dominant position of white men in a revalidated patriarchal system. More than any other genre, the flourishing genre of science fiction contributed to the shoring-up of white masculinity by resorting to the hallmarks of hypermasculinity, that is to say the extreme glorification of masculine attributes, including an emphasis on physical strength and aggression.[9] However, hypermasculinity has negative connotations for many psychologists, such as Donald Mosher and Mark Sirkin, who devised, as early as 1984, a Hypermasculinity Inventory to 'measure the macho personality constellation', comprised of three elements: 'Calloused Sex Attitudes'; 'Danger as Exciting'; and 'Violence as Manly'.[10] As Erica Scharrer has stated:

> the hyper-masculine male eschews and even ridicules 'soft-hearted' emotions, celebrates and views as inevitable male physical aggression, blocks attempts by women or others to appeal to emotions by belittling sexual relations or women in general, and exhibits sensation-seeking behaviors that bring a welcome sense of vigor and thrill.[11]

Analysing science fiction films through the lens of hypermasculinity can reveal a more complex and nuanced portrayal of masculinity than the more manichean and univocal hard body. This chapter insists on the complexity of hypermasculinity in 1980s science fiction films. If films like *The Terminator* (James Cameron, 1984), the *RoboCop* trilogy (*RoboCop*, Paul Verhoeven, 1987; *RoboCop 2*, Irvin Kershner, 1990; *RoboCop 3*, Fred Dekker, 1993), *Predator* (John McTiernan, 1987),[12] *Total Recall* (Paul Verhoeven, 1990), *Terminator 2* (James Cameron, 1991), *Universal Soldier* (Roland Emmerich, 1992) or even *The Fly* (David Cronenberg, 1986) seem, at first, to present an enhanced masculinity especially in terms of bodily strength, which could therefore be seen as the masculinist realisation of the hypermasculine ideal, the male bodies in these films often experience a process of transformation that presents them as vulnerable because penetrable by an Other, whether it be a machine or an animal as small as a fly. The films are actually built on a tension between the need to restore hegemonic masculinity through the showcasing of the 'hard body', that is to say the hypermasculine built-up male body, and what can be seen as a strategy of victimisation, which insists on the suffering and vulnerability of the male body. Many of the hypermasculine heroes of American science fiction movies of the 1980s paradoxically derive their power from a fundamental traumatic experience, legitimising them as victims. However, this paradoxical masculinity, apparently invulnerable yet penetrable, transformed and fragmented, can also be seen as a questioning of the hypermasculine ideal and the drive to impose a normative hegemonic masculinity which, pushed to the extreme, reveals itself as an unnatural construction or even a monstrosity.

Reclaiming Hegemony Through Hypermasculinity

Displaying the male body

The most striking aspect of the big blockbuster science fiction films of the 1980s is the visibility of the male body. This can be explained in part by the context, described by Jeffords as 'an era of bodies',[13] when even such politicised and countercultural figures as Jane Fonda turned away from political battles to focus, in fitness exercise videos, for example, on the individual body. Yet given the possible homoerotic overtones associated with the spectacle of masculinity, as underlined by Steve Neale,[14] the extent to which male bodies appear naked or half-naked on screen remains a surprising fact. *Total Recall*, for example, begins its narration with a shot of Arnold Schwarzenegger waking from a bad dream and sitting up in bed, his bare torso progressively revealed and enhanced by light streaming in (his wife – played by Sharon Stone – conveniently opens the blinds), by a change in camera position that cuts from a frontal close shot of his shoulders to a medium-long shot of his whole body shown in profile, muscular arms extended, pectorals bulging, and finally by his wife's titillating playfulness, pulling the sheets so as to offer a glimpse of Schwarzenegger's buttocks (Figure 1.1). In fact, Schwarzenegger had already appeared *au naturel* a few years earlier, in the opening scene of *The Terminator* showing the arrival of a cyborg sent back in the past unarmed and unclothed, a scene paralleled within the film by the arrival of his human opponent,

Vulnerable Hypermasculinity

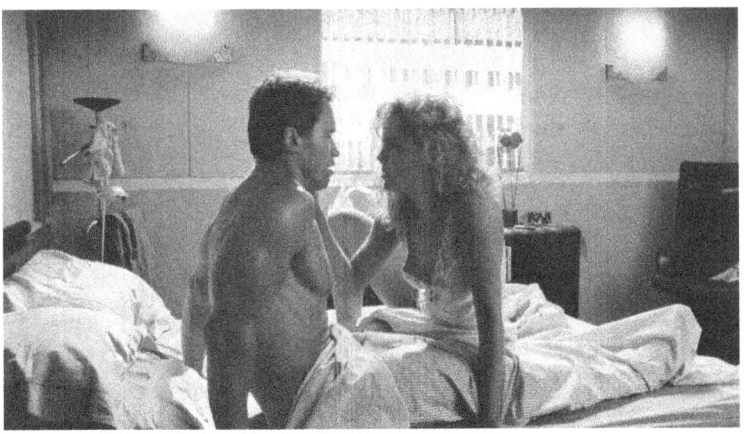

Figure 1.1 Doug wakes up in *Total Recall*

played by Michael Biehn, also presented stark naked. As we shall see, this seminal scene had further ramifications in *The Fly*, where Jeff Goldblum is revealed in the nude, and of course in *Terminator 2*, where the arrival scene is reprised and Schwarzenegger's nudity commented on humorously by a reverse shot of a waitress nodding appreciatively when the disrobed Terminator walks into her bar.

Why are there so many scenes of male nudity in science fiction films of the 1980s? Male nudity in the previously mentioned scenes is always heavily loaded, with a strong emphasis on muscles, especially biceps and pectorals, seen as more specifically male. A synecdoche for the display and control of the male body, muscles function as visible and natural male attributes, connoting physical strength and activity, and are as such central to the construction of hypermasculinity. Muscles are constantly foregrounded, even in the simple handshake between Dutch (Schwarzenegger) and Dillon (Carl Weathers) in *Predator*, which immediately turns into an arm-wrestling match framed in close-up, biceps bulging out of the two men's short-sleeved shirts, or in *RoboCop*, which showcases sculpted titanium pectorals in Robocop's metallic armour, reproducing a bodybuilt torso. Within an ideology that associates masculinity with activity, the emphasis on bodybuilding as a process of physical training and transformation allows male stars to display their bodies without being feminised, since, as Richard Dyer puts it, '[t]he muscle man is the end product of his own activity of muscle-building'.[15] Hypermasculinity thus appears as the net result of the male actors' often highly publicised bodybuilding and physical training efforts, especially in Schwarzenegger's case, but also in those of Carl Weathers and Jean-Claude Van Damme, even though the process itself is never shown onscreen. Thus, the heroes' physical strength remains 'natural'. Despite its constructedness through bodybuilding, hypermasculinity paradoxically goes back to an essentialist definition of masculinity as both active and naturally powerful. Furthermore, according to Dyer, muscles are read as *signs* of male power, hence naturalising male hegemony:

> The potential for muscularity in men is seen as a biological given, and is also the means of dominating both women and other men who are in competition for the spoils of the earth. The point is that muscles are biological, hence 'natural' … The 'naturalness' of muscles legitimises male power and domination.[16]

The visibility of the male body in hypermasculine science fiction films can be seen as reinforcing and justifying male hegemony, which is something men have actively strived for and therefore somehow 'deserve'. In this way, hegemonic masculinity is praised for being 'hard', both resistant and difficult to attain.

Scenes of male nudity are also often used to stage a rebirth. In *The Fly*, Seth Brundle (Jeff Goldblum) is first seen naked when he enters the telepod that will fuse him with a fly, creating a new mutant creature. It is interesting to see how this teleportation scene echoes in many ways the arrival of the Terminator in the 1984 film. Both scenes are filmed as fantastical and even mystical events, with lightning and mist announcing and delaying the revelation of the transformed male body. The latter is finally revealed by a cold white light contrasting with the surrounding darkness, creating a chiaroscuro effect that makes the male body stand out. Most striking is the similarity between the positions of the male body and the camera movements used in both scenes. The naked body is first shown crouching in a foetal position, then slowly deploys itself while the camera zooms in and tilts to end on a magnifying low-angle close shot

Vulnerable Hypermasculinity

Figure 1.2 Low-angle shots of the naked Goldblum and Schwarzenegger in *The Fly* and *The Terminator*

underlining the protagonists' torsos, especially their well-defined pectorals (Figure 1.2). These echoes from *The Terminator* – Seth's foetal position in the womb-like telepod and the final low-angle shot – all contribute to announce the arrival of a new, more masculine hero who can meet the standards of hypermasculinity.

Indeed, Seth's rebirth initially appears as a hegemonic regeneration and masculinisation, underlined by the enhancement and display of the male body. Goldblum worked out intensively before being 'exposed', as he puts it himself,[17] after the teleportation, thus giving the impression of a suddenly beefed-up body. And exposed he is, appearing repeatedly unclothed in the scenes following the teleportation: in bed with Ronnie (Geena Davis), performing incredible acrobatics half-naked, wandering around in his underwear after lengthy intercourse. In fact, the teleportation initially transforms Seth into the man he always wanted to be, as he remarks when he grows coarse hair on his back: 'I've never been hairy enough, always too boyish. I'm looking forward to a hairy body.' His costumes also reflect this masculinisation, with the film utilising a leather jacket which functions as a fetishistic expression of virility, again in an interesting echo of *The Terminator*'s famous 'I'll be back' scene, where the Terminator 'mans up', putting on a leather jacket and sun glasses before attacking the police station. In *The Fly*, the jacket is repeatedly associated with virile sexual performance: Ronnie buys the jacket for Seth after their first night together; she is followed in the shop by her ex-boyfriend who snatches it from her in a jealous rage and comments sarcastically on Seth's 'big cock'. After his teleportation, Seth always wears the jacket to go out, most visibly when he leaves Ronnie in search of a new female partner, ranting on about 'penetration beyond the veil of the flesh' while putting on the jacket over his bare chest.

These films, especially those featuring a transformation, show the protagonists' 'hypermasculinisation' through the display of masculine attributes and a special emphasis on the male body. This is central and quite specific to the 1980s, even though displays of the male body can be found in a few science fiction films of the 1960s and 1970s, especially those with Charlton Heston, such as *Planet of the Apes* (Franklin Schaffner, 1968) or *The Omega Man* (Boris Sagal, 1971). Comparing *The Fly* to its original, directed by Kurt Neumann and released in 1958, is particularly relevant in this respect. Whereas Cronenberg's film is centred on the male body, its transformations and wonderful/terrifying abilities – the scene where Seth shows off his acrobatics is centrally positioned in the narrative as a purple patch of masculinity – the original film hardly shows the male body at all. Indeed, the main character in Neumann's film is not the male scientist, André (David Hedison), but his wife, Hélène (Patricia Owens), who is also the narrator of the central flashback explaining her husband's misadventure. Hélène's emotions, traumatic experience and possible guilt are the driving force of the narrative, and she is thus onscreen for most of the time: the film repetitively uses close-ups of her expressive face, and her beauty is highlighted thanks to make-up, elegant dresses and revealing negligees. As for André, he only appears onscreen after 27 minutes, emerging in the upstairs light from his dark laboratory in the basement of his home, where he will remain for the rest of the film. Far from being on display, the male body is hidden and shielded from sight; confined in the dark, it is constantly covered, first by a scientist's long coat later used to hide his fly claw, to which is added a black cloth draped over his fly head. Apart from one three-minute episode of destructive rage in full sight, the mutant body appears only briefly and rarely, helpless under its black sheet and lacking a voice, forced to ask for his wife's help even to commit suicide. The body can only be glimpsed in death: a black claw hangs from the metallic press, the only visible part of André's crushed body, otherwise hidden from view by a pillar at the end of the flashback, while André's scarred leg is uncovered by the police so that his brother can identify the body at the beginning of the film.

Defying death

Thirty years later, American science fiction films had adopted quite a different representation of the male body and its death, influenced by the new aesthetics of the action film and its 'choreographed mise en scène of death'.[18] The films of the 1980s often feature lengthy scenes of bodily feats performed in the face of death, as in *Universal Soldier*'s grand finale combat scene between Jean-Claude Van Damme and Dolph Lundgren, both dressed in sleeveless open military jackets. The whole film seems to be geared towards this scene, which lasts for over ten minutes to the sound of rhythmic and stirring music, and boasts a whole series of spectacular kickboxing moves, including a long jumping sidekick filmed in slow motion, followed by Van Damme's trademark helicopter kick and a rapid triple sidekick which pushes his opponent onto metal spikes and crucifies him in gory fashion. No bodily restraint here: the point of the film is physical performance. This feature had become so essential in the early 1990s that it was systematically tacked onto the narrative, for instance in *RoboCop 3*, where the display of body feats inspired by martial arts actually seems to be the only function of the strange Japanese robot, a sword-wielding samurai figure first seen bare-chested who spends the rest of the film attacking Robocop in somersaults.

Hollywood science fiction thus responded to the popularity of the action film and to the dominant Reaganite discourse of indomitable omnipotence by promoting hypermasculinity and its glorification of masculine strength through the featuring of invulnerable heroes. The films indeed insist on the male protagonists' quasi-invulnerability, as their bodies stay whole while their opponents' are pierced through, as evidenced by the Terminator's punch through the hooligan's body at the beginning of *The Terminator*, Robocop's bullet through a woman's skirt to reach her rapist's groin, or the infamous arm-wrestling match in *The Fly* where Seth breaks his opponent's wrist in two. Furthermore, the films are replete with challenges to the male bodies that are met with defeat: knives that do not penetrate the flesh, blows that hurt the aggressor, bullets ricocheting off, fires from which male bodies emerge unsinged. Interestingly, invulnerability to fire is underlined in comparable scenes in *The Terminator* and *RoboCop*, where the two eponymous characters are engulfed in a fire lit to destroy them but from which they materialise unharmed, in similar low-angle shots of glinting metallic bodies striding purposefully through the flames to the sound of loud triumphant music and to their opponents' dismay, highlighting the underlying resemblance between two morally opposed characters.

Invulnerability is best embodied by the cyborg figure, which became omnipresent in American science fiction films of the 1980s. Since the cyborg is the focus of an excellent book by Sue Short,[19] I will not develop the subject at length here, but I would like to insist on how the cyborg embodies the ideal of a fusion between machine and man that gives concrete expression to hypermasculinity, reinforcing an ideal of toughness and aggressiveness visualised in the male body as machine. The films literalise the fantasy of a perfect machine-like body, constantly highlighting the long-lived associations between men and their bodies with machines. Robocop's body is thus made of titanium, and his mechanical aspect is reinforced by Peter Weller's change in acting style after Murphy's transformation. He moves stiffly with a heavy gait, emphasised by the resonating sound of his footsteps in the police station when he first walks in as Robocop – Weller was indeed coached by a mime artist named Moni Yakim, who is credited in the film for developing the character's 'Robomovement'.[20] In *The Terminator*, man and machine are associated in the first sequence through the editing and camerawork, which draw a close parallel between the Terminator and a garbage truck. The first shot opens on the truck, which seems to have a life of its own, as the driver is shown only after several close-ups of its arms and fork, and since its headlight, shot in close-up like an eye, goes out suddenly and unexpectedly. The driver becomes useless as he cannot turn the engine back on, so that the truck, shot as a whole in a medium-long shot and lit up by lightning, seems to generate on its own the figure that appears next to it, the two machines being directly linked by a pan from the truck to the Terminator. On the soundtrack, the noise of the truck gives way to the Terminator's theme, the same note repeated four times on percussions, the absence of any melody and the repetition of the same sound likening it to the automated sound of a machine. These cyborg films thus participate in the warrior ideal of man becoming one with the machine, a fantasy symbolised at its worst by Robocop's gun arm in *Robocop 3*, when Robocop's titanium arm is cut off by the samurai but replaced by Robocop himself with a gun, which allows him to blow the samurai away, proving that the male body is a weapon in and of itself.

White hegemony

Yet what is striking in these films is that the invulnerable body is a feature of white males. Cyborgs were exclusively white until the release of *I, Robot* in 2004, with Will Smith as its main cyborg character (which I'll come back to in Chapter 4). More generally, all science fiction films featured white heroes, with non-whites as antagonists or as supporting characters who usually disappear or die during the course of the action. In *Predator*, for example, Dutch (Schwarzenegger) is aided by a group of soldiers including two black men and a Native American who are all killed, leaving the white hero to fight the Predator on his own in the third and final act of the film. Most of the soldiers are killed swiftly and their bodies are removed by the Predator, so that they disappear instantly from the screen, but the film resorts to slow motion for the attack on Dutch's African-American partner, Dillon (Carl Weathers), who is brutally slaughtered onscreen. The black body thus provides the thrilling gruesome effects central to 1980s science-fiction/action cinema: Dillon's arm is shot off, leaving a visible bloody stump, and he is then gored by the Predator, the scene ending with a close-up of his contorted face screaming with pain. The non-white members of the team act as sacrificial figures: African-American Mac (Bill Duke) decides to go after the Predator alone to avenge the death of his white friend; he is followed by Dillon, who also seeks revenge and hopes to delay the Predator so that the others can reach the helicopter in time; their deaths in turn seem to motivate Billy (Sonny Landham), the Native-American scout, to take a stand, staged as a human self-sacrifice, as he strips himself of his military gear, throws his gun in the river and waits for the enemy half-naked and exposed, alone on a wooden bridge. His death occurs off-screen, but is signified to the remaining survivors (and to the audience) by a terrifying scream resonating through the jungle. Indeed, apart from Dillon and especially Dutch, all the soldiers are killed without being able to see their enemy clearly, much less fight back: they are shown as vulnerable prey, while the Predator remains invisible, creeping up on his victims and striking without warning. Only Dutch is able to see him fully, when he himself has become invisible to the Predator thanks to a mud bath. Indeed, there is an interesting play on visibility/invisibility, whiteness/blackness throughout the last part of Predator: the white male is paradoxically able to escape from the Predator when he covers his skin with mud, passing as black through blackface makeup. However, only when his blackface is washed away to reveal his white and therefore visible skin does the Predator recognise Dutch as a worthy adversary, literally weighing him up and examining his features up close before challenging him to a technology-free, hand-to-hand face-off. Even though *Predator* seems at first to be inclusive, encompassing two bodybuilt black men (Carl Weathers and Bill Duke) in its celebration of hypermasculinity, in the end, non-whites do not measure up. Only the white hero survives to fight back, while non-whites are eliminated instantly, as if they had no power of agency: all they can do is rant or scream. The hypermasculine white male is presented as 'naturally worthy' through a physical examination, and recuperates minority attributes that enable him to defeat the Predator, blending in with his environment like Billy or the racially hybrid Predator.

Science fiction films of the 1980s acknowledged the generalised integration of blacks in American society and especially in the entertainment industry – with such figures as Richard Pryor, Eddy Murphy, Michael Jackson or Bill Cosby – by routinely including non-whites as supporting characters, often in minor roles. For instance, *RoboCop* and *The Terminator* both feature the traditional and ubiquitous African-American police captain, well-meaning but powerless and ineffectual (and also nameless): refusing to believe in the Terminator's dangerousness, the captain is killed and does not succeed in protecting Sarah Connor, while in *RoboCop* the captain is brushed aside in his own police station by corporate executive Bob Morton, who tells him insultingly to 'get lost' while his team marches into the station to set up Robocop's headquarters. As James Chapman and Nicholas J. Cull remark,[21] *RoboCop* tries to be racially balanced and includes several African-American policemen and one executive (the only black face in the corporate meetings), many of whom reappear and are fleshed out in the sequels – especially Johnson, the black executive played by Felton Perry. *RoboCop 2* even features a black, if rather goofy and feckless, mayor. However, these characters have little screen time and few lines, and consequently no real impact on the narrative. As in *Predator*, minority characters do not have any agency,[22] except as villains: the Predator's dark dreadlocked hair disturbingly conjures up a Jamaican heritage, while the gang in *RoboCop* is composed of ethnically marked criminals. Indeed, what is especially striking in *RoboCop*, despite its progressive credentials and its satire of the Reagan era,[23] is the way it participates in the demonisation of ethnic and racial minorities through its portrayal of its 'bad guys', a gang of sadistic drug-trafficking criminals responsible for hundreds of deaths. The gang, headed by a bespectacled white man, otherwise includes an African American, a Hispanic, an Asian American and an ethnic white whose name, Emil Antonowsky, emphasises his foreign origin. All are associated to the 'soft body', defined by Jeffords as an 'errant body containing sexually transmitted disease, immorality, illegal chemicals, "laziness"'.[24] The African American poses and laughs hysterically, and is stereotyped as a 'stud' when he distracts Murphy's female partner by showing her his penis and then boasting about his feat. The Hispanic is arrested by Robocop in a nightclub full of undulating and scantily clad bodies. All deal in and consume cocaine. In a striking and gory image, the degeneracy of these criminal bodies is underlined at the end of the film when Emil crashes into a tank of toxic waste and transforms into a monster, his shredded body liquefied by the acid.

The gang is moreover constantly associated with the decay of Detroit, plagued by violent crime. Their headquarters are in a dilapidated industrial zone and they take great pleasure in destroying the city during the police strike: Emil breaks the window of a TV shop only so he can listen to his favourite show while the African American burns down a car to test his new 'toy', a military mortar. So although the film criticises Reaganite America by emphasising the corruption of elites who are in collusion with the drug-traffickers, it nevertheless clearly associates the decay of America's downtowns with a rising criminality attributed to ethnic minorities. Indeed, *RoboCop* directly refers to the financial crisis affecting US cities in the 1980s, abandoned by those who could move to the suburbs and deeply affected by the federal cuts to urban renewal subsidies approved by Reagan, where insecurity became a major issue. For Roger Ebert, reviewer for the *Chicago Sun-Times*, part of the film's social satire comes from the proximity between Robocop and Bernhard Goetz,[25] a white man who killed four black men in 1984 in a New York subway because he thought they were going to attack him. Goetz, who gave himself up to the police while pleading self-defence, was dubbed 'the subway vigilante' and became a hero in the eyes of many New Yorkers and Americans sick of the rising criminality and the inefficiency of the police.[26] In spite of itself, *RoboCop* falls partly into a Reaganite discourse by opposing a hypermasculine white protagonist to ethnically marked criminals, in a context of violence where lone vigilantes are celebrated as heroes.

Science fiction films of the 1980s that celebrate hypermasculinity through the showcasing of the white male body's invulnerability and physical prowess, including the *Terminator* and *RoboCop* franchises, *Predator* and *Total Recall*, could, like *Rambo* and *Rocky IV*, be seen, in Valerie Walkerdine's words, as 'fantasies of omnipotence, heroism and salvation', which provide 'a counterpoint to the experience of oppression and powerlessness'[27] felt by many white men, as their position of dominance became threatened by the progress of women and non-whites. In 1983, for instance, the number of economically active white men fell below 50 per cent for the first time, compared with 52 per cent of women, the same year that Martin Luther King's birthday became a federal holiday.[28] This fantasy is even expressed as such in *Total Recall*, where Doug, an ordinary construction worker who dreams of another life, pays to have memory implants of an espionage mission on Mars. The salesman assures an enraptured Doug that 'by the time the trip is over you get the girl, kill the bad guys and save the entire planet'. The humour lies in the bombastic and clichéd nature of the salesman's pitch, but also in the film's self-reflexivity, since it will follow precisely this narrative, enacting a fantasy of heroism and omnipotence for both Doug and the wider audience. These hard-bodied science fiction films could thus be seen as masculinist, as they were indeed by some critics like Claudia Springer[29] or Susan Jeffords,[30] since they seem to promote the ideal of aggressive and invulnerable hypermasculinity so conspicuous in the 1980s.

Vulnerability as a Path to Victimhood

A structuring tension between invulnerability and vulnerability

However, as Yvonne Tasker develops in *Spectacular Bodies*, there is a tension in the action movie 'between the hero as a powerful figure ... and the hero as a threatened figure, in need of the protection that only the developed body can offer'.[31] Yet even the body fails the heroes of science fiction films, which regularly include prolonged scenes of suffering where the male body's vulnerability and capacity to feel pain are emphasised. The films are, in effect, structured on an underlying tension between invulnerability and vulnerability, with the male body constantly open to attack, penetration and alteration. Many of these films feature altered male bodies (the *Terminator* and *Universal Soldier* franchises for instance), while a few actually thematise the process of transformation, like *The Fly* and *RoboCop*. In these 'mutant body films', the male body is penetrated by something other, whether it be machine or animal, so that the body is no longer contained and bounded, hence eminently vulnerable. In *Universal Soldier*, for example, the universal soldiers are repeatedly shown lying naked in reclining medical chairs, as their bodies are cooled down and treated with drugs. In their first such appearance, their passivity is underlined by their expressionless faces and their complete obedience to orders, since they press the button to inject a memory clearance serum themselves. Their vulnerability is further highlighted by a tracking shot that ends on the back of their necks, while the mechanically activated syringes are positioned a few inches away. The anticipated yet disquieting moment when the needle penetrates the flesh is thus emphasised first by being delayed, then by a close-up and finally by the soundtrack, which underlines the release of the serum by foregrounding and musically amplifying the mechanical sound of the needle's trigger and release. The soldiers exemplify the tension between invulnerability and vulnerability at the heart of hypermasculine science fiction, since this scene, which presents them as utterly passive and vulnerable laboratory rats, follows immediately after their heroic and physically straining rescue of terrorist-held hostages.

The repeated display of the hypermasculine male body discussed above opens a serious breach in the contained nature of masculinity, since the male body becomes an object of the gaze. The body's vulnerability is indeed expressed by its 'to-be-looked-at-ness', a concept applied by Laura Mulvey to the status of women in classical films[32] but which becomes a defining characteristic of male characters in hypermasculine films. Men can be eroticised and made desirable by the gaze, as in the acrobatic scene in *The Fly* when Seth's feats are watched admiringly by Ronnie, who acts as focaliser in this scene, the camera mediating the female gaze in this instance. The eroticisation of the male body is further enhanced by the camerawork and the soundtrack: the camera alternates between long shots of the whole body performing acrobatic feats and medium close-ups, often low-angle, of the chest and head, while the general silence, broken only by Seth's heavy breathing, focuses the viewer's attention on the body at work. The scene ends on a beautiful still shot outlining Seth's torso with shafts of soft light on his gleaming and well-delineated muscles, and the erotic appeal of the male body is finally confirmed by a reaction shot of Ronnie's smile and the return of music.

However, as Pat Kirkham and Janet Thumim have pointed out,[33] men's objectification is usually linked to suffering and endurance rather than desirability. As Neale had already argued in 'Masculinity as Spectacle', the display of the male body creates a form of homoerotic anxiety that has to be alleviated, most often through ritualistic violence, so that 'the repression of any explicit avowal of eroticism in the act of looking at the male seems structurally linked to a narrative content marked by sado-masochistic phantasies and scenes'.[34] This is exemplified in science fiction films in scenes showing the body in pain, where the visibility of the naked body is counterbalanced by the visibility of the body in pain. In *Total Recall*, Schwarzenegger's naked appearance in bed at the beginning of the film is inextricably linked with an experience of bodily pain in the opening dream sequence on Mars. This is emphasised by the editing, which cuts from a close-up at the end of the dream of Schwarzenegger's contorted face, eyes popping and tongue sticking out, to his bare torso as he wakes up, with continuity being established primarily through his scream. It is as if nakedness stemmed from pain and vice versa, since it is the breaking of the spacesuit's glass visor and the consequent exposure to Martian atmosphere that triggers the pain. This specific experience of pain, represented by the bulging eyes and the scream, will recur throughout the movie, at Rekall, then at Cohaagen's and finally in the last sequence, which exactly reprises the original dream scene.

More often than not, then, nakedness comes at a price, as the body's exposure is linked to its suffering. Contrary to the Terminator's invulnerability in *The Terminator* – even naked, he easily disposes of three mocking punks – Kyle's arrival in the present is far from painless. Instead of appearing on his feet, ready to rise, Kyle's naked body is thrown from above at great speed into a concrete backstreet full of garbage. Lying on his side, his back to the camera, Kyle has difficulty standing up and can only manage to get on his knees at first, trembling and groaning from the pain. A sense of physical pain permeates the scene: the visual and audible shock of a body hitting the ground is followed by extreme close-ups of a sweaty, scarred and huddled-up body. Unlike the Terminator, Kyle is unable to stand fully erect and remains bent in pain, limping to a wall to regain his balance, with visible scars on his back. This difficult and chaotic arrival in a cluttered setting contrasts with the Terminator's calm and smooth rise in a landscape cleaned of any debris, a contrast further emphasised by the camerawork, which favours fluid tracking shots for the Terminator, while using a succession of slightly unstable fixed shots for Kyle. Nakedness is thus used in two completely different ways in *The Terminator*: on the one hand, it underlines the Terminator's invulnerability when his naked flesh resists the punk's knife; on the other, it highlights Kyle's vulnerability, as, bare-chested, he is hunted down by the police. The tension between invulnerability and vulnerability is split across two characters whose naked bodies are positioned in direct contrast.

Nowhere is this tension between invulnerability and vulnerability as centrally structuring as in the *RoboCop* trilogy. Indeed, the first film is built on repeated scenes of pain and suffering inflicted on its protagonist, which are then reprised in the two sequels, where Robocop's metallic invulnerability is constantly counterbalanced by his sadistic destruction, followed by an operation to reconstruct him. Murphy's execution is the seminal scene. It occurs in the first instalment after a relatively brief 20-minute introduction where his character is barely developed: all we learn is that he has been transferred from a quiet neighbourhood to 'hell', as his colleagues warn him, and that he has a son for whom he wants to be a good role model. He represents the stereotype of the decent policeman and loving father, out of place in a chaotic environment, whether it be the disorderly police station where everyone brawls or the criminals' lair in a run-down warehouse, a maze in which Murphy moves with extreme caution, while the criminals feel at home enough to watch television slouched on a sofa. As Murphy nears the criminals, his isolation is further emphasised by his repeated and concerned calls to his partner Lewis (Nancy Allen), who is unable to respond after having been knocked out, and the recurrence of high-angle shots showing first a deserted room, then a sequestered and overpowered Murphy, as two gang members appear on the stairs above him and point their guns at him. He is trapped, his vulnerability underlined as more and more gang members enter the room and encircle him. Utterly surrounded, he is disarmed, his helmet is removed and he is brought to his knees by a violent blow.

The criminals' cynical sadism, visible in their broad smiles, mannered postures and ironical remarks – the gang's leader, Clarence, nonchalantly takes off Murphy's helmet and puts it on a subordinate's head while asking him whether he is 'a hot shot' – contrasts with Murphy's proper, even slightly prim, behaviour as a policeman. Indeed, Clarence makes fun of his 'good cop' attitude that led him to believe he could take out a gang all by himself and means '[he] probably [doesn't] think [Clarence] is a very nice guy', while Murphy vindicates him in a way when he gives an inexpressive, old-fashioned and corny reply: 'Buddy, I think you're slime', at which all the gang members burst out laughing. Furthermore, whereas Murphy only shot one gang member in self-defence, attempting to handcuff another, Clarence sadistically tortures Murphy, slowly moving his gun above him in feigned suspense before shooting off his hand point blank. Murphy's inability to express himself – he cannot even utter a scream when his hand explodes – is again contrasted with Clarence's sarcastic wit, when he exclaims: 'Well give the man a hand!' Murphy is, in fact, deprived of any agency, be it verbal – he has no real voice and is denied the oneliners so popular in cop shows and films such as *Dirty Harry* (Don Siegel, 1971) or *Miami Vice* (Michael Mann, 1984–9) – or physical, since he is pushed around, his passive body offered repeatedly in close-up as a fixed target. Indeed, his final execution transforms him into a sacrificial victim, as emphasised by the references to Christ's martyrdom – the blown-off hand as stigmata, his final vertical position with arms extended evoking a crucifixion – and by the scene's extreme brutality; his body is riddled with bullets, twitching at every impact, while he screams continuously to the amusement of his sadistic torturers, who are shown several times in medium close-up to highlight the smiles on their frenzied faces. The scene ends on another cruel remark, a mocking Shakespearean end quote: 'Good night sweet prince',[35] triggering widespread laughter, which comments on and contrasts with the close-up of Murphy's mutilated body and dead silence.

This brutal scene constitutes Murphy's original trauma and will resurface several times in the film and in its sequels. It first comes back as a memory reactivated by pain when Murphy is lying in hospital. The electric shocks given by the doctors trying to reanimate him trigger a set of flashbacks reprising the brutal images seen in the previous scene, stressing again their harrowing impact: Murphy's last mental images are those of the smiling criminals and their hateful leader shooting him in the head. The repetition of these images establishes a continuum of pain that prolongs Murphy's suffering at the hands of the gang well into the hospital scene, even though he is now unconscious. His bodily pain is emphasised by the camerawork and the editing, with repeated medium close-ups of his bloody chest twitching after each shock, followed by the images of his killers, a juxtaposition that equates the defibrillation-induced twitches to those endured during his execution, reactivating his pain. The seminal scene of Murphy's murder constitutes a reference point for the numerous subsequent scenes of torture inflicted on Robocop, which recycle many of its visual elements. In the first film, after being beaten up by ED209, Robocop is cornered by his fellow police officers, who encircle him much like the criminals did. Robocop is in the same position as Murphy: he is unarmed, disoriented, jerking his head every time a new opponent appears, trapped in a circle of hostile guns that are likened to an execution squad as they move in, firing continuously, their gun flashes contrasting with their darkened silhouettes. The already bruised and battered Robocop is again brought to his knees, forced to crawl away since he cannot fight back. However, yet another scene of torture awaits him: the film ends on a final confrontation with Clarence Boddicker's gang, which does not showcase Robocop's invulnerability and superior strength but just the opposite, his vulnerability, even as a machine. Robocop is hunted down by the criminals, who can locate him thanks to a tracking device implanted in him, and have acquired massive weapons which clearly outgun him. They manage to pin him down, crushing him under huge metal planks so that he is again trapped and powerless. When Clarence hits him with a metal rod, each clanging blow is magnified on the soundtrack by a strident chord played sforzando, which suddenly gives way to Robocop's resounding howl, as Clarence pierces his metallic body, reviving Murphy's pain and spine-chilling scream during his execution.

By constantly referring to Murphy's human pain, *RoboCop* downplays the machine's invulnerability and formidable strength to insist on its vulnerability and ability to suffer instead. These characteristics will be further developed in the sequels through repeated scenes of torture and agony where the camera highlights and lingers on the body in pain, going beyond its metallic nature. Indeed, there is a desire in the *RoboCop* films, as in other American science fiction films of the period, to see what is inside the machine, to go beneath the armour and reveal the inner workings of the mechanical body, as when the Terminator takes out his mechanical eye to repair it.[36] The *RoboCop* franchise constantly focuses on 'the chinks in the armor', comparing the mechanical body to a human one and insisting that even a metallic body is penetrable: it does not prevent torture but only prolongs it. Thus, *RoboCop 2* replays Murphy's execution as a brutal three-and-a-half-minute-long attack on the now-metallic body of Robocop. The hero is again trapped in a factory by a criminal gang who blow his hand off, revealing not blood but his inner circuit, with electric wires coming out of his maimed arm, while his body goes into spasm with electric sparks. He is then electrocuted, paralysed by a magnet and strapped to a roller table, where he is methodically broken down with hammers, stakes and drills piercing through his body, his limbs falling to the ground, his electrical wires pulled out of his body like entrails, with blood (or rather oil) spurting out onto his face. The visual shock of a human body being riddled with bullets is transferred onto a machine being slowly ripped to pieces, with some of the shock value coming from a brutal soundtrack composed of a series of unpleasant sounds – hammering, drilling, sawing, electronic interference – that make the scene a painful experience for the viewer as well as for Robocop, encouraging identification with the cyborg character. Robocop's body parts are then dumped in front of the police station, revealing the insides of his body as cables stick out of him and unrecognisable parts are scattered across the floor like discarded organs (Figure 1.3). His armour having been 'stripped', as one of the policeman exclaims, and his helmet removed, his body appears exposed and vulnerable, his torso suspended and fed by tubes, wires coming out where his legs used to be, his contorted face expressing pain through uncontrollable twitches and groans, his eyes rolled upward. The camera gaze here insists at great length on the protagonist's agony, since the scene lasts for more than four minutes and is dominated by medium close-ups, zoom-ins and close-ups of the body, fragmented by the camera.

Figure 1.3 Robocop's suffering in *RoboCop 2*

Robocop as victim

The *RoboCop* franchise consistently insists on the vulnerability and powerlessness of Murphy/Robocop (*RoboCop 3* features another painful operation), while at the same time showcasing Robocop's metallic invulnerability, alternating between pathetic scenes of suffering and exciting action scenes. From this perspective, the franchise, and especially the first two films, can be read as a melodrama, following Linda Williams' revised definition of the genre.[37] Williams first emphasises melodrama's 'quest for an old space of innocence'.[38] This is at the core of the two films: Verhoeven himself acknowledges that 'the idea of lost paradise was part of the attraction of the script'.[39] Robocop continuously longs to return to his previous unproblematic identity as Murphy, going back to his former home in the first film or watching his wife from afar in the second. Each return to the location of his human identity triggers a series of flashbacks depicting an idyllic family life with loving wife and son, always set in the closed environment of the home. The flashbacks therefore operate as melodramatic markers, conjuring up the image of a perfect family only once it has been destroyed, and underlining the protagonist's impossible wish to go back to a (possibly imagined) happier time, narrative devices that are reminiscent of the family melodrama. Furthermore, the flashbacks create pathos by highlighting what the hero has lost, as in the scene where Robocop visits his former home. The editing juxtaposes past images of a joyful and animated home where his wife and son rush to greet him, expressing love and admiration, and a lonely and sorrowful present in a now-deserted house where wife and son have been replaced by a computerised real estate agent. As in the staple family melodrama *Written on the Wind* (Douglas Sirk, 1956), the home is the locus of frustrated desires and emotions, which the male hero can only express through anger: in an uncharacteristic emotional outburst, Robocop punches through the computer, silencing its cold, inhuman and materialistic palaver. The flashbacks thus enable Robocop to regain some of his human identity through the return of emotions, although the anger and sorrow displayed by Robocop contrast with Murphy's gentle smile and twinkling eyes in the opening scenes and in the flashbacks. The quest for lost innocence will be partly fulfilled at the end of the first instalment, when Robocop presents himself with a smile as 'Murphy', the film's Rosebud-like last word.

The *RoboCop* films are structured according to a 'dialectic of pathos and action'[40] characteristic of the melodrama according to Williams. For instance, the two parallel scenes of execution, by the gang and by the policemen, are both followed by a pathetic aftermath where physical pain is complemented by emotional suffering. Murphy's execution triggers the first flashbacks during his hospital defibrillation, which highlight Murphy's severed human connections, his son's question ('Can you do that Dad?') and wife's exclamation ('I really have to tell you something') remaining open or inconclusive. The bond is definitely cut in the last image, which shows them waving a final farewell while the camera zooms out at great speed, signifying Murphy's imminent death. The pain of losing his loved ones resurfaces after the second attack, when Robocop nurses his wounds in an abandoned factory. After removing his damaged helmet to reveal his post-operation head, Robocop asks Lewis about Murphy's wife and son, only to find out that they moved away. Both scenes associate the damaged body with emotional loss, revealing a core vulnerability that marks the male body not only with physical scars but also emotional trauma. The factory scene represents a paroxysm of pathos, as Robocop acknowledges his transformation and his lost 'space of innocence', asking about Murphy in the third person and realising that he cannot remember his wife and son. Pathos is further conveyed by the setting (a deserted factory), the camerawork (long still shots contrasting with the fast-paced action scenes) and the music (soft strings in a minor key).

Both an active hypermasculine hero and a suffering victim, Robocop can therefore be seen as a melodramatic character, one of the numerous 'male victim-heroes' whose 'hard bodies' or hypermasculinity should not overshadow the 'melodramatic moments of masculine pathos', as Williams herself points out.[41] However, Williams does not fully develop the political implications of the use of melodrama to create male victim-heroes. Indeed, melodrama and its concurrent victimisation of the hero shift the male hero into a minority position, giving him a moral authority traditionally associated in melodrama with blacks or women.[42] Indeed, scenes of suffering help turn the white male body into a body marked by physical pain and emotional trauma. Sally Robinson denounces these 'images of physically wounded and emotionally traumatised white masculinity', arguing that 'the figure of the wounded white male enables an erasure of the institutional supports of white and male dominance'.[43] Through pathos and melodrama, then, the white male Robocop can claim to be a victim, decentring hegemonic masculinity to recentre it as a minority category, whose moral high ground allows it to claim visibility and power.

Moreover, scenes of pathos prepare the viewer for 'the exhilaration of action': the victim-hero's suffering justifies his active response and even his use of violence as understandable retribution, 'allow[ing] the white man to engage in the same violently aggressive behaviour that earned him his reputation as the world's chief oppressor, while freeing him from guilt by recoding that behaviour as justifiable acts of vengeance'.[44] Robocop's suffering can, then, be seen as actually reinforcing hegemonic masculinity, since it allows the white man to retain a central position, to have a voice in the midst of growing multiculturalism; it also validates his violent actions and even his masculinity as a proof of his ability to endure pain,[45] while at the same time distancing him from a position of power by portraying him as a victim.

Questioning Hypermasculinity

However, one could also argue that in *RoboCop* the hero is actually a victim of an ideal of hypermasculinity that is imposed on him. Indeed, Murphy does not choose to become Robocop; he is transformed by OCP, the corporation that runs the police and is looking to build a 24/7 police officer. As one executive in the Robocop team puts it, '[Murphy] signed a release form, so we can do pretty much what we want'. What is striking throughout the franchise is his constant passivity during the recurrent operation scenes where he is fixed or altered. This is emphasised by his position, lying down under the care of doctors and laboratory technicians, and the repetition of low-angle point-of-view shots showing his caretakers leaning over him. Robocop is placed in a child-like position where he has no voice and is dominated by others, often female doctors in motherly roles – this aspect is especially developed in the sequels, where the doctors in charge are all women. In the first film, this mother-child relationship is exemplified when, at a party celebrating Robocop's birth, a female technician bends over her 'new-born' to give him a kiss, in a low-angle POV shot which stays on the lipstick smudge left on Robocop's face, that is, the screen, a slightly erotic play on the hackneyed image of a lipstick kiss on a boy's cheek. In *RoboCop 2*, it is no longer Murphy but Robocop who is shown lying on an operation table, dominated and controlled by a female psychologist changing his psychological profile via a computer. As she types in what she says, he repeats her words ('I type it, you think it' – 'You type it, I think it'), having lost any will of his own, so that the scene again ends on a low-angle POV shot where Robocop is congratulated by this controlling-mother type doctor.

Robocop's personality and appearance are thus imposed from the outside and reflect the desires of his creators, first and foremost those of OCP executive Bob Morton (Miguel Ferrer). An aggressive and ambitious yuppie, Morton is indeed the one who insists that Robocop be entirely metallic, yelling at the female technician for trying to save Murphy's human arm: 'I thought we agreed on total bodily prosthesis, now lose the arm!' He smiles excitedly when the new arm is displayed, made entirely of very hard titanium, and is duly impressed when he shakes a hand that could 'crush every bone

Masculinity in Contemporary Science Fiction Cinema

Figure 1.4 Hegemonic masculinity is imposed on Robocop

in [his] body', exclaiming: 'He's got a hell of grip!' Like a father mentoring his son, he bends down over Robocop, in another low-angle POV close-up, projecting his own hypermasculine fantasy when he tells him: 'You are going to be a bad motherfucker' (Figure 1.4). These POV shots show how Robocop's very identity is shaped by other people's desires and fantasies, so that the stern and broad-shouldered Robocop is a far cry from Murphy's slim body, soft face and gentle expression.

Hybridity and instability

Nevertheless, Robocop's new identity is fundamentally unstable, as Cynthia Fuchs points out: 'simultaneously meat and matrix, Robocop is manifold, charged up, violently dislocated from himself'.[46] These words are particularly apt to describe Robocop's evolution in *RoboCop 2*, where his body is treated as 'meat', violently butchered and his personality as 'matrix', reprogrammed by a computer so that he is completely changed. His movements become haphazard, his language high-flown to the absurd and his behaviour erratic: he stays in the car instead of helping Lewis in a firefight, then shoots at a man for smoking. An object of ridicule and sensing his own 'trouble', as he puts it, Robocop feels so alien to himself that he 'charges up', that is, electrocutes himself to erase his cumbersome programme. Robocop thus embodies the instabilities inherent in Donna Haraway's beloved cyborg figure,[47] a 'mulatto' character who 'exposes hybridity', as celebrated by Leilani Nishime.[48] This is especially apparent in a crucial scene analysed by both Nishime and Fuchs, the moment when Robocop removes his helmet to expose a fractured head – a mechanical skull made of metal casing, wires and earpieces surprisingly attached to a human face. The incongruous juxtaposition of shiny blue metal with the texture of his skin emphasises the instability of Robocop's body as well as his identity. Indeed, when Robocop looks at himself in the mirror, the cinematography underlines the strangeness and artificiality of the human face, which is shown second, after the metal skull, and as a small, distanced and hazy reflection in the mirror. The well-delineated face looks like a cut-out, a human mask covering an electronic brain, so that it is now the human elements of Robocop's body that seem fake (see Figure 1.5).

The cyborgs' hybrid bodies reflect their fragmented identities, most visibly in scenes of intimacy when protagonists inspect their transformed bodies, recognising them as radically Other. As David Roche remarks in his article on Cronenberg,[49] such scenes play on and develop Freud's insight that the subject perceives his as a foreign body, visually

Figure 1.5 Reverse shot of Lewis looking at Robocop's fractured head

displaying and transferring the dichotomy between body and soul onto a hybrid or fragmented body as the locus of a fragmented identity. The examination of the transformed body leads to the realisation that the self has become Other, especially in mirror scenes, which can be found in many science fiction films, particularly those involving transformations like *RoboCop*, *RoboCop 2*, *The Fly* and *The Terminator*. *RoboCop 2* indeed reworks the first episode's mirror scene to play up the fracture of the protagonist's identity. Robocop is spying on his former wife and child when memories of his old life as the human Murphy come rushing back: the camera adopts Murphy's point of view in subjective shots of his wife, until he follows her in the bathroom and appears on-screen as a reflection in the mirror. As soon as Murphy sees himself in the mirror, he gives a start, his smile fades and the scene cuts back to Robocop. The mirror thus emphasises the identity split, since the eyeline match brings a shot not, as we could expect, of the smooth-faced human Murphy, but of a helmeted Robocop sitting in his police car. Robocop's dual identity in the first film has become split into two distinct identities separated by a mirror that presents his former self as an entirely different person. The scene creates a jarring and disheartening effect, as the camera switches from POV shots of Murphy in soft lighting and fleshy pastel colours to a medium close-up of Robocop framed and distanced by the car window, his metallic blue armour shining in a bright light, while the only visible portion of his face, his mouth and jaw, is left in the shadow.

In *The Fly* and *The Terminator* the line of fracture and the boundary between the different bodies and identities disappear, so that the films veer into body horror, as human bodies are scrutinised and brutalised into revealing a hidden inhuman core. Contrary to the mirror scene in *RoboCop*, where Robocop's fragmented body is distanced and delineated by the camera so that the spectator can better see and understand, the mirror scene in *The Fly* uses extreme close-ups to collapse the line between human and fly, provoking the spectator's disgust at the disintegration of the body and its inhuman reactions, when for example Seth loses his fingernails and spurts goo from his fingers onto the mirror. Hybridity as blending rather than juxtaposition provokes fear and horror at the collapse of a body contaminated by an Other and no longer contained and predictable.[50] In fact, mirror scenes are particularly interesting because they are both moments of diegetic self-awareness for the protagonist and moments of distance for the spectator, when identification is broken by distanced monstration or disgusting proximity. The scenes generally insist on the unnaturalness of the protagonists' bodies, mourning the loss of a whole and 'natural' male body as the repository of an equally 'natural' male identity while at the same time highlighting the falsity of this concept.

Indeed, Sue Short remarks about the potentialities of cyborg films that 'perceiving the body as unfixed, unstable and unnatural is a potentially radical idea because it upsets the logic that links identity to a biological hierarchy of abilities and dispositions'.[51] Hybrid and unstable bodies question the fixity and superiority of one model of hegemonic masculinity. In fact, science fiction films often present several versions of their protagonist, which embody different versions of masculinity, highlighting the fact that masculinity is not an unchangeable essence but a construction that can change with time and circumstance. *The Fly* opposes the new incredible Seth to the old introverted and gentle Seth; *RoboCop* constantly underlines what separates Robocop from his previous human identity as Murphy; *RoboCop 2* centres on the possibility of programming men and cyborgs at will, reprogramming the cyborg to be a more sociable but ineffective public servant, while casting a criminal drug addict to be the next Robocop; *Total Recall* opposes the ordinary well-meaning Douglas Quaid to his previous corrupt, cynical and chauvinist self, Douglas Hauser; finally, the *Terminator* series famously refashions the first film's brutal Terminator into an attentive protector in the second instalment. In so doing, these science fiction films acknowledge that there is not one single type of masculinity but a whole range of masculinities, and even suggest that hypermasculinity is not the best version: Ronnie comments negatively on the new Seth who 'look[s] bad' and 'smell[s] bad', ordinary citizens complain in *RoboCop 2* about Robocop's 'destructive behaviour' (criticism which is, however, dismissed by the film as spineless and inept), while Hauser betrays Quaid to subjugate minorities (the mutants as well as his girlfriend, whom he wants to make 'respectful, compliant and appreciative') and reinstate an autocratic patriarchy.

A critical perspective?

Can we then say that these films are critical of hypermasculinity? If the invulnerable machine-like body is first presented as a triumph of masculine toughness, science fiction films also point to the dehumanising potential of this ideal whereby machine-like bodies are literally reified to become actual machines. They are objects denied any will of their own, as emphasised by the use of digital screens with computer commands to represent the protagonists' vision and thinking process in *The Terminator* and *RoboCop*. Cynthia Fuchs analyses the repetition of what she calls '"robovision" shots – indicated by grid screens, blinking instructions, and targeting mechanisms' as expressing 'a loss of (self-)control through ... an impossible point-of-view camera'.[52] Yet more than sharing Robocop's trauma, as she suggests, the recurrent POV shots underscore his subjugation through the repeated low-angle close-ups of dominating father or mother figures, analysed above. They also underscore his reification, that is to say the impossibility of an independently thinking self. Indeed, when Robocop tries to arrest OCP's vice-president, Dick Jones, his digital screen indicates that he is in 'arrest mode', and he accordingly moves forward to enact the command. However, as 'Product violation' appears on the screen, Robocop is stopped in his tracks, his body as product ultimately controlled by electronic commands and directives programmed by others. The 'robovision shots' here express both his reification, since his screen vision is blurred by static, and his subjugation, as Dick Jones appears in a low-angle close-up. The mechanisation of the body is therefore tantamount to its reification, which is also demonstrated in *The Fly*. Seth's transformation is indeed computer-generated, and the first insect hairs tellingly grow in a wound caused by a microchip, as Seth becomes incredibly strong and indefatigable, resembling the Terminator. This latent mechanisation is ultimately and ironically underlined by his final transformation, which fuses him with a telepod, his mutant body twisted around wires and spiked with metal shards. It is as if the end goal of hypermasculinity was always to produce a machine, as evidenced by *The Terminator*, where underneath the skin of hypermasculinity's muscled forearms lie the pistons of a well-oiled machine.

Vulnerable Hypermasculinity

The Terminator and *The Fly* indeed show how the hypermasculine fantasy can become a nightmare, mixing horror with science fiction to criticise hypermasculinity. The Terminator is not the hero but a terrifying antagonist who 'doesn't feel pity, or remorse or fear and will not stop until [Sarah] is dead', as Reese explains. Schwarzenegger's machine-like body was meant to inspire fear, as James Cameron underlined in an interview: 'I think [the public] see him from the beginning as this implacable, sexless, emotionless machine – in the form of a man, which is scary, because he's a perfect male figure.'[53] *The Terminator* explores the dark side of hypermasculinity, revealing how absolute invulnerability is, in effect, dangerous and horrific. This is underlined in the nightclub scene where Sarah first sees the Terminator, unable to understand his hostile intentions and indomitable nature. In a terrifying repeat, the Terminator gets back on his feet twice after being shot several times at close range. His resurrection is displayed first for the spectator in spine-chilling close-ups of his moving fingers, opening eyes and head rearing up. The shot is then reprised as a long shot from Sarah's perspective and is followed by a reverse shot of an astonished and frightened Sarah, who cannot understand how the man could survive such gunshots. The repetition of the shot amplifies the viewer's fear, as it is shared and mediated by Sarah's, propelling the film into the realm of horror. The Terminator is likened to a zombie, rising up from the dead again and again, which puts him squarely in the category of monsters.

The Terminator thus highlights the negative aspects of hypermasculinity, exemplifying the categories defined by Mosher and Sirkin in their Hypermasculinity Inventory ('Calloused Sex Attitudes', 'Danger as Exciting' and 'Violence as Manly'),[54] to which J.A. Hall adds 'toughness as self-control over emotions'.[55] The Terminator embodies the 'fantasy of robotism as emulating what we most fear, by abandoning emotion so as to live forever'.[56] Schwarzenegger maintains the same grim, impassive and determined expression throughout the movie, never registering any emotion (so that critics applauded his casting, despite what many saw as his poor acting skills[57]). Even Kyle Reese, in spite of the emphasis on his physical suffering, is partly contaminated by robotism. Traumatised by the rise of the machines, he behaves like one, aping the Terminator's every move. He steals his clothes from a weaker human being, a homeless man, finds a gun and tracks down Sarah, who reacts with fear at this menacing stalker. Only when he shoots the Terminator is it made clear that he is on her side, but even then he is unable to understand human emotions, such as Sarah's initial fear and confusion and then her growing attachment. When she asks what women of the future are like, Kyle answers, 'Good fighters', to which she replies with a sigh: 'That's not what I meant.' Kyle evaluates all humans in terms of combat ability, even Sarah, with whom he falls in love because she trained her son to become a great military leader. Kyle can therefore be seen as the Terminator's contaminated human double, displaying some of the same hypermasculine traits: physical strength, skill with weapons and stunted emotions.

However, what distinguishes the Terminator as a 'hypermasculine monster' is his cruelty towards his female victims, echoing sociological and psychological research on hypermasculinity that associates it with physical and sexual aggression against women.[58] Acting on his mission to kill Sarah Connor, he proceeds by methodically killing all the Sarah Connors listed in the phone book, as well as Sarah's roommate, Ginger, whom he mistakes for her. His attacks on the first Sarah Connor and on Ginger are presented in a much more detailed, violent and frightening way than his attack on men, in the police station for example. In both cases, the Terminator forces entry into these women's homes, remaining calm and composed before every obstacle (dog, boyfriend), while the women react with terror. Their terror is underlined by the close-ups of their frozen faces and the use of slow motion to depict the Terminator's movements, as he points his gun at them and shoots repeatedly, even after they have fallen to the floor, standing high above their agonised bodies. The Terminator's coldness, dominating position and casual use of violence clearly echo the categories of the Hypermasculinity Inventory developed by Mosher, Sirkin and Hall.

In the same way, Brundlefly (post-transformation Seth) is presented in *The Fly* as dominating and even threatening, as he seeks to assert power and control over the women around him. After his transformation, the hypermasculine Seth becomes aggressive towards women, relentlessly dragging them towards the telepod to transform them into perfect partners who will satisfy his increasing sexual needs. He manhandles Ronnie and yells at her when she refuses to go in the telepod, before leaving her to roam the bars in search of a more willing sexual and teletransportation prey, to the sound of powerful brass music signalling his new-found aggressiveness. His callousness is revealed when he bets on a woman in a bar, treating her like a prostitute who can be bought in an arm-wrestling match. Yet as the scene moves on, he becomes creepy and menacing, first when he declares that he 'takes bodies apart and puts them back together again', then when he stops and watches the girl intently as they arrive at his deserted warehouse. The gothic setting – a loft converted into a mad scientist's laboratory – finally bears out what had only been hinted at in previous scenes, as the characters get out of the taxi in the rain and smoke and climb the dark stairs to the isolated apartment, on a soundtrack of rapid discordant string music: this is the lair of a psychotic madman whom all should fear, as Ronnie states at the end of the scene: 'Be afraid, be very afraid.' Indeed, both *The Fly* and *The Terminator* equate the hypermasculine male to a serial killer, explicitly in the case of the Terminator, described as a 'one day pattern killer' by the police, and implicitly in *The Fly* through location and atmosphere, thus assimilating hypermasculinity to a dangerous psychosis producing violent and deviant men, if not monsters. In fact, hypermasculinity in *The Fly* is the first stage in a moral and physical deterioration that transforms a gentle and touching protagonist into a frightening and monstrous predator. As Fabien Boully suggests, the film could therefore be seen as an ironic take on the superhero,[59] especially in the penultimate sequence where Brundlefly breaks through the window of a doctor's office to carry Ronnie back to his apartment – his impressive jumps, the way he carries Ronnie, her arms around him, and his insect nature are all reminiscent of a putrescent Spiderman. Criticising the American obsession with bodily prowess and physical strength, *The Fly* presents hypermasculinity as a transient and delusive fantasy that leads only to violence and decay, as the hard body decomposes to reveal the brutal insect within.

American science fiction films of the 1980s have participated, to a large extent, in the reconstruction of hegemonic masculinity by promoting white muscular bodies capable of withstanding any threat. As such, the films can be seen as both producers and products of the hypermasculine ideal of the 1980s, an ideal of muscular masculinity that reflected anxious concern with national military strength as well as individual bodily strength. This body of films presents *fantasies* of hypermasculinity, which can be cathartic and empowering – part of what the Terminator represents, according to James Cameron[60] – but also cautionary, shown as delusive and even debilitating, as in *The Fly* or *RoboCop*. Indeed, the films are structured on a central tension between invulnerability and vulnerability where the body on display is often a body in pain. Furthermore, science fiction films of the 1980s repeatedly feature transformations or mutant bodies that emphasise the male body's hybridity and instability, with hypermasculinity being only one face – or phase – of multiple masculine identities. Thus, hypermasculine science fiction films are more ambivalent than critics like Claudia Springer, Susan Jeffords or Pauline Kael have acknowledged. Like Yvonne Tasker, I find it 'more appropriate to frame an analysis in terms of "both/and"' by following her argument that the muscular heroes of action films both enact and call into question the masculine qualities that they embody.[61] Indeed, as genre films, these movies have what Thomas Schatz calls the 'capacity to play it both ways',[62] enacting the fantasies of the audience by upholding the ideal of hypermasculinity through iconic heroes but also criticising hypermasculinity as a monstrous mutation, perhaps as a soothing response to the anxieties of the male audience faced with an unrealisable masculine ideal of invulnerability and bodily prowess. In so doing, these films could be seen as prolonging the men's movements of the 1970s, highlighting the ways in which men, too (or rather *especially*, women being pushed to the sidelines) are victims of hegemonic masculinity, in terms of physical expectations as well as economic power, as we will see in Chapter 2.

2

Dystopia and Class War

While a strand of 1980s science fiction provided 'escapism' and 'good feelings',[1] including some of the most successful science fiction films of the decade such as *The Empire Strikes Back* (Irvin Kershner, 1980), *Return of the Jedi* (Richard Marquand, 1983), *ET* (Steven Spielberg, 1982) and the *Back to the Future* trilogy (Robert Zemeckis, 1985, 1989, 1990), 1980s science fiction also encompassed a series of much darker, even visibly dystopian films. These films have rarely been discussed as a specific cycle,[2] most critics focusing either on the generally upbeat renaissance of the genre as a whole in the 1980s[3] or on bleak outliers, especially the iconic *Blade Runner* (Ridley Scott, 1982).[4] Yet a dystopian streak is apparent in such diverse films as *Escape from New York* (John Carpenter, 1981), *Outland* (Peter Hyams, 1981), *The Terminator* (James Cameron, 1984), *RoboCop* (Paul Verhoeven, 1987), *The Running Man* (Paul Michael Glaser, 1987), *They Live* (John Carpenter, 1988) and *Total Recall* (Paul Verhoeven, 1990),[5] all set in decadent worlds blighted by the consequences of ultra-capitalism and dehumanised by ubiquitous technology. In these iniquitous democracies or totalitarian corporate regimes, the authorities are at best inefficient, more often corrupt, no longer a support system for the heroes as they were in American sci-fi films of the 1950s like *Them!*

Masculinity in Contemporary Science Fiction Cinema

(Gordon Douglas, 1954) and *The War of the Worlds* (Byron Haskin, 1953), but opponents to be vanquished. Dystopian films of the 1980s thus remain in the paranoid/narcissistic spirit of the 1970s described by Christopher Lasch in *The Culture of Narcissism*,[6] and reflect the continuing post-Watergate distrust of Americans in their leaders[7] that had featured so prominently in 1970s science fiction, as in *Soylent Green* (Richard Fleischer, 1973), *Rollerball* (Norman Jewison, 1975), *Invasion of the Body Snatchers* (Philip Kaufman, 1978) and of course *Alien* (Ridley Scott, 1979), with its all-powerful Company more than willing to sacrifice individual lives to further its economic interests.

Indeed, more often than not, 1980s dystopias specifically target the economic elites as greedy and corrupt, in a critique of the 'greed is good' ideology of the Reagan era and its economic policy promoting lower taxes for the rich, deregulation of the economy and investment in technology. The heroes are presented as marginalised outcasts victimised by self-seeking and untrustworthy magnates only interested in their own gain at the expense of the rest of humanity. A form of class resentment can therefore be felt in this body of films, that of white male workers buffeted by the economic and social changes of the 1980s. Indeed, as major industries like defence or automobile continued to downsize and information technology transformed the economy, many semi-skilled working-class and lower-middle-class men lost their well-paying jobs.[8] The wages of male production workers remained stagnant,[9] while unemployment rose to almost 10 per cent in 1982–3,[10] with the fastest-growing occupations in the mostly feminised low-paid service sector (waiters and waitresses, nurses, janitors, cashiers).[11] Many of these men felt they had lost not only their economic status but also a sense of masculine worth, since, as Joseph Pleck underlines, industrial working-class jobs are at the foundation of a 'traditional' masculinity associated with physical labour.[12]

This chapter argues that Hollywood science fiction dystopias of the 1980s address the concerns of working-class males (an often-forgotten segment of film audiences but an important audience for science fiction) by highlighting the alienating nature of (American) capitalist society and revalidating working-class masculine identity against decadent elites. To this end, the films oppose two different structures of hierarchy: the corporate structure that scorns working-class men and places them at the bottom of the ladder is offset by a hierarchy of masculinities in which the working-class representatives of traditional masculinity appear as the only reliable safeguards in disintegrating dystopian societies. The chapter will thus analyse the structures of power *within* masculinity by focusing on the intersection of masculinity and class.

Interestingly, class is rarely mentioned by American film critics who, when they do review science fiction films, tend to focus mainly on the films' special effects. It could be argued that this blindness to very visible class tensions was part of a more general denial in public discourse of class inequalities in a country that extols social mobility, particularly during the Reagan era. To remedy this erasure of class, also found in academic discourse on science fiction,[13] this chapter will show how dystopian films of the 1980s are structured on a clash between working-class men and the political and economic elites. In a nightmarish version of our post-industrial societies, working-class men are abandoned by the powerful and left to wander in urban landscapes where technology is replacing them. Like the technology they support, decadent elites are completely dehumanised, obsessed with profit at the expense of their fellow men. Science fiction dystopias work therefore to revalidate a besieged working-class male identity, by staging its rebellion against the perverted type of masculinity embodied by the elites, but also by opposing it to 'others' constructed as beneath it. Dystopian films can then be considered as subversive to the extent that they visibly criticise contemporary society, especially in the way they question relations of domination within capitalism, following the dystopian literary tradition best exemplified by George Orwell's *1984*. But this chapter will finally argue that their inscription within the genre of science fiction works to paper over the cracks and resolve class tensions through generic conventions. As a genre, science fiction is indeed both a space of negotiation where the fears of a certain category of population can be expressed and social tensions exorcised and an ideological tool that, in the end, maintains the status quo.[14]

Dystopian Societies
Urban decay

In 1980s dystopias, the future always appears gloomy: the cinematography of films like *Escape from New York*, *Outland* or *Blade Runner* is characterised by darkness, with most scenes having been shot at night or in dimly lit sets. This is particularly striking in *Escape from New York*, since the events are supposed to take place over a 24-hour time period, yet the film includes very few daytime scenes: the beautiful panoramic shot of the New York skyline at daybreak contrasts starkly with the rest of the film, set mostly within the murky city and its decrepit buildings. Nature is practically absent from films that take place in urban landscapes, be it the mining colonies of *Outland* and *Total Recall* or the decayed cities of *Escape from New York*, *Blade Runner* and *RoboCop*. The cities have become claustrophobic nightmares where freedom can be found only in natural areas that appear completely artificial and unreal, for instance in the quasi-psychedelic final scenes of *Total Recall* and the original version of *Blade Runner*. These utopian endings appear all the more improbable as bright colours suddenly fill the screen, and stand out in otherwise gritty films dominated by grey and black hues. The city appears as a place of corruption and decadence, a traditional theme in classical Hollywood cinema[15] but one that had particular resonance for 1980s audiences.

Indeed, many American cities, especially in the Northeast and Midwest, were deeply in trouble in the early 1980s, as a result of a sharp demographic and industrial decline which began after the war and accelerated dramatically in the 1970s. As vital industries moved away and those who could left for the suburbs, cities like New York, Chicago, Boston and Cleveland experienced great financial difficulties in the 1970s,[16] aggravated in the 1980s by the budget cuts imposed by the Reagan Administration as a means to reduce federal spending. Cities thus had to cut spending not only in infrastructure and education, but also in law enforcement, which led to a critical increase in crime rates, for instance in New York, where they reached their highest point in 1981 and remained high for the rest of the decade.[17] The alarming rise of crime is at the basis of Carpenter's idea for *Escape from New York*, which begins with an all the more frightening statement since it only exaggerated a known reality: '1988. The Crime Rate in the United States Rises 400 Percent'. The transformation of New York into a prison where criminals reign supreme perfectly reflects the urban crisis of the 1980s and the resulting fears aroused by the city. The film was shot in St Louis, which, as Carpenter explains, had been partly destroyed by fire and could not be rebuilt as it was in the middle of a recession. The city was in ruins, and had let the crew cut off the electricity, set fires and put trash everywhere.[18] In his review, Vincent Canby stresses the relevance of a film that 'works so effectively as a warped vision of ordinary urban blight that it seems to be some kind of hallucinatory editorial'.[19] This nightmarish vision of cities in decay can also be found in *Blade Runner* and *RoboCop*, which present cities devastated by the effects of capitalism and industry. *RoboCop* is purposely set in emblematic Detroit, the symbol of urban breakdown due to deindustrialisation, while *Blade Runner* takes place in Los Angeles, pointing the finger at urban sprawl and its environmental consequences. The latter film opens with an aerial night shot of the sprawling city, lit up sporadically by factory chimneys spitting fire. The city dominates the screen throughout the film, the towering skyscrapers forbidding escape. Omnipresent advertising on huge talking screens and constantly falling acid rain further contribute to creating an oppressive and unpleasant environment. The film thus evokes recognisable urban problems, including overpopulation, pollution and poverty,[20] in a dark blending of science fiction and *film noir* that has had a great impact on science fiction since.

Alien invasion

Dystopian films underline how ultra-capitalism threatens the social fabric by dividing the population into two disconnected groups: a marginalised underclass living in the cities' slums and a powerful elite shut off from the rest of society. The division is especially apparent in *Escape from New York*, where it is horizontal – the deviant criminals are relegated to a circumscribed zone clearly delineated on a map in the film's introduction – and in *Blade Runner*, where it is vertical[21] – the industrial magnate Tyrell lives alone on the last floor of an empty skyscraper and communicates only with replicants (i.e., mechanical androids) or via videophone, while the streets of Los Angeles swarm with people of mixed origins. In both films, the elites have deserted the cities, which are invaded by racial and ethnic aliens demonised as potentially subversive 'monsters' in what Michael Rogin has called American political demonology.[22] *Blade Runner*'s Los Angeles crawls with lowly Asian workers who barely speak English, from the noodle shack cook to the artificial eye-maker. Communication is difficult: the cook does not understand what Deckard (Harrison Ford) wants at the beginning of the film, while the eye-maker will not answer the replicants' questions, repeating that he only makes eyes. No identification is possible with these characters, who are usually pushed to the background and presented as incongruous and fundamentally other: the Asian eye-maker for instance is particularly strange, talking to himself and letting out odd little cries, dressed in a bizarre fur coat attached to cables. Furthermore, the film repeatedly associates the immigrant workers with the animal world: Deckard asks an old Asian couple to analyse a snake scale and is sent to an Arab artificial snake-maker, making his way through a miscellaneous throng of people and animals. Every time Deckard or Roy, the two white heroes, confront an immigrant, the same thing happens: the foreigner seems not to understand English, therefore cannot answer their query, then eventually answers in English under duress. This scenario confirms the oft-repeated accusation xenophobes make against immigrants, suspected of pretending not to speak English so that they can circumvent the rules of dominant society. An impassable barrier thus has to be maintained between such degraded aliens and the white workers embodied by Deckard and Roy – even though the replicants are presented as exploited labourers and compared to blacks in the original version's voice-over (Deckard translates 'skinjobs' by 'niggers'), their physical appearance associates them clearly with the Aryan ideal of a 'master race'.[23] Hence, the recurrent use of shop counters as a line of demarcation between the foreign lumpenproletariat and Deckard.

Whereas *Blade Runner*, inspired by *Metropolis* (Fritz Lang, 1927),[24] is rather critical of a deeply unequal society where workers are exploited and forced to work in deplorable conditions (the smoke of the noodle shack, the extreme cold of the laboratory), *Escape from New York* is much more ambivalent in its presentation of those excluded from American society.

Dystopia and Class War

Indeed, it conjures up the nightmarish fantasy of a barbaric America as a society dominated by blacks, resorting to a savage imagery pertaining to 'a distinctive American political tradition fearful of primitivism and disorder that developed in response to peoples of color'.[25] The character of the Duke (Isaac Hayes) is especially ambivalent, as Vincent Canby underlines with unease:

> Mr Hayes [is] very impressive as the flamboyant Duke. Is it a coincidence that when he exhorts a crowd of followers about their coming freedom, he sounds more than a little like the Rev. Dr Martin Luther King Jr? The fact that he's the film's principal villain may not sit well with some audiences, but then perhaps they'll respond to his style.[26]

The Duke encapsulates the racial anxieties of white America by combining the charisma and oratory style of the most respected civil rights leader with the violence of the 'Brutal Black Buck'. In fact, the character superimposes many layers of stereotypes: 'the big baadddd nigger'[27] (the presence of Hayes is an homage to blaxploitation), the aggressive Black Power activist, as well as the fearsome 1980s drug dealer, so that the combination of black activism and ghetto violence plays with the fears of white spectators, reminding them that African Americans could one day demand reparation for 400 years of oppression. The Duke, indeed, behaves like a statesman or an African potentate, driven around in a limousine adorned with chandeliers, all the more luxurious as gas has become scarce in the blighted city, addressing the crowd from a balcony before a boxing match like a Roman emperor opening the Games and forcing the US president (Donald Pleasance), his hostage, to bow before him and shout: 'You're the Duke of New York, you're A number one.'

The rule of the Duke is, in effect, a distorted reflection of the 'legitimate' president's power. His barbarous methods (boxing fights to the death, human-target darts) parallel those of a pseudo-democratic regime that jails for life all those who do not follow its rules. The brutal and sarcastic character of the Duke enables us to question some of the American institutions that oppress a large part of the population, notably African Americans, by taking away the aura of one of the main pillars of US democracy, the

President of the United States. According to Carpenter, this aspect was at the heart of his original screenplay in 1974 and was one of the reasons for its delayed production, as the studios 'felt it was a too mocking film' in the aftermath of the Watergate scandal and Nixon's resignation. Donald Pleasance was purposely chosen by Carpenter to play the bumbling president after his interpretation of a similarly 'emasculated and tortured' character in *Cul-de-sac* (Roman Polanski, 1966).[28] The virile Duke is thus opposed to a president who is continually humiliated, for instance when he is tied to a chair and forced to wear a blonde wig. His emasculation symbolises the breakdown of US institutions, which is expressed visually by the disintegration of his body. Indeed, the President, a short, fat and bald man, is shown trembling and sweating throughout his captivity, constantly sagging and unable to stand tall. In a mocking scene, the Duke shoots at the President whose flabby bound body has become a live target, shuddering at each shot while his terrified eyes seek assistance in vain (Figure 2.1). The confrontation and reversal in power satirically points to the proximity between a white America that sees itself as legitimate and a tyrannical regime dominated by blacks and based on the survival of the fittest.

Yet such a proximity between democracy and anarchy, blacks and whites, is so disquieting that the film has to distance the black alien in order to isolate white masculinity from any 'contamination' by the racial Other. It falls on the hero, Snake Plissken (Kurt Russell), to clearly demarcate white masculinity from black masculinity and ensure the superior

Figure 2.1 The President's humiliation in *Escape from New York*

status of the former over the latter. Snake Plissken is strongly masculinised throughout the film, exhibiting many of the attributes of hypermasculinity described in the previous chapter. His muscular body is enhanced by his costume, which includes tight camouflage pants and a sleeveless black undershirt soon removed to reveal a sculpted chest and an impressive snake tattoo. His character draws, somewhat satirically, on the archetypal strong silent type who never flinches under pain, as evidenced in the unequal boxing match opposing Snake to an ogre-like gigantic bearded skinhead who beats him mercilessly with a baseball bat. His virile status puts him on the same level as the Duke, yet the two men never really come into contact. They meet only once and exchange just a few words; Snake gives the Duke a smouldering look to which the latter nonchalantly replies: 'I've heard of you, I thought you were dead', before hitting him on the head with his cane. There is no verbal or physical connection between the two men, who are constantly separated in the editing through repeated crosscutting. Although Snake is also an outcast, he is set apart from the Duke, whose rebellion he does not help even though it could benefit him. Forced to collaborate with the authorities who have inserted explosives in his neck as an 'incentive' to rescue the President, Snake never considers taking sides with the socially excluded and liberating the prisoners.

As such, he participates in the racial demonisation that has always prevented white workers from uniting with black workers against the dominant class, a persisting phenomenon in the 1980s, as evidenced in the interviews of white working-class men led by Michelle Fine, Lois Weis, Judi Addleston and Julia Marusza at the end of the decade. The interviewees defined themselves in opposition to 'Others', mainly blacks and white women, whom they blamed for their economic degradation, in an effort to 'sustain a *place* within the [gender/race] hierarchy and secure the very *hierarchies* that assure their place'.[29] Indeed, rather than challenging the political decisions that led to the devaluation of all workers and fighting for more equitable social conditions, white working-class males have been holding on to a hierarchy which offers them little reward. Symptomatically, Snake only associates with white partners to maintain the powers that be, helping the President cross the bridge and scale the wall that separates the powerful from the powerless, while preventing the Duke's escape. The

President can then have his revenge: he shoots the Duke from the top of the wall, vengefully shouting back the same words he was humiliated into uttering ('You're the Duke of New York, A number one') as a means of recovering his lost honour. The violent Black Buck has to be punished at the end of the film, which maintains the status quo: America's racial Others remain caged in, and the white authorities stand untouched.

All's well that ends well? In fact, the sarcastic tone of the film calls into question such an orderly restoration by ridiculing the President until the very end. His revenge against the Duke is so extreme that he appears more like a madman than a respectable statesman, repeating the same humiliating words over and over again, his nasal squawking turning into a halting low voice as his body sags onto the railing. Moreover, the low-angle long shot is used here not to magnify the character, as is usually the case, but on the contrary to underline the President's short height and plumpness by placing him behind a guardrail that stretches across the frame, cutting him in half and widening the screen. The President appears worn out and almost deranged in his torn and dirty shirt. This image contrasts starkly with his return to power in the following scene, which shows him seated and surrounded by watchful bodyguards as he is being shaved and made up by dexterous assistants. The scene comments sarcastically on the vanity and vacuity of political leaders, confirmed by the President's canned answer to Snake's question about those who gave their lives for him: 'Well, I wanna thank them, huh, this nation appreciates their sacrifice.' The fact that he hesitates, clearing his throat after the first part of the sentence, and that he avoids making any eye contact with Snake, looking at himself in the mirror instead, confirms what the film has suggested all along: that the authorities are utterly indifferent to the fate of those they are supposed to represent, including those who sacrificed their lives to protect them.

Marginalised heroes

The President's indifference justifies Snake's final decision to substitute a jazz tape for the tape supposed to save humanity from annihilation, which he carefully destroys in the last scene of the film. Snake refuses to be part of legitimate society and become humanity's saviour. He presents himself as a criminal with his leitmotiv 'Call me Snake', a nickname evoking the mob rather than the Army to which he once belonged, and spurns the police chief who asks him to join and informally calls him 'Snake', replying: 'The name's Plissken', a way of claiming his dignity as a free man who no longer has to collaborate with a brutal police force. However, Snake's rejection of any commitment prevents his redemption, since he prefers to remain alone, retreating in individualistic nihilism. Like the antisocial heroes of westerns such as *The Searchers* (John Ford, 1956) or *High Plains Drifter* (Clint Eastwood, 1973), Snake's hero status is announced by a reputation that precedes him (every character recognises the famous thought-to-be-dead Snake Plissken) but is complicated by his self-willed marginalisation and unfeeling hostility to all. The last scene evokes the traditional ending of a western, with Snake leaving on his own and smoking a cigarette, but its meaning is profoundly altered by his destruction of the tape and the fade-to-black that ends the film. Instead of an open landscape suggesting possible salvation, there is no horizon, no prospect of redemption because the hero has deliberately thrown away his opportunity to save humanity, underlining the artificiality of many Hollywood endings that insist on reconciling the hero with society. Snake remains an outcast from beginning to end, as underlined by his pirate's limp and eye patch, which suggests that he sees the world from a single self-centred perspective. The eye patch partially blocks the hero's eyes and prevents the audience's total identification, already made difficult by his chosen marginality and an ironic distance on the part of the character as well as the film.

The heroes of *Escape from New York* and *Blade Runner* are therefore marginalised both within the story, as they distance themselves from corrupt authorities, and in the films, where they are not always the centre of attention and the focus of audience identification. Indeed, easy identification is complicated by the heroes' questionable moral status as well as uncertain identity and goals. Snake's past is blurry, either criminal, as suggested by his nickname and tattoo, or military, as mentioned briefly at the beginning of the film. The same is true of Deckard, whose occupation is, in addition, morally reprehensible, as Peter Ruppert underlines:

> Deckard's function as a blade runner puts him clearly in the service of corporate interests, and, since replicants are explicitly

compared to runaway black slaves, makes it difficult for us to identify with him at this point in the film.[30]

Over the course of the film, Deckard will waver between his duty as a blade runner, that is, an assassin working for the authorities, and his growing compassion for those he is hunting down, but his evolution and point of view are somewhat eclipsed by the other plot line of the film, the replicants' quest – especially in the version Ridley Scott originally defended, the director's cut, where Deckard is not given a voice-over. In fact, Deckard is completely absent from long scenes featuring the replicants, who are much more spectacular in terms of physique, costume and behaviour.

Indeed, as David Desser argues, Roy (Rutger Hauer) could be seen as the central character of the film.[31] His evolution is very dramatic, climaxing in a mesmerising scene of redemption opposite a completely ineffectual Deckard. In this final confrontation, Roy is transformed from a savage and frightening creature who licks his dead partner's blood and howls like a wolf, into a divine prophet who points out Deckard's moral and physical deficiencies. Roy is laden with biblical symbols: resembling Christ when he drives a nail into his hand to stay alive, he then appears God-like with a dove in his hand,[32] to the sound of ringing bells and filmed in a magnifying low-angle shot. Roy becomes a guiding prophet, showing Deckard the path to redemption and a superior state of being, both physically and morally. Whereas Deckard nearly misses his jump, painfully landing on a protruding beam, Roy gracefully jumps across to the other building – in general, Roy's fluid yet controlled movements contrast with Deckard's breathless contortions. Roy also initiates him to higher morals, expounding the fearful slave-like condition of the replicants ('Quite an experience to live in fear … That's what it means, to be a slave') before saving his life. Contrary to the death-giving Deckard, Roy chooses to preserve life beyond his own death, which he eventually accepts.[33] His death constitutes the most memorable scene in the film through its visual beauty, poetic dialogue and emotional intensity. The spectacular shots of Roy stand in sharp contrast with those of Deckard, sunk against a column in the dark, petrified and mute, while the former stands erect in the light, majestic and lyrical.

In fact, as many critics have underlined,[34] Roy is the one who brings emotion into the film, notably in his last poetically riveting monologue, accompanied by a magical flute: 'I've seen things you people wouldn't believe. Attack ships on fire off the shoulder of Orion. I watched seabeams glitter in the dark near the Tanhauser gate. All those moments will be lost in time, like tears in rain.' As death sets in, the lines are spoken with more and more difficulty, and the monologue ends with Roy gracefully lowering his head, his blond hair lit up like a halo, and releasing a dove, the symbol of the soul and ultimate proof of his humanity. Roy embodies a superior masculinity, poetic and visionary, because he is able to understand and go beyond his destiny. Thus he becomes an icon, as underlined by the prolonged reverse shot of an awe-struck Deckard. The final dissolve and superimposition of the men's faces emphasise their proximity and the revelatory impact of Roy's death on Deckard, who finally becomes clearsighted and sides with the replicants against the authorities to save the last android.[35] Nevertheless, Roy remains the most fascinating and complex hero of the film, the 'light that burns twice as bright' and illuminates the dark world of *Blade Runner*.

More generally, Deckard tends to be eclipsed by the visually impressive futuristic world of *Blade Runner*.[36] The audience is less interested in his story than in contemplating a new world full of mesmerising objects, including the entrancing half-mechanical replicants, for instance when they perform for Sebastian. The scenery relegates the main character to the background. This 'excessive scenography'[37] reinforces the marginalisation of a hero without any clear identity, who becomes another detail in a richly elaborate *mise en scène*. Deckard is repeatedly lost in a diverse crowd (e.g. in the Arabic bar) or decentred in wide-angle shots of spectacular sets, at Tyrell's for instance. His first appearance presents him as a man in the crowd, submersed in an oppressive environment. The scene opens with a long shot presenting the urban setting: towering skyscrapers supporting huge advertising screens, flying cars and airships blaring out the benefits of life in the colonies. The camera tracks into the city, focusing again on an advertisement, a dragon neon restaurant sign, while the people jostle through the crowd hidden under umbrellas. Beyond the crowd sits Deckard, waiting for a seat at the noodle shack, singled out by the camera

Figure 2.2 Deckard's first appearance in *Blade Runner*

as it tracks forward and pauses in a medium-long shot, where he is backlit against glaring neons and repeatedly hidden from view by passers-by in the foreground (Figure 2.2). A second fixed shot establishes his character status, yet lasts only three seconds before the film cuts to a reverse shot of the advertising airship. Eventually, the Chinese cook calls Deckard, who is just another customer in an anonymous crowd.

The dystopian worlds of *Escape from New York* and *Blade Runner* are dehumanised environments where the heroes are misfits. Both films begin with lengthy scenes unveiling the setting, while the main character's entrance is delayed and played down. Just like *Blade Runner*, *Escape from New York* starts with an introductory intertitle, followed by an interactive map of Manhattan explaining how the island has been transformed into a maximum-security prison. After a short scene showing the brutal methods of the police against a backdrop of New York landmarks in the dark (the skyline, the Statue of Liberty), the camera stops in the Security Control base that guards the prison, lingering on the helicopter landing area. A bus enters the frame in the background, and we see Snake get off, surrounded by three policemen. Like Deckard, the medium shot that establishes his character status is very brief and decentred: he appears at the edge of the shot, which is dominated by the glaring lights of the bus in the foreground, as an ordinary prisoner who has just been arrested. The following scene systematically shows him in medium-long shots that include elements of the prison, denying him any close-ups. Snake walks through the prison under police escort, hemmed in by the alienating structure of the prison; his body is crisscrossed by a metallic staircase, then framed by a narrow white corridor where a loudspeaker blares repressive orders and policemen watch him intently.

Escape from New York and *Blade Runner* both relegate their heroes to positions of secondary importance to focus on dark inhuman worlds. In both cases, the reviews paid much more attention to atmosphere and scenery than to the characters, even criticising their weakness: Vincent Canby only briefly mentions Snake Plissken, while Janet Maslin finds Harrison Ford to be 'a colorless hero' for a movie which she praises as 'darkly fanciful'.[38] In fact, the films denounce a widespread loss of identity in contemporary post-industrial and technologically advanced societies, which affects first and foremost the hegemonic position of men, who are sidelined from their traditional status as heroes at the centre of the narrative. The films explore the harrowing consequences of a dehumanised but also demasculinised world, where male leaders are emasculated and indifferent to the plight of their more masculine subjects, leading to their rebellion. These consequences would be further explored throughout the 1980s, notably in dystopias featuring cyborgs, where technology and corrupt authorities have replaced men with machines, in a process of literal dehumanisation.

Worlds Devoid of Humanity

On top of their general critique of contemporary society, Hollywood science fiction films of the 1980s also address specific anxieties linked to the social and economic upheavals of the Reagan era in the United States, especially the obsession with technology and the materialistic greed that characterised the era. The Reagan Administration, indeed, encouraged technological innovation both on a military level in the context of the Cold War, with for instance the Strategic Defense Initiative put forward by President Reagan to build a shield against missiles in space (a project widely thought to be unrealistic and derisively nicknamed 'Star Wars'), and on an economic level, to increase productivity and competitiveness with the Japanese. The Reagan era was also dominated by ostentatious materialism, summed up in the famous phrase 'Greed is healthy',[39] formulated by Ivan Boetsky, a reckless businessman who made the cover of *Time* in December 1986[40] and was later convicted of insider trading; Boetsky inspired the character of Gordon Gekko and his iconic 'Greed is good' speech in *Wall Street* (Oliver Stone, 1987). Such upheavals contributed to undermining the esteem in which white working-class men were held, since their position was weakened by automation and the celebration of white-collar professionals over blue-collar workers. The cyborg dystopias can therefore be seen as addressing their concerns first by expressing a deep fear of technology, and then by denouncing heartless elites, via cyborg characters that appear alternately as horrific monsters and defenders of a threatened working-class masculinity.

Technophobia

Contrasting with the sense of wonder expressed in some 1950s films such as *Destination Moon* (Irving Pichel, 1950) and *Forbidden Planet* (Fred Wilcox, 1956) or in the space adventures of the *Star Wars* trilogy, dystopias of the 1980s exhibited a nightmarish vision of technology. As such, they reflected and perhaps even exorcised the fears created by the appearance and democratisation in the 1980s of a host of new machines that transformed the daily lives of Americans, such as the answering machine, the VCR, the remote control and especially the computer, which became the first object to be elected 'Man of the Year' by *Time* in 1982.[41] The working class felt especially threatened by the development of automation in industrial sectors like the automobile industry, which, under pressure from Japanese competition, had to restructure, leading to massive lay-offs.[42] American car companies adopted the methods that they thought accounted for the success of Japanese car manufacturers, especially the key concept of 'flexible production', 'utilizing unspecialized, quickly reprogrammable computer-controlled machinery and cross-trained, diversely skilled workers who could move rapidly from job to job as production requirements dictated'.[43] Robert F. Arnold shows how the promise held out by industry leaders that 'the industrial robot would free workers from the drudgery of repetitive, dangerous, mind-numbing and back-breaking assembly-line jobs', unsuccessfully concealed a more cost-conscious agenda that sought to cut labour costs by replacing workers with cheaper robots; this resulted in a fear of robotisation that 'reached epidemic proportions in the early 1980s', exemplified by a 1981 Carnegie-Mellon study predicting that, over the next 20 years, three million more jobs would be lost to industrial robots.[44]

This widespread technophobia is clearly visible in Hollywood science fiction dystopias of the 1980s, notably in *The Terminator* and *RoboCop*. Indeed, *The Terminator* features innumerable machines, and begins with a bleak pre-credit sequence showing a future dominated by massive robots that shoot humans with laser beams and crush their skulls under caterpillar tracks. Every machine is potentially dangerous, and the film repeatedly links the machines of the present with those of the future. For instance, the destructive laser beams of the future are already featured in the high-tech gun sold to the Terminator by a praiseful salesman: 'The beam comes on, you put the red dot where you want the bullet to go. You can't miss.' The irony being, of course, that the salesman will be killed a few seconds later by his expert customer. Similarly, Kyle's falling asleep next to a construction site full of innocuous tracked excavators triggers a nightmare linking them within the same shot to the murderous machines of the future. The camera tracks forward and pans down slightly so that the stones underneath the tracks are revealed to be skulls, and the monotonous purr is suddenly punctuated by the sound of cracking bones. The camerawork intensifies the terrifying aspect of the machines by using close-ups which break them into generic, thus interchangeable, parts: an excavator becomes a war machine through a close-up of its caterpillar tracks. The same is true for the garbage truck at the beginning of the film, the close-ups of its arms, fork and headlight giving it a life of its own (see Chapter 1). Today's trucks may become tomorrow's war machines, as heralded at the time by the car manufacturers' promotion of unspecialised, multifunctional industrial robots. As a matter of fact, apparently harmless machines have a nefarious impact on their users throughout the film. For instance, Sarah's roommate does not hear the telephone ringing or her boyfriend fighting against the Terminator because she is glued to her Walkman, while Sarah inadvertently tells the Terminator where she is by leaving the address on her own answering machine whose message turns out to be especially ironic given the circumstances: 'you're talking to a machine, but don't be shy, machines need love too'.

However, the film presents a significant evolution in the relations between humans and machines, which tends in the end to soothe technophobic anxieties. If the film opens with a seemingly animated garbage truck and its old black driver, a man so worn out and degraded by a dangerous and mind-numbing machine job that he can only grumble a few words before running away, embodying the humiliating fall of status feared by the white working class, the last sequence of the film reverses the oppressive domination of machine over man.[45] Indeed, to get rid of the Terminator's terrifyingly self-willed metallic endoskeleton, Sarah relies on the old-fashioned, specialised machines of an assembly line, reasserting human power and control: crawling out of a press where the Terminator has followed her, she shuts the gate manually and reaches out to the control button, pushing it with the tip of her fingers, so that the Terminator is finally crushed. The Terminator's glistening metallic arm and hand contrast with Sarah's sweaty human hand, shown in close-up, but also with the basic geometrical shapes of simple push button-activated machines. Technophobia is thus exorcised by the scene's reassuring demonstration that machines can be useful to humans as long as they remain under the latter's control. As Robert F. Arnold notes, *The Terminator* finally argues that humans cannot be replaced by robots and that even automated factories require human supervision.[46] The end of the film can be said therefore to celebrate the satisfying victory of humans over robots, at the same time as it reconciles the audience with machines whose simple shapes eventually appear reassuring in comparison with the horrific skeleton of the fleshless Terminator.

Anxieties concerning automation and robotisation can also be found in *RoboCop*, purposely and ironically set in Detroit, which, as Julie F. Codell remarked, stood for 'technological incompetence and the deficit in [US] exports and imports of the automobile'[47] at the time of the film's release (and still does today, so that the film remains topical 30-odd years later). In addition, Detroit represented the collapse of the city, plagued by financial problems and rising crime, a perfect location for Verhoeven to explore and critique the implementation and consequences of the Reaganite policies of deregulation and privatisation. In *RoboCop*, the city is under contract with a big corporation, OCP, to manage a certain number of public services, including the police. The film starts with the death of three policemen, arousing anger among their colleagues, who blame OCP and their budget cuts for these deaths. This proves right when Murphy and his partner call for backup in vain and are outnumbered by a group of criminals, who shoot Murphy dead. Priding itself in having 'gambled in markets traditionally considered non-profit', OCP seeks to cut its labour costs by developing 'a twenty-four hour-a-day police officer, a cop who doesn't need to sleep or eat', in short, a machine. Privatisation and robotisation go hand-in-hand: OCP takes over an entire wing of the police precinct without notifying the police captain, in order to set up their own police officer, Robocop. The policemen understandably fear being replaced, which is strikingly expressed in the scene at the shooting range. The officers are practising target shooting when an unusual noise attracts their attention. The camera tracks forward on a much longer gun, firing in regular bursts, held by a gloved hand at the back of the frame. Instead of making more or less accurate holes in the cardboard target, Robocop destroys it entirely, chopping off its arms then its chest to leave only the head. Dwarfed by Robocop's stature and accuracy, the policemen are impressed but also concerned about their own fate, as one of them bleakly states: 'What are they gonna do, replace us?'

In fact, humans are being replaced by machines on many levels in *RoboCop* since Robocop is him/itself an artificial body created out of and in the end substituted for a human one. Murphy's transformation shows that the body itself, the locus of human mortal essence, can be stripped of its humanness. Murphy's salvaged left arm is thus replaced by a titanium prosthesis, an operation foreshadowed at the beginning of the film in a fake advertisement for artificial hearts, thereby suggesting that the gradual replacement of organs or limbs by prostheses logically results in the creation of cyborgs. Robocop's artificial nature is at first a source of humour, his lack of emotion and simple sentences contrasting with the difficult situations that confront him. He thanks storeowners who have just been robbed for their cooperation, and mechanically tells a young woman whom he saved from rape that she 'has suffered an emotional shock' and that he will 'notify a rape crisis centre'. His lack of empathy is at odds with the traumatised victims' gratitude and his status as a superhero revered by the entire city. Even after having recovered some of his human identity, his articulated movements remain very mechanical and his sentences terse, in a parody of action hero one-liners, for example, his warning to drug traffickers as he busts their cocaine factory: 'Come quietly or there will be [pause] trouble.' Furthermore, the gesture that allows Lewis to recognise the human Murphy under Robocop's armour, when he spins his gun before putting it back in its holster, is borrowed from a fictional hero in a TV show cited earlier in the diegesis, T.J. Lazer. Far from being an individual idiosyncrasy, the gesture is a common trope, itself borrowed from innumerable westerns and police shows. In *RoboCop*, humans tend to disappear under layers of artificial replacements: the policemen are replaced by a cyborg, who is substituted for a human, whose singular identity is in fact made up of common movie tropes.

However, like *The Terminator*, *RoboCop* also opposes two types of machines in order to redeem one of them. The humanoid Robocop is indeed opposed to ED209, a huge bug-like and threatening machine incapable of thought. The fight between Robocop and ED209 brings to mind the one between Sarah and the Terminator. The much bigger and powerfully weaponised ED209 marches determinedly towards Robocop and hurls him to the other end of the room. Like Sarah, Robocop is powerless before such an implacable and invulnerable foe and can only fight back through ruse: he uses one of ED's gun arms to destroy the other and runs down the stairs, where ED's bulk is a hindrance – its 'feet' are too big for the stairs so that it falls over, squealing uncontrollably as it struggles in vain to get back on its feet. In comparison with ED's grotesque awkwardness, Robocop's rigid articulated movements appear much more human. While the camera zooms in on Robocop's face, with an extreme close-up of his eye suggesting an emotional reaction close to fear, the close-ups of ED underline its monstrosity, with a loudspeaker for a head, guns instead of arms and palmed feet likening it to a giant duck. *RoboCop* adopts the same method as *The Terminator* to soothe technophobic anxieties, opposing an out-of-control inhuman machine to one that works to help and protect humanity.

Inhuman elites

The fear of robotisation is associated in *RoboCop* to the dangers of privatisation, which the film sharply criticises by presenting the corporate environment as a dog-eat-dog world where only the ruthless reach the top. As Robocop gradually recovers his human identity and attracts the viewers' sympathy as a hero full of pathos rather than an invulnerable machine, OCP's executives, who created him and control him, appear more and more inhuman. The film is indeed openly satirical of the materialistic cutthroat business culture of the Reagan era, denouncing the pernicious effects of 1980s neoliberalism that *Blade Runner* had already exposed and that Verhoeven would go back to in *Total Recall*.

Reagan himself had set the tone by declaring in 1983 that he wanted above all to see that the United States remained 'a country where someone can always get rich'.[48] Ronald and Nancy Reagan restored glitz and glamour to the White House, contrasting with the Carters' simplicity. The President's inauguration was followed by a series of lavish receptions, for which the First Lady was rumoured to have spent $25,000 on her wardrobe.[49] The Reagan era promoted wealth while condemning the poor – it was the era of 'yuppies' obsessed with social and material success, when TV shows on the rich and powerful, like *Dynasty* (ABC, 1981–9) and *Dallas* (CBS, 1978–91), attracted a wide audience, and real estate magnate Donald Trump's autobiography (*The Art of the Deal*, 1987) became a bestseller. This obsession with making a profit can also be found in the proliferation of mergers and acquisitions: in the 1980s, one out of five Fortune 500 companies was either taken over, merged or forced to go private.[50] Mark C. Carnes describes how the culture of work changed because of increasingly fierce competition that forced well-established companies like IBM or GM to lay off thousands of workers: well-paying, unionised lifetime employment virtually disappeared in the 1980s. For instance, IBM, whose unofficial slogan was 'a job for life', laid off 80,000 workers between 1985 and 1994, that is to say more than a third of its workforce. Many companies downsized or moved abroad, such as Nike, which closed its American shoe factory and moved its operations to Indonesia. Thus, corporate ethos changed radically: companies were no longer seen as harmonious family-like communities where loyal workers would spend their whole lives, but became places for personal ambition and individual promotion, where workers competed against each other for status, maximum profitability and productivity.

RoboCop clearly draws on this context to present an extreme version of the Reagan era's reckless materialism and ruthless competition, which are inextricably bound to rampant sexism. For instance, the recurrent TV show featuring an old pervert surrounded by tall big-breasted giggling blondes repeats the same joke over and over again – 'I'll buy that for a dollar' – explicitly linking consumerism and women's objectification. The show is watched by several male characters, who burst out laughing at the host's continual sexist remarks. The film also links materialism and sexism through the character of the ambitious yuppie Bob Morton, who celebrates his promotion to vice-president by inviting two female 'friends' to his house to share champagne and cocaine. The women are dutifully impressed by his new position (one says: 'I love the way it sounds: "vice-president"', to which the other adds: 'It just turns me on'), while he ironically tells these stereotypical bimbos in glittering dresses that he 'loves intelligent women'. Moreover, Bob Morton belongs to a clearly patriarchal structure, OCP, where two old men, the stern but fatherly 'Old Man' (Daniel O'Herlihy) and his iron-hearted vice-president, Dick Jones (Ronny Cox), dominate an exclusively male executive hierarchy. Only men compete to reach the top, while women are relegated to secretarial positions deemed inconsequential: when visiting Jones in his office, drug dealer Clarence Boddicker cockily tries to pick up the latter's secretary before gluing his gum on her name plate.

OCP is presented as an extremely competitive environment, which can be read in the spatial distribution of its headquarters. The conference room where the executives meet the directors is at the top of the building, and can be reached by glass elevators that display and at the same time constrain users, who are visible to all. Even the toilets reflect hierarchical distinctions: Bob Morton's promotion gets him a gold card that allows him to have access to nicer toilets or what the company has called the 'executive lounge'. Verhoeven uses this vulgar setting to ridicule corporate competition, staging the crucial confrontation between Bob Morton and Dick Jones in the toilets. The camerawork emphasises the satirical tone of the

Dystopia and Class War

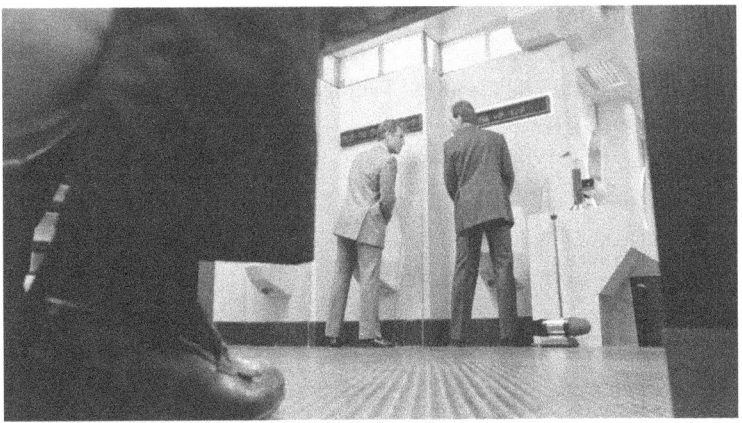

Figure 2.3 The toilet scene in *RoboCop*

scene by opening with a floor-level shot showing in the foreground Jones's pants around his ankles (he is sitting on a toilet seat in a cubicle) and in the background Morton and his colleague standing in front of the urinals (Figure 2.3). The scene then underlines the executives' cowardice: they all leave the toilets in a hurry as soon as Jones's name is mentioned, with Morton's colleague zipping up his fly before he has actually finished urinating, making a stain on his trousers. The competitive ethos is scraped of any glamour to reveal its darkest demons; Jones abuses Morton physically and verbally, pulling his head back and threatening him crudely: 'You just fucked with the wrong guy.' Jones will actually eliminate Morton by having him assassinated, validating the expression Morton had used so nonchalantly in the toilets: '[Jones]'s got this killer rep, but it's a smoke screen.'

Indeed, the expressions that were so common in the American business world of the 1980s, like 'out for the kill' or 'hostile takeover', are taken literally in the film: Jones forces Morton to bow in front of his image by sending a henchman who shoots him in both knees while comparing the competition between them to a poker game: 'It helps if you think of it as a game. Every game has a winner … and a loser. I'm cashing you out, Bob.' The film exposes the metaphor of the business world as a competitive sport: the goal is quite simply to eliminate your competitors. Science fiction films show, in effect, how the twin goals of competitiveness and profit-making, which were so dominant in the Reagan era, actually create inhuman elites ready to 'off' their opponents to keep their power. Jones's overweening ambition is only the result of the ideology of success at any cost; money and power have driven him out of his mind. His crazed megalomania is expressed by his repeated appearances on television screens, ending with his face appearing on dozens of OCP screens and viciously declaring: 'I killed Bob Morton because he made a mistake.' Jones is a caricature of the businessman so obsessed with power and money that he has lost any consideration for human life.

This character is reprised and developed in *Total Recall*, with the same actor (Ronny Cox) playing an all-powerful leader who has both political and economic authority. Vilos Cohaagen is at the same time the governor of Mars and the president of the mining corporation that provides a strategic ore needed for war on Earth. Jones and Cohaagen dwell in similar settings: a spacious office at the top of a tower from which they dominate and watch over their planet (Detroit or Mars) across large plate glass windows. The settings reproduce the type of architecture predominant in the corporate world: tall hierarchical glass and metal buildings where the presidents sit on the top floor with a panoramic view of a world to conquer. Moreover, Jones and Cohaagen both act tyrannically, abusing their employees, over whom they exercise absolute power: Jones causes the death of a young executive in the middle of an OCP meeting without expressing any remorse, while Cohaagen screams at his head of police, expressly forbidding him from thinking on his own. They personify a patriarchy which also oppresses men: Cohaagen repeatedly erases and reconfigures the memory of his favourite special agent, Hauser, first to turn him into an ideal mole, Doug Quaid (Arnold Schwarzenegger), and then, once the mission has been accomplished, to give him back his original personality, that of a 1980s senior executive with a nice car, a nice house and a nice girlfriend. He gives the captive Quaid and his girlfriend Melina an outrageously patriarchal and sarcastically comforting little speech that spells out the sexist implications of unashamed materialism: 'Relax, Quaid, you'll like being Hauser ... He's got a big house, a Mercedes. [Melina]'s gonna be Hauser's babe', adding, to Melina: 'We're having you fixed. You're gonna be respectful, compliant and appreciative. The way a woman should be.'

Both Jones and Cohaagen seek to maintain a corrupt social order which ensures their domination and control over the population. Jones defends his own mechanical creation, ED209, in spite of its obvious deficiencies, because he won a 25-year supply and maintenance contract with the Army, and is revealed to be the head of the criminal gang responsible for the deaths of dozens of policemen. Cohaagen takes advantage of his mining monopoly to assert his power over Mars by controlling the supply of oxygen and its market value. Greed replaces any kind of concern for ordinary citizens, as Cohaagen tells Quaid when he is being transformed into Hauser: 'In five minutes, you won't give a fuck about the people.' Cohaagen's inhumanity is encapsulated in a rare instance of Soviet montage juxtaposing a scene where he knocks down a bowl full of fish, who die out of the water, and a shot showing the people of Mars lying on the floor and unable to breathe because of the lack of oxygen cut off by Cohaagen. The montage offers a brief radically progressive moment focusing on the people rather than the hero, drawing attention to Cohaagen's callous disregard for human beings, whom he views with the same indifference as he sees fish. Deregulated capitalism thus gives excessive power to a small elite who loses its humanity in its obsession for profit-making. Such a patriarchy exploits women as well as men, leading to a break between the men of the upper-class elite and working-class men and resulting in the latter's revolt.

Defusing Class Warfare

Showing class conflict

Even though, according to Patterson, 'class resentments did not flourish in the 1980s',[51] an era dominated by the celebration of wealth and the belief in the American Dream, class conflict is very apparent in the decade's science fiction films, perhaps as a way to manage and even exorcise such tensions. Every film set in the near future includes a confrontation scene between a member of the dominant elite and a member of the working class. *Blade Runner*, *RoboCop* and *Total Recall* all oppose, in a neoliberal context, top executives who have economic but also political authority, to workers who are deprived of their human rights so as to become mere products. The three films show the rebellion of these workers, who demand from their employers-cum-designers their unalienable rights. The confrontations reveal how the elites have betrayed their workers by inscribing in their very bodies their submission to an iniquitous economic order, and end with the workers (always white men) coming back on top and expressing their frustrations through revolt.

In *Blade Runner*, for instance, Roy, an android worker manufactured by the Tyrell corporation to be a slave in a space colony, seeks out his designer to ask him to prolong his life. But Tyrell is well protected and not easy to find: he lives in a luxurious apartment far above the dirty, teeming city streets, at the top of a pyramid accessible only by an elevator under video surveillance. Tyrell (Joe Turkel) embodies a decadent elite, giving stock orders from his bed in a lily-white bathrobe, propped up by enormous pillows and surrounded by draped curtains, antique furniture and numerous lit-up candelabras. Roy finally manages to penetrate this golden ghetto, but Tyrell has designed a built-in safeguard against an android rebellion, limiting their lifespan to four years. *Blade Runner*'s economic system thus resembles contemporary America's, in which workers are treated as human resources of limited durability, any attempt at rebellion being stymied by the threat of discharge. However, the film inverts the economic hierarchy by giving Roy moral and physical superiority over his designers. Tyrell and his employee J.F. Sebastian are indeed both weakened by a natural or pathological ageing process, and seem small and puny next to the tall and princely Roy. Moreover, Roy's desire to prolong his life appears natural and human, whereas Tyrell's scientific jargon (e.g. 'to make an alteration in the evolvement of an organic life system is fatal') hides a more essential economic truth stated in the end by Roy: 'You were made as well as we could make you', Tyrell explains, to which Roy adds: 'But not to last ….' This confrontation in a way justifies Roy's reaction: the slave worker finally vents his frustration by taking hold of his master's body, as Roy takes Tyrell's head in his hands and squeezes it until it cracks. Furthermore, the preceding kiss, Roy's pained expression and tears, as well as the tragic musical score, tend to offset the brutality of the murder, which is not presented as an immoral act but more as the expression of Roy's rage at being powerless to change his own pre-defined fate.

Dystopia and Class War

In the same way, Robocop is a product designed and manufactured by OCP with built-in computer instructions protecting the senior management of the company. Indeed, when Robocop discovers that OCP's vice-president, Dick Jones, is working with drug dealer Clarence Boddicker, and walks naively into OCP to arrest Jones, his computer system suddenly breaks down. Robocop goes from humanised policeman to mere electronic product, as evidenced by the changing instructions on his screen: the first instructions pertain to the law and his status as a policeman ('arrest mode', 'penal code violation'), whereas the following belong to the field of electronics, revealing his electronic essence ('product violation', 'directive 4'). Robocop suffers from a conflict between on the one side, his organic body and his role, which impel him to arrest Jones, and on the other, his computerised core, which prevents him from doing so, resulting in incompatibility problems and breakdown. Jones had indeed built 'a little insurance policy' into Robocop's operating system, a directive leading to shutdown at any attempt to arrest a senior officer of OCP. Robocop's screen vision therefore becomes blurry; he drops his gun and falls to his knees at Jones's feet. His disintegration contrasts with Jones's cool and detached attitude, as he belittles and objectifies him: 'What did you think, that you were an ordinary police officer? You're our product. And we can't very well have our products turning against us, can we?' Jones has complete control over Robocop, which he designed in order to maintain the corrupt economic order that ensures his domination and the subjugation of others. Robocop thus literally embodies the alienated worker who cannot control his own body, since he is only a means of production controlled by the ruling class.

Indeed, Robocop's links with the city of Detroit and the world of machines associate him with blue-collar workers, as underlined by the film's producer and visual effects team, who saw and designed the Robocop suit as 'a sleek product of Detroit'.[52] The policemen in *RoboCop* are equally presented as an exploited working class, who finally go on strike to protest against dangerous working conditions and the scornful indifference of OCP management towards their plight. Robocop's humiliation and degradation are even worse, since he is objectified, attacked and betrayed by those who created him as well as his fellow officers. As both an industrial product and an exploited worker, or a worker become product, Robocop personifies the complete alienation of the worker. He can therefore be seen as a character specifically addressing the anxieties of the working class, and more particularly of working-class men aggrieved by America's deindustrialisation and economic transition into a transnational order dominated by information technology.[53] In this framework, his triumphant return at the end of the film reads as a cathartic expression of blue-collar rebellion against white-collar control, as Verhoeven himself implies in an anecdote about a preview in an ethnic, blue-collar theatre of New York, where the whole audience yelled 'Murphy!' in response to the Old Man's final question: 'Nice shooting, son. What's your name?'[54] One of the film's scriptwriters, Michael Miner, further describes Robocop as an empowering blue-collar individual fulfilling the desires of an unempowered audience.[55]

The end of the film indeed allows Robocop to take his revenge on the glittering yet inhuman white-collar corporation, asserting his own identity against the corporate privatisation of bodies, spaces and services. He first destroys the monster guarding the building, ED209, which tries to arrest him for 'illegally parking on private property'. Whereas Robocop is almost fully humanised – he is not wearing his helmet so we see his human face smiling for the first time, conveying a positive human emotion – ED209 appears in a low-angle shot underlying its 'utilitarian stupidity',[56] since its severed legs continue to move forward without a main body, before toppling over definitively. Cutting immediately from ED to Dick Jones presenting his conqueror's vision to the OCP board, the montage emphasises Jones's inhumanity, further underlined by his words ('We will meet each new challenge with the same aggressive attitude'), his rigid movements and his hardened expression, with jaw moving aggressively forward like a shark moving in for the kill. However, Jones is interrupted by Robocop's triumphant entrance, framed by the heavy doors of the meeting room. Robocop's impressive height and strength are emphasised by a low-angle forward tracking shot and the exclamations of the diegetic audience, the men and women sitting around the board table, who mediate the excitement of the non-diegetic spectators. Indeed, Jones backs away into the background, appearing all the more distanced as he is seen through Robocop's striated screen vision and stands in the background of a deep-focus shot, at the other end of a very long table spread across the frame. Robocop is finally in control of the situation, and is able to overcome his electronic limitations through self-awareness. His final shooting of Jones thus expresses his acceptance of himself, as well as his mastery over others. The scene is particularly gory, in part to express a sense of triumphant delight, but also to echo another gory scene in the same room, the death of a junior executive under ED209's fire, described callously by Jones as a 'minor glitch' in ED's program. Jones's execution and literal expulsion from the scene (he is shot out of the window and falls from the top floor to the ground) works as a joyful reversal of power, eliciting the cheers of the audience. Furthermore, Robocop's violent act is validated as just retribution by the widening smile and facetious thumbs up of the only African-American executive at OCP (another oppressed character?), in a fixed medium close-up. Robocop is finally admitted into the world of the dominant class and can reclaim his original identity from the company's president. The famous 'Murphy' that concludes the film is celebrated as a victory, with a true smile on Robocop's face and the reprisal of his musical theme at a faster tempo, a brass victory march.

The figure of the working man oppressed by a multinational corporation also appears in *Total Recall*, in which control is maintained by manipulating his brain rather than his body. Doug Quaid (Arnold Schwarzenegger) is a construction worker who dreams of another destiny but is constantly put down and told to be content with his simple but unfulfilling life. The first scene mentions several times Quaid's wish to start again on Mars, which his wife (Sharon Stone) dismisses, suggesting a leisurely cruise to Saturn instead. Quaid embodies a stereotypically American model of masculinity, that of the ordinary man wanting to succeed by exploring a new frontier. His character draws on the archetypal pioneers that conquered the West in the nineteenth century, spurred on by the idea of America's 'Manifest Destiny', a destiny of expansion that triggered the space race of the twentieth century. The beginning of the film emphasises American ordinariness: Quaid prepares his breakfast in a blender, watches the news on TV and finally expresses his frustration in hackneyed lines: 'I feel like I was meant for something more than this. I want to do something with my life, I wanna be somebody', to which his wife gives the standard mawkish answer: 'You are somebody: the man I love.' In fact, Quaid's 'ordinary working man' character is so visibly clichéd because it was artificially built by Cohaagen to control him. To escape from such stifling banality, Quaid decides to buy virtual memories of a trip to Mars from a company named Rekall, which sells implants advertised as being 'cheaper, better and safer than the real thing' to those who cannot afford the trip. In fact, Rekall sells dangerous escapism (the procedure can lead to lobotomy), causing psychological alienation, as underlined by the option humorously named 'ego trip' that the salesman suggests to Quaid – the opportunity to 'take a vacation from yourself'. Quaid is thus tied to a chair and subjected to brainwashing radiations, to which he reacts badly, developing a 'schizoid embolism'. He has, in fact, recovered his 'true identity', that of a secret agent, before having had his fake secret agent 'ego' implanted. By playing on 'true' and 'false' identities, the film highlights how the dominant class controls others by limiting and narrowly defining the types of identities available, as well as assigning each and every one to a certain type. To this end, a Rekall salesman passing as a doctor, therefore given legitimate authority, is sent to Mars to bring Quaid back to 'reality', that of a humdrum daily life as an ordinary married man. Using pseudo-scientific jargon, this 'doctor' in fact tries to make him accept his condition as a construction worker, from which he could only have escaped through an illusory 'ego trip':

> What's bullshit, Mr Quaid? That you're having a paranoid episode, triggered by acute neuro-chemical trauma, or that you're really an invincible secret agent from Mars, victim of an interplanetary conspiracy to make him think he's a lonely construction worker? Stop punishing yourself, Doug. You're a fine upstanding man, you have a beautiful wife that loves you. Your whole life is ahead of you. But you've got to want to return to reality!

The doctor's sarcastic speech aims at maintaining a social order in which one cannot better one's condition and any attempt at transgression leads to psychosis or lobotomy.

However, Quaid rebels and kills the doctor, signifying his new-found resistance to psychological manipulation: his 'schizoid embolism' actually represents his willingness to fight against those in power, Cohaagen and his agents. A second brain operation, this time at Cohaagen's, reprises the scene at Rekall's and exposes the alienating drive at the heart of the business world, whether it be a small company like Rekall or a big corporation like Cohaagen's mining operation on Mars. Quaid is forcibly transported by Cohaagen's team and sat in a chair, which looks just as much like an electric chair as the one at Rekall's, his hands tied down with metallic handcuffs rather than Velcro straps, and his head in a vice, in order to subject him to radiations that this time are not only undesirable but also unwanted. The parallel between the two scenes highlights the two-pronged alienation of consumer citizens, who are deprived of any free will in a society dominated by economic interests and so alienated from the structures of power that they actually seek self-alienation.

A progressive subtext?

Nevertheless, Quaid's working-man muscle and secret agent skills help him free himself from the straitjacket chair, kill the technicians and accomplish his destiny, as announced by the Rekall salesman: 'You get the girl, kill the bad guys and save the entire planet.' Although Quaid is a humorously self-reflexive action hero – played once again by Schwarzenegger, whose lines and fate are highly predictable – he differs from the traditionally individualistic hero by becoming the leader of an oppressed community, the mutants. The mutants represent the ultimate Other, repulsively deformed humans turned into monsters by the rapacious Cohaagen, who built cheap housing that was not radiation-proof. Fred Glass refers to them as an 'underclass', an interesting term that suggests a more ambivalent political stance than what Glass himself sees: 'The role of the "other" … is assumed in *Total Recall* by the mutant underclass. Once just like the other humans, they make the film's moral/political point that otherness is not license for abuse.'[57] Indeed, the term gave rise to two interpretations of poverty – cultural and structural.[58] The first interpretation, which was very present in both neoconservative discourse and the media in the 1980s, sees the underclass as the result of a 'culture of poverty' that leads individuals to adopt nefarious behaviours setting them apart from the rest of society. The underclass is held responsible for its poverty and reviled as frightening criminals or freeloading spongers. For instance, a 1987 article in *Fortune Magazine* insisted on what it described as a behavioural problem: 'What primarily defines [the Underclass] is not so much their poverty or race but their behaviour – their chronic lawlessness, drug use, out-of-wedlock births, non-work, welfare dependency and school failure.'[59] The second interpretation, defended by liberal sociologists, considers that the formation of an underclass is due to structural problems linked to changes in the US economy. They include in the underclass all those left behind by the 'new economic order' created by the decline of manufacturing in the United States, blacks as well as whites, the working poor as well as the unemployed. The 1980s were dominated by the first discourse, which vilified the unemployed as criminals and stigmatised first and foremost African-American males, as underlined by Carole Marks: 'In a ten-year period, the underclass has been transformed from surplus and discarded labor into an exclusive group of black urban terrorists.'[60]

The ambivalence at the heart of the notion of underclass can be found in *Total Recall*'s vision of the mutants, presented as criminals on the one hand, but also as an oppressed population. In the morning news at the beginning of the film, the mutants are described as 'terrorists' and are accused by Cohaagen of 'undermining trust in the government'. They do not have their say, only appearing briefly in a clash with Martian police, depersonalised in their guerrilla uniforms. Just as the members of the underclass are seen by the proponents of the culture of poverty as '*alien* beings who cannot be assimilated and hence must remain beyond the pale',[61] the mutants in *Total Recall* are presented as radically Other, confined to a ghetto, Venusville, where they are kept out of sight from the rest of society. Nevertheless, the 'terrorists' quickly turn into liberators fighting an oppressive and corrupt government, as underlined by the graffiti reading 'Kuato lives' in the Mars arrivals terminal and the comparison made by a police captain between Kuato and George Washington: 'The Martians love Kuato. They think he's fucking George Washington.' Seen by some as terrorists and by others as liberators, the mutants bring to mind the many revolutionary movements that made the headlines in the 1980s, such as the Sandinista National Liberation Front in Nicaragua, the IRA in Ireland or the ANC in South Africa, reminding the viewers that the oppressed, including the frightening

Dystopia and Class War

underclass, can fight back. Like the uprising of colonial Americans against British tyranny, their rebellion is, in the end, seen as justified, and succeeds, under Quaid's leadership, in toppling the political tyranny of the economic elite.

Quaid, however, is not one of the mutants: he is their superior leader, embodying a recurrent Hollywood type: that of the white saviour who fights for an oppressed minority. Indeed, the mutant leader, Kuato, who is fundamentally Other since he comes out of another man's stomach, is assassinated by a traitor who is also a mutant and just happens to be black. Benny (Mel Johnson Jr), the taxi driver who leads Quaid to the mutants, personifies the vilification of the underclass. First, his recurrent complaint that he has five children to feed evokes the stereotypical vision of African-American households teeming with children, unable to apply Malthusian rationalism and dependent on government support. Moreover, this complaint turns out to be a lie, and Benny is revealed to be much worse than an inveterate procreator: he is a remorseless criminal who will do anything to make money, including betraying his own people. When he kills Kuato, the signs of his poverty become, in effect, signs of his criminality: alongside his machine gun, his wide smile revealing fake silver teeth, his leopard print shirt and his gloves hiding a physical deformity summon up the cliché of a violent ghetto gangster (Figure 2.4). The real heroes of *Total Recall*,

Figure 2.4 Benny in *Total Recall*

RoboCop and even *Blade Runner* are, in effect, the white working-class men, whose moral integrity and righteous rebellion are vindicated in contrast with the untrustworthiness of a degraded underclass. We have seen how, in *Blade Runner*, Deckard distances himself from the lowly immigrant workers, while the androids stand out by their physical beauty and disturbingly white-and-blond Aryan superiority; similarly, the criminals in *RoboCop* are all ethnically marked in comparison to the blond Murphy.

Moreover, these heroes embody a superior masculinity, evidenced by their physical strength. Robocop and Quaid both display all the hallmarks of hypermasculinity defined in Chapter 1. Such a display tends to obscure any progressive subtext in support of social rebellion, since the heroes are seen more as fantasies of invulnerability than as political agents, as an anecdote related by Glass underlines. He saw *Total Recall* in a working-class suburban multiplex, where the young male viewers highly approved of Schwarzenegger's violent acts and were prone to 'misreading' certain scenes as misogynistic, for instance Quaid's execution of his wife followed by the famous quip: 'Consider this a divorce.' Consequently, Glass interprets Schwarzenegger's presence as 'an unconsciously presented male member',[62] a reassuringly hegemonic model of masculinity for a working-class audience. The white male heroes of *Blade Runner*, *RoboCop* and *Total Recall* thus also stand as victorious bulwarks against those held responsible for the decline of the white working-class, African Americans and other ethnic minorities, as well as women. In a dog-eat-dog world, they can finally impose their rule over the underclass as well as the upper class.

Indeed, stressing the heroes' muscular strength reasserts the value of working-class masculinity, seen as righteous, contrary to the seamy underclass, and solid, contrary to debilitated white-collar executives. Working-class bodies stand erect while those of upper-class characters cannot withstand physical assaults. In *RoboCop*, Bob Morton falls to his knees before his killer, begging him to spare him, while the bodies of Dick Jones in *RoboCop* and Vilos Cohaagen in *Total Recall* are literally expelled from their sphere of influence. Jones, as we have seen, is shot out of the window of the OCP meeting room, while Cohaagen cannot withstand the blast of the explosion he triggered himself, so that he is expelled from the city's oxygenated dome into the Martian desert. In contrast, Quaid's strength allows him to climb back up a rope and start the oxygen reactor, so that he survives. The films thus remasculinise their heroes by associating them with physical strength and labour, while denigrating upper-class men who break down when they are no longer supported by the power of money. Science fiction films work on the symbolic level to rehabilitate working-class men facing a difficult economic transition by featuring hypermasculine characters who show that 'real men' are to be found among blue-collar workers. Criticising the white-collar elite is a way to vindicate traditional masculinity and to exorcise the fears of a group that was feeling more and more marginalised in a new deindustrialised economic order where manual labour was being replaced by service jobs and where, therefore, masculinity was no longer associated with physical labour.[63]

Using science fiction to deflect class resentment

However, class warfare is channelled by the generic conventions of science fiction, which deflect the challenge to the political and economic order onto a more metaphysical questioning over what constitutes a human being. Class conflict is, indeed, assuaged by being diverted towards what Annette Kuhn sees as a traditional theme of science fiction stories: 'the conflict between science and technology on the one hand and human nature on the other'.[64] Even if they highlight the problems and inequalities of contemporary society, Hollywood science fiction films of the 1980s tend to ease social tensions by confronting humans (men, in fact) with machines: class resentment is transformed into technophobia. The elites' inhumanity is both highlighted and hidden by the presence of non-human machines. The conflict between oppressor and oppressed is often redirected towards a conflict between human and machine, as in *Blade Runner*, where the confrontation between Deckard and Roy follows immediately that between Roy and Tyrell and overshadows it completely, being much longer and much more spectacular. The authorities' incompetence (especially that of the police) is also forgotten halfway through *The Terminator* to focus on Sarah and Kyle's struggle against the machine to ensure humanity's survival. Once the machine is destroyed, any mention of inefficiency disappears, and Sarah is taken care of by policemen and doctors who have come a little late to her rescue.

Even in the very caustic *Total Recall*, the end of the film surprisingly sidelines the struggle against Cohaagen to display spectacular pyrotechnics celebrating the survival of humanity thanks to an oxygen-producing turbine. By foregrounding special effects, the final scene returns the viewer to what Steve Neale calls the 'fetishistic aspects of the fantasy genre' and its ability to 'astonish the senses'.[65] The expected fight between Quaid and Cohaagen is literally blown aside by the blast of the machine, which threatens to expel all the characters. The latter then struggle not against each other, but against a hostile environment dominated by a powerful technology – the final techno-volcanic eruption that shatters the dome protecting Mars explicitly evokes the fear of a nuclear explosion. Moreover, the film ends with another trope of the science fiction genre, a narrative metalepsis blurring the boundary between the different narrative spaces of the story and questioning Quaid's hero status: is he really the saviour he thought he could be, or is he only a working man dreaming that he rose above his station and escaped from his dreary daily life, as the doctor from Rekall suggested? In *Total Recall*, alienation is first economic, then psychological and finally metaphysical, when Quaid suddenly wonders about the world he has been living in: 'I just had a terrible thought: what if this is a dream?'[66] The musical notes that call into question the perfect chord traditionally expected at the end of a film, along with a fade to white, thus prevent any simple and joyful identification with the triumphant working-man-turned-hero, going back to the doubts expressed by the authorities questioning Quaid's ambitions.

RoboCop features an even greater compromise with the authorities. Indeed, resentment is transferred from the elites onto the machines in the very first confrontation between Robocop and Jones, who steps aside to let ED209 enter and face Robocop, leaving him outside the frame; ED then throws Robocop out of Jones's office, so that Jones can watch the fight between the two machines in peace from the landing. Moreover, the end of the film is especially disappointing since it maintains the status quo against all odds. Robocop does eliminate Jones but remains under the control of OCP and of its CEO, who is perhaps less corrupt than Jones but as callously materialistic. The patriarchal corporate structure is even validated by the CEO's last sentence – 'What's your name, son?' – which integrates Robocop into this very structure. As Glass underlines, Robocop can only kill Jones after the CEO has fired him, so that Jones is no longer protected by the directive that prohibited Robocop from harming any senior officer of OCP, 'but the injunction itself remains intact'; Glass therefore denounces 'a nauseating political compromise beneath the surface of the happy ending'.[67] Science fiction heroes are, in fact, hampered by their own hybrid and uncertain status in a genre that delights in continual questioning. The anxiety felt by white working-class males is thus channelled towards ontological meditation,[68] and their resentment redirected towards an Other embodied by the non-human machine. The Marxist alienation of the working class is transformed into a more generally human metaphysical alienation by the conventions of science fiction and its openly stated focus on the human.

Furthermore, the technophobia resulting from the transfer of class conflict is itself counterbalanced by one of the defining characteristics of science fiction films, the exhibition of technology through special effects. For Annette Kuhn:

> Cinematic codes specific to science-fiction as against other film genres are seen to be at work especially in special effects of sound and vision ... The technology of cinematic illusion displays the state of its own art in science-fiction films.[69]

Science fiction films appeal to their audiences by creating imaginary worlds where the most advanced forms of technology are on display, like cyborgs, which are fascinating because they blend the human and the machine but also because they represent the acme of technology. What are cyborgs made of? As science fiction films, *RoboCop* and *The Terminator* answer the question by showing the creative process behind the cyborg. The transformation of Murphy into Robocop is at the heart of the first film, with an emphasis on questions of identity but also on the material composition of the cyborg, a computerised brain with titanium limbs. The film's 'making of' in fact comments at length on the design and production of Robocop and the 'Robosuit', from the models originally sculpted by Rob Bottin to his final idea of having a flexible undersuit with a harness over it, on which to hang the solid pieces of the fibreglass exoskeleton.[70] In the same way, a cult scene from *The Terminator* shows the inner structure of the Terminator and what it is made of. The scene when the Terminator repairs itself in a hotel room can, in effect, be interpreted as a *mise en abyme* of science fiction's reliance on special effects. Indeed, the apparently human Terminator cuts its arm open to unblock the rods in its forearm, then gouges out its eye, where an electronic red light continues to shine, so that its mechanical structure is revealed onscreen. The scene draws a parallel between this revelation and the exhibition of the film's special effects by spotlighting the artificial nature of the cyborg through the visible use of an animated puppet to replace Schwarzenegger. The special effects thus reinforce the viewers' terror in front of the cyborg, but also their fascination for a technological creation that is pure science fiction. These revelatory scenes and the detailed explanations given in the DVD extras cater to eager (often male) science fiction fans especially interested in the creative process behind the films' inventions and special effects. While outwardly technophobic, science fiction films actually put technology on show to mesmerise their audiences, so that the cyborgs appear as technological objects of wonder. As Michael Stern puts it: 'SF foregrounds technology as a special effect – magical, socially ungrounded – while naturalising the technologies of domination themselves.'[71] Deeper social issues recede in the background in the process.

Hollywood dystopian films of the 1980s call into question the power structure of post-industrial capitalist societies, highlighting the alienating effects of ultra-capitalism and drawing attention, often through satire, to the nefarious consequences of Reaganism, the drive towards privatisation and deregulation and the growing gap between the rich business elites and the working class. Consequently, the films can be seen as an expression of the concerns of working-class white males at their increasing marginalisation in a liberalised economy seeking maximum profit through automation. These films portray inhuman worlds where workers have been replaced by machines or abandoned by callous authorities. They dramatise the rebellion of these workers, systematically staging their confrontations with members of the ruling classes, in order to revalidate a hard-working, 'hard-bodied' masculinity, traditionally associated with the working class and physical labour. Castigating the elites' masculinity as ultimately 'soft' and weak, these films, however, also attempt to differentiate working-class masculinity from ethnically marked 'inferiors' who are presented as 'others', so that white working-class men appear as the last embodiments of a traditional masculinity emphasising strength and decency. Nevertheless, class warfare and the working man's rebellion are eventually overshadowed by the conventions of science fiction, channelling a potentially subversive challenge to the social order toward ontological meditations on the human. Resentment against the elites is transferred onto the machines, while the resulting technophobia is counterbalanced by the display of technological wonders and special effects. These Hollywood dystopias are thus particularly fascinating because they use genre to both criticise contemporary society and smooth away social tensions, revalidating and finally integrating working-class masculinity in this very same society through the rituals of genre.

3

Sidelining Women

The success of the *Alien* franchise and of the first two *Terminator* films, and the resulting cult status of their remarkably tough female protagonists, Ellen Ripley (Sigourney Weaver) and Sarah Connor (Linda Hamilton), often obscures the fact that women rarely play more than a bit part in Hollywood science fiction films, which are centred almost exclusively on male heroes. Ripley and Connor have attracted so much critical analysis[1] that little attention has been paid to the status and role of women in the genre as a whole,[2] thus skewing the debate in favour of 'action heroines'. In 1993, Yvonne Tasker announced the arrival of muscular action heroines taking on the physical and narrative attributes of masculinity, as 'a response of some kind to feminism',[3] a forecast confirmed in 2007 by Silke Andris and Ursula Frederick in *Women Willing to Fight*: 'The 1980s and 1990s heralded the arrival of powerful muscular heroines the likes of Ellen Ripley (*Alien* quartet (1979, 1986, 1992, 1997)), Sarah Connor (*The Terminator* trilogy (1984, 1991, 2003)) and GI Jane (*GI Jane* (1997)).'[4] Yet, interestingly, what Andris and Frederick overlook is that Sarah Connor has died and does not appear in the third instalment of the *Terminator* films (*Terminator 3*, J. Mostow, 2003), which focuses primarily on a young John Connor aided by an old Terminator and a shrieking ex-girlfriend pitted against a devious female Terminatrix: the woman with the gun has become the antagonist.

In fact, examining masculinity in science fiction as a genre and thus focusing on a large corpus leads to the striking realisation that there are very few centrally positioned action heroines or 'female heroes', to use Christine Cornea's more revealing expression.[5] Out of approximately 130 top-grossing Hollywood science fiction productions between 1980 and 2015, there have been only 18 female-led films, that is to say less than 14 per cent of sci-fi production.[6] Women appear mostly as supporting characters, enhancing the male hero's central status in the narrative, as well as validating his masculinity. Rather than focusing solely on what is, in the end, an exception, this chapter aims at deconstructing the mainstream narrative, where the woman's role is to help and support the *male* hero while remaining a subordinate sidekick.

This is not to say that there have not been any changes in women's roles. Even though women have been a central feature of the genre from early on (for instance in the silent shorts by Méliès or famously in Fritz Lang's *Metropolis*), they never engaged in combat, even when cast as intelligent scientists in such 1950s invasion narratives as *Them!* (Gordon Douglas, 1954), *Attack of the Crab Monsters* (Roger Corman, 1957) or *It Came from beneath the Sea* (Robert Gordon, 1955).[7] After somewhat of an eclipse in the 1960s and 1970s – there are no women for instance in *2001: A Space Odyssey* (Stanley Kubrick, 1968) and *Silent Running* (Douglas Trumbull, 1972), while they appear mainly as objects of desire in *Planet of the Apes* (Franklin Schaffner, 1968), *Soylent Green* (Richard Fleischer, 1973) and *Logan's Run* (Michael Anderson, 1976) – the 1980s saw the emergence of active gun-wielding women, who sometimes even triggered the narrative. Even though the 1980s can be seen as a decade of 'backlash'[8] against American women, major science fiction films of the 1980s like *RoboCop*, *The Fly* or *Aliens* did take into account the demands and achievements of Second Wave feminism, positioning women no longer as sexual objects but as prominent decision making characters with a will of their own. This phenomenon became even more visible in the 1990s, when a growing number of women entered the public sphere, notably in US media and politics. However, and this is even more the case today, women have mainly been cast in supporting roles, with the central hero being a man. This chapter thus raises two main questions: why include women as supporting characters? Does the inclusion of active female characters destabilise men's hegemony?

I will first analyse the emergence of active sidekicks in science fiction films of the late 1980s, focusing on Lewis (Nancy Allen) in the *RoboCop* franchise, Veronica (Ally Walker) in *Universal Soldier* and Ronnie (Geena Davis) in *The Fly* to determine why a woman was chosen to replace the traditionally male sidekick and what role these female characters play in relation to the hero's masculinity. Then, attention will be paid to the few female heroes of the 1980s and 1990s, Ripley, who will be discussed briefly given the amount of work already published on the subject, Sarah Connor, but also Dizzy (Dina Meyer) and Carmen (Denise Richards) in *Starship Troopers* (Paul Verhoeven, 1997), as well as Lt. Melanie Ballard (Natasha Henstridge) in *Ghosts of Mars* (John Carpenter, 2001), to determine if women need to be masculinised to be heroes. Finally, this chapter will explore the disappointing legacy of 1990s female heroes, with the narrative sidelining of female characters given only apparent power in supposedly postfeminist worlds.

Women as Sidekicks

Women with agency

The 1980s witnessed a shift in the roles given to women: no longer cast as remote princesses or love objects who die, leaving the hero lonesome but heroic, as they were in the 1970s – for instance in *The Omega Man* (Boris Sagal, 1971), *THX 1138* (George Lucas, 1971), the remake of *Invasion of the Body Snatchers* (Philip Kaufman, 1978) and even in the *Star Wars* trilogy – female characters now participate in the action and live to see the end of the film. They are presented at first as competent and cool-headed professionals, as active as or even more so than the male protagonists. In *RoboCop*, for instance, Ann Lewis is first shown in mid-combat, high-kicking and punching a criminal to the ground, while Murphy looks on with admiration. The scene insists on her physical strength and downplays her gender since she wears a police uniform and helmet. Only when she removes her helmet does it become clear that she is a woman, as she swings her head sensuously. Despite Murphy's initial gaze and praising comment, Lewis is desexualised throughout the film. Always in uniform, with short hair and an androgynous physique, she is portrayed first and foremost as a police officer, who is systematically called by her last name: she is a buddy, not a love object. The police force is indeed presented as an egalitarian gender-neutral environment, where all officers, men and women alike, face the same difficulties and risks. Like brothers and sisters, they even change in the same locker room, the camera panning from one bare-chested officer to the next without any difference being made between men's torsos and women's breasts, all covered in the end by the same uniform. Sexual difference tends to be erased throughout the *RoboCop* franchise, so that Lewis knows that something is wrong when Robocop calls her Ann and comments on her hair in *RoboCop 2*.

However, Lewis becomes more and more feminine in the sequels: her hair is longer, blonder and always neatly bobbed in the second film, while in *RoboCop 3* her first appearance is delayed, her face hidden behind a newspaper creating a sense of expectation as if she were the film's true star. Moreover, she hardly ever wears her helmet so that emphasis is put on the long strawberry blond curls that were the hallmark of Nancy Allen's early career as a glamorous and sensual beauty, notably in Brian De Palma's *Carrie* (1973), *Dressed to Kill* (1980) and *Blow Out* (1981). Even her uniform is more flatteringly 'feminine' in the third instalment, with an open collar and a waist belt highlighting her curves. Nevertheless, Lewis's feminisation goes hand in hand with her loss of agency in the two sequels: in *RoboCop 2*, she arrives on the first crime scene *after* Robocop, as his back-up and is, tellingly, ordered to drop her gun so that Robocop can shoot the criminal while she catches the baby that was being held hostage – she is positioned as a mother rather than a police officer. After being overpowered by a young boy who calls her a 'bitch', she does not participate in the pursuit of the film's criminal mastermind, Caine, and is mostly absent from the second half of the film. She is further downgraded in the third film, since, after being insulted by a sexist motorist, she has to be rescued by Robocop, then gets shot without a fight and dies in his arms, a sacrificial victim laid at the foot of an altar, thus disappearing from the remaining two-thirds of the film.

Like Nancy Allen, Ally Walker, who achieved fame in the late 1980s for her role in the TV show *Santa Barbara*, was also cast against type in *Universal Soldier* as Jean-Claude Van Damme's intrepid buddy. Veronica is actually the first character in the film to be shot in close-up at the beginning of the opening sequence, after the pre-credit sequence in Vietnam, where she stands out as a female civilian in a decidedly military opening full of male soldiers in fatigues. She is presented from the outset as bold and confident as she honks her car horn aggressively to get through a police checkpoint, arriving 20 seconds before she is to go live on camera. The film humorously emphasises her unglamorous, even masculine, attire, which evokes classic (male) reporters in the Tintin tradition, but is unsuitable for a female TV reporter, thereby exposing the codes of femininity imposed by mainstream television: she has to take off her felt hat, put a jacket over her khaki shirt, drop her cigarette and be shot waist-high so her dusty sneakers do not show on camera. Despite her lateness and inappropriate clothes, Veronica is nevertheless very professional and gives a smooth, clear and confident report that goes off without a hitch.

Driven solely by professional curiosity, Veronica is a daredevil maverick willing to break the rules to get a good story, thus triggering the narrative as she breaks into the military compound and discovers the universal soldiers. She constantly takes the lead over men who are less daring or less intelligent than her, for instance dragging her unwilling cameraman into the restricted military zone and ignoring his repeated attempts at holding her back. His constant moaning, his panicking and ensuing crash when they try to escape, and his inability to speak up when humiliatingly brought to his knees – while Veronica speaks decisively and holds her own in front of two fearsome universal soldiers – inevitably leads to an early death: he is the weaker of the two and, accordingly, quickly killed off. Veronica also takes matters into her own hands with GR44/Luc Devreux (Jean-Claude Van Damme), replacing the colonel in charge and taking over his authority when she throws out the headphones through which Luc receives orders – a transfer of power from man to woman that the colonel resentfully acknowledges by calling her a 'bitch'. Veronica represents a threat to the authorities since she is constantly breaking the rules, including the norms of feminine behaviour – and is thus turned into a wanted criminal for her actions. Her energy and feisty spirit are opposed to Luc's docile behaviour, as he follows her around like a child. She is the one making decisions (for instance, visiting the doctor who operated on him) and handling the money, so that Luc is at a loss without her, as in the diner where he goes blank when asked to pay for the enormous quantity of food he has just eaten. She becomes the figure of authority to which he defers, as exemplified by the question he asks her in a small voice in the diner: 'Do you think you can help me?' The invincible universal soldier relies on a female partner for guidance and financial support.

The transformation of female characters into independent and active partners in the 1980s is particularly apparent in the 1986 remake of *The Fly* by David Cronenberg. Whereas in the 1958 original, Hélène (Patricia Owens) is a housewife who has no real input into her husband's research and stays at home for most of the film, telling the story from her bed, Ronnie (Geena Davis) appears *in medias res* as a journalist in search of a good story at a science convention, bold enough to follow an interesting stranger to his isolated laboratory. In the first part of the film she repeatedly asserts herself over the men around her: she kicks her ex-boyfriend out of her apartment, treats his jealous rage with contempt and challenges him when he releases an article on Seth (Jeff Goldblum) without her consent. The only character to have a car, she literally drives the action at the beginning of the film, creating interest in Seth's findings and initiating a romance that will lead him to his breakthrough. Until Seth teleports himself in her absence, she is present in every scene and the narration centres on her, focusing on her emotions, from her initial excitement when she gets her story to her attraction to, then love for Seth. Indeed, she is the desiring subject in their relationship: while he is passively lying on the bed, she comes and sits next to him, bending over to kiss him and finally lying down on top of him. It is this initiation into the secrets of the flesh that helps Seth understand how to teleport living beings, by teaching his computer 'to be crazy about the flesh', just as Ronnie taught him. Ronnie plays a decisive role in his research process on the flesh, even asking 'what have *we* proved?' after their experiment on steaks: she is in fact the trigger for his final discovery.

Marginalised onlookers

However, despite their feisty personalities and active participation in the narrative, Lewis and the two Veronicas are all sidelined during the course of the action. Lewis and *Universal Soldier*'s Veronica are evicted from the driver's seat early on: Veronica is never shown driving after her first appearance, while in *RoboCop* Murphy insists on driving their police car immediately after partnering up, even though he is new to the area. In *Universal Soldier*, Luc constantly saves Veronica from being shot, protecting her with his body and clearing an escape path for them. She never holds a gun and, like Lewis, is tied down during the last battle, so that she is completely marginalised while Luc fights his foe (Dolph Lundgren) on his own. The scene insists on her powerlessness as Luc is being badly beaten up: she is gagged and tied down by ropes, then unable to do anything but scream 'Luc' in despair after liberating herself, before being finally thrown out of the way by a grenade, so that the spectacular final ten-minute martial arts fight happens entirely without her. Even Ronnie, surprisingly, ends as a damsel in distress in *The Fly*: in tears throughout the second half of the film, she has to be consoled and finally saved by her ex-boyfriend Stathis (John Getz) after being kidnapped by the monstrous post-transformation Seth. The *mise en scène* of the kidnapping, with Ronnie being lifted by the superhuman Brundlefly and carried, helpless, in his arms, as if she weighed nothing, indeed brings to mind the numerous damsels in distress on the posters of 1950s science-fiction B-movies like *Forbidden Planet* (Fred Wilcox, 1956), *Creature from the Black Lagoon* (Jack Arnold, 1954) or *Tobor the Great* (Lee Sholem, 1954). Left on the roof of his laboratory, she cannot prevent Brundlefly from maiming Stathis and finally manages to kill him only because he begs her to.

So if they are sidelined from the action and romance is cut short, what role do these women actually play? Significantly, the two Veronicas are journalists, dedicated to observing and recording. As such, they bear witness to the male protagonists' transformations: Veronica takes pictures of a dead soldier suddenly opening his eyes at the beginning of *Universal Soldier*, then observes Luc's gunshot wound heal almost instantly with astonishment. In *The Fly*, we see Seth's deteriorating condition primarily through

Ronnie's eyes: her two consecutive visits highlight the rapid changes he has undergone, underlined by the numerous reaction shots of her face expressing in turn horror, compassion and despair. Her role as professional observer – and no longer as active participant – is emphasised by the interview she does of him on camera, the video screen working as an additional screen distancing her from the action. Although she is not a journalist, the same goes for Lewis, who is cut off from the action to be positioned as an observer. Distracted by the sight of a criminal's penis at the very beginning of her first onscreen investigation, she is knocked out (subdued by penis envy), and thus cannot respond to Murphy's calls for help in his confrontation with the gang, resurfacing only to see him being brutally executed by them. She first hears Murphy's howl, then witnesses his execution behind bars that prevent her from helping him. The brutality of the execution and Murphy's suffering are intensified by the reverse shots of her face and horrified expression, eyes wide open, hands gripping the bars that work, again, as an additional screen keeping her at a distance from the action.

From then on, Lewis becomes the witness of the protagonist's physical and emotional pain, the only one to recognise the human Murphy under the metallic armour of Robocop. She is the medium through which the male protagonist's suffering can be visualised and laden with compassion, a supporting character in every sense of the word, providing assistance to Murphy, but also – and perhaps mainly – offering empathy and compassion. When he is attacked by his fellow officers, she picks him up in her car and helps him recover in an abandoned factory, where she bears witness to Murphy/Robocop's physical trauma as he unscrews his helmet to reveal a fractured head. Her vision of a pathetic hybrid abandoned by all, family and colleagues, is reflected in the mirror she holds up for him, while the numerous reverse shots of a sorrowful Lewis highlight Robocop's physical and emotional trauma by systematically including his fractured head (see Figure 1.5 in Chapter 1). Reworking Mulvey's famous concept of the man as 'bearer of the look' in classical Hollywood films,[9] *RoboCop* casts a woman as bearer of the look, a role which is confirmed when Lewis helps Robocop fix his targeting system by aiming for him, literally substituting her human eyes for his digital vision. The desiring male gaze is replaced by a compassionate female gaze that places women as observers rather than active participants.

As Yvonne Tasker argues, women are 'rendered increasingly marginal' since the male figure is both active and passive: 'he controls the action at the same time as he is offered up to the audience as sexual spectacle'.[10] Men have become objects of the gaze but the gaze is now mediated by women. These women could be seen as a means of facilitating (heterosexual) audience identification by removing, somewhat unsuccessfully, any hint of homoeroticism, what Tasker calls 'the fixing of difference and heterosexual desire'.[11] This is especially apparent in *Universal Soldier*, where the final hand-to-hand combat sequence in the rain and mud between Luc and Scott is justified in the narrative by the need to protect Veronica (with reverse shots of her struggling and screaming), then avenge her supposed death once a grenade has conveniently tossed her offscreen. However, these women facilitate identification mainly because they mark the heroes as human despite the films' insistence on the latter's inhumanity or hybridity: Ronnie repeatedly takes Seth in her arms in spite of his repulsive appearance, while Veronica is embarrassed by Luc's nakedness even though he is not really a man. Their expressive faces reflect the human weakness and vulnerability of otherwise supra-human heroes, so that their role is embodied by the reaction shot: providing emotion while watching the action.

In so doing, the presence of women points to a major weakness in the male heroes: their sexual impotence. Women are, in effect, cast as buddies because of the impossibility of sex. In the scene described above, Lewis is a witness to Robocop's suffering but also to his pathetic 'loss of manhood', as symbolised by his inability to shoot straight and sorrowful question about his former self's wife and son ('Murphy had a wife and son. What happened to them?'). The faithful partner is a mother rather than a lover, taking care of him and bringing him baby food. The impossibility of sex is dealt with very candidly in *Universal Soldier*, where scenes with erotic potential are completely defused to become comic. The humour indeed lies in the absence, even impossibility, of sexual desire between Luc and Veronica, who systematically recoils when confronted with his naked body, first in front of the motel, then in the toilets of the service station: in

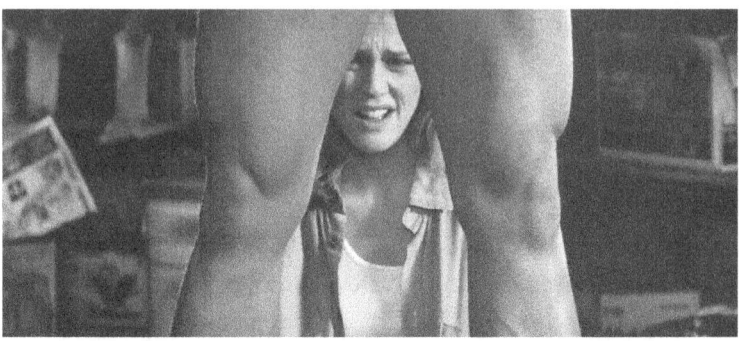

Figure 3.1 Veronica's head between Luc's legs in *Universal Soldier*

the second instance, she agrees only reluctantly to feel his body in search of a tracker, looking awkward throughout. Both scenes humorously play on the contrast between Veronica's disgusted expression and Van Damme's beautifully sculpted body on display, most emphatically in the shot of her repulsed face appearing between his muscular legs in the second scene (Figure 3.1). The point is obviously to underline Van Damme's muscular physique, shot naked in the foreground while she stands in the background fully clothed (she is even hidden behind him in the second scene), but within the narrative his nakedness stands for vulnerability. On both occasions Luc strips off his clothes as a cry for help, first because he needs ice to cool down, then because he needs her to remove his tracker. The impossibility of sexual desire is played for laughs, but there is something pathetic in this man-child who does not know if his penis is 'supposed to be there'. Like Lewis in *RoboCop*, Veronica, who answers reassuringly: 'Yes it is. It's very normal', is therefore positioned as his mother, not his lover. The very idea of a lover for Luc (called GR44 by the military) appears incongruous, as expressed in Veronica's question: 'Is there a Mrs 44 waiting for you someplace?' As in *RoboCop*, it is the presence of a woman which triggers the realisation of sexual impotence and emotional loneliness, highlighting the male heroes' pathetic dimension in scenes when the narrative suddenly comes to a halt, for instance when Robocop takes refuge in an abandoned factory in *RoboCop* or when Luc suddenly gets out of the car in *Universal Soldier*: both scenes interrupt the dialogue to replace it with plaintive music and present the male heroes alone in long shots, while reverse shots of concerned female faces (Lewis and Veronica) arouse pity and compassion.

Sex is much more present and explicit in *The Fly*, bearing the stamp of Cronenberg's obsession with the body and the flesh. Unlike *RoboCop* and *Universal Soldier*, the film shows sexual desire and enhances Geena Davis's sex appeal rather than hiding it. She is portrayed as glamorous and alluring from the very beginning, when she slowly takes off her stocking for Seth's experiment, and is repeatedly shown naked or half-naked when she makes love to Seth. The film was seen by many critics[12] and by the cast themselves[13] as a romance, a love story within a context of science fiction. However, as William Beard notes, 'human closeness, romantic attachment, sexual intimacy, are all seen as leading inexorably to visceral horror',[14] with sex turning into a nightmare when Ronnie becomes pregnant with Seth's possibly mutated baby. Despite Ronnie's helplessness and marginalisation from the action after Seth's transformation, the second half of *The Fly* nevertheless retains her point of view, most emblematically in the abortion nightmare sequence. In this scene, the viewers are immersed in Ronnie's female anxieties, the fear of giving birth foremost, but also the sense of being pressured by others and not being able to make your own decision. In the dream, Stathis and the doctors counter her fears and encourage her to have the abortion, telling her to push out what turns out to be a monstrous maggot; the next night she has to insist that she wants an abortion on the spot, and to maintain that wish in the face of the reluctance of the men around her, Stathis, the doctor and of course Seth. Her female point of view thus denounces male desire to control the female body, especially when faced with Seth's increasingly threatening pleas to keep the baby. Finally, Seth seeks to reassert control over the woman's body by fusing it with his own, in order to create 'the ultimate family, a family of three joined together in one body'. Symbolically castrated when he starts losing body parts, Seth turns away from biological sex and back to science, at the expense of the woman's body. Male impotence becomes horrific as intercourse between two desiring subjects is replaced with the fantasy of complete fusion with and absorption of the female Other. *The Fly* exposes a major theme of the science fiction genre, most commonly discussed from a hegemonic male point of view: how to control reproduction and bypass the woman's body. The film finally ends on the woman's perspective and chronicles her resistance to male domination as she pushes Seth away, scrapping his last human features to reveal the monster inside. Her final action, pulling the trigger on a completely deformed and dehumanised Seth, is represented as an act of love, Ronnie standing tall while the two men lie crushed on the floor, so that one can conclude, as Pam Cook does, that 'there is no doubt that the future will be better left to Veronica than either Seth or Stathis'.[15] *The Fly* thus differs from *RoboCop* and *Universal Soldier* in that it keeps the woman's point of view until the end of the film and gives her a final say on the action. By contrast, in the latter films, the female characters disappear from the endings, which are focused on the male protagonists' triumphant comeback against male enemies. Their compassionate gaze is no longer needed since the men have won.

The Fleeting Rise of Action Heroines

The major exception to the marginalisation of female characters in 1980s science fiction is, of course, the character of Ellen Ripley in the *Alien* saga. Her success in *Alien* (Ridley Scott, 1979), and even more so in the second opus, *Aliens* (James Cameron, 1986), triggered the rise of the action heroine insofar as 'it signalled to the industry that female-centred, big-budget, action-adventure films were a viable option'.[16] Ripley's elevation to the status of main protagonist can be read as a Hollywood strategy to attract female spectators to the traditionally male science fiction genre, but it is also linked to societal changes, as briefly underlined by Ximena Gallardo and C. Jason Smith: 'Ripley is the product of 1960s and '70s Second Wave feminism ... Without feminism, there would be no Ripley.'[17] Ripley's success at the box office indeed has to be considered in a context of increased visibility and presence of women in the public sphere. Census numbers reveal striking changes concerning women in the 1980s, first in the labour force: paid males in federal civilian employment outnumbered females by almost 2:1 in 1980, while in 1992 the ratio had dropped to 1.3:1; the percentage of women in the labour force grew from 43.3 per cent in 1970 to 57.9 per cent in 1993.[18] The same could be seen in politics, too; the number of women elected to Congress almost doubled from 1978 to 1992, from 17 to 33.[19] Furthermore, in 1990–1, the Gulf War saw the largest deployment of military women to a combat theatre, so that women on duty wearing military uniforms appeared regularly on the evening news, watched by millions of Americans.[20] Hollywood finally caught on to the mainstreaming of women in the public sphere, including in a military setting, in the 1990s. The decade indeed saw the rise and fall of the 'action heroine', which Raphaëlle Moine defines as a female character who overcomes the trials facing her through her physical abilities and combat techniques.[21]

Equality in hypermasculinity?

Indeed, Ripley, the surprisingly cool-headed and resourceful survivor of *Alien*, emerged as a true action heroine in *Aliens*, which is particularly interesting since it endows its female heroine with the attributes of hypermasculinity developed in Chapter 1, celebrating aggressiveness and strength through the fusion with machines. Ripley is strongly militarised in a film that draws heavily on images from the war in Vietnam and subsequent Vietnam War films. Recruited as a civilian technical advisor, Ripley becomes more and more warrior-like as she spends time with the Marines sent to destroy the alien. Like the soldiers, she is only called by her last name, and ends up taking command of the mission when the lieutenant in charge loses his grip. Beating him off, she takes control of the military tank in order to rescue his team under alien attack. In this scene, Ripley seems to merge with the machine, as the camera goes back and forth between the tank moving forwards and the determined expression on Ripley's face at the steering wheel, as if Ripley's iron will was being translated into the machine's brute force. She is so welded to the machine that she cannot let go of the steering wheel, clinging on to its mechanical power.

Ripley becomes even more of a warrior by learning to handle a wide range of weapons; for instance, she insists on learning all the possibilities of a sophisticated rifle and grenade launcher, remarking to her cautious instructor that '[she] can handle [her]self'. The mastery of machines is a crucial element of her hypermasculinisation, maximising her strength and indicating her ability to fight. Her readiness for combat is affirmed when she prepares to confront the aliens alone, taking all the weapons she can carry, two guns slung across her shoulder and grenades in her pockets. She goes through all the motions of a warrior preparing for combat: loading her weapons decisively with a loud click, taking off her jacket to reveal a sweaty undershirt, slinging the weapons around her neck and steeling herself, standing solidly on her two feet. In so doing, she is able to face and destroy the alien queen, suddenly filled with a warrior rage reminiscent of Vietnam War films[22] when she lights the queen's eggs on fire (like the Americans burned down the forests to uncover the Vietcongs) and starts shooting frantically, howling and snarling, destroying everything in her sights with her machine gun, grenades and flame thrower (three weapons commonly found in images of the Vietnam War). Ripley's fusion with machines is completed by her blending with a power loader in her last confrontation with the alien. When the camera slowly tilts to follow the opening of the steel door, the loader is backlit, silhouetted to enhance its gigantic yellow fork arms. Only Ripley's face is lit, the rest of her body disappearing in the machine so that she is engulfed in its mechanical shape, transformed into an invincible robot. Ripley's strength and determination have taken shape in a mechanical armour, recalling the Terminator's hypermasculine invulnerability. Ripley's movements indeed resemble a machine's as she moves slowly, jerkily but inexorably towards the camera until her face appears in close-up and she challenges the alien to a fight. Her face embedded in metal, Ripley has hardened into a live weapon able to engage in hand-to-hand combat with the alien, taking on hypermasculinity's 'hard body'.

Ripley's striking masculinisation in *Aliens* – a comparison between the iconic final confrontations with the alien in the first two films is especially revealing, with Ripley's mechanisation in the power loader contrasting with her stripped-down slim and graceful body in underwear in the first film – was criticised by many who saw it as reactionary, or even masculinist, like Andrew Ross, who denounced Ripley's assimilation into the 'western-masculinist posture' of the Marines.[23] Indeed, Ripley was derisively nicknamed 'Rambolina'[24] or 'Fembo'[25] by the American press, underlining her appropriation of the codes of hypermasculinity, as evidenced in the film's poster showing her in military gear carrying a child in one arm while holding a huge rifle in the other hand, with grenades slung around her shoulder; Walter Goodman of *The New York Times*, for instance, sneered at her 'blasting away with a flame-spouting, grenade-launching weapon capable of wiping out a small zoo', seeing it as 'a Rambo joke'.[26]

Ripley's transformation into a female warrior of the future bears the influence of director James Cameron, who had started to outline a similar character in *The Terminator*, released the previous year, but the success of *Aliens* clearly had, in turn, a major impact on the evolution of the *Terminator* franchise and especially on that of Sarah Connor in *Terminator 2: Judgment Day* (James Cameron, 1991). Indeed, Connor's masculinisation comes not only from her opposition to, and subsequent association with, the hypermasculine Terminator, but also from her inscription in a traditionally masculine iconography. The last scene of *The Terminator* stands in stark contrast to the rest of the film, moving from a sprawling urban setting to the Mexican desert, the traditional setting of the western. From harassed waitress in pink, Sarah Connor has become a lone cowboy ready to face the incoming storm, with a bandana in her hair and a gun in her lap – a Madonna for the NRA headquarters, as suggested by Sean French[27] – her big jeep contrasting with the tiny scooter she drove to work in her first appearance. The end of the film positions her as the (female) hero, whose iconic photographic image will travel through time and whose voice on recording now dominates the narrative.

Sarah's first appearance in *Terminator 2* confirms and intensifies the change announced in the first instalment, transforming her into a hypermasculine action heroine. Sarah is presented as an outlaw imprisoned in a psychiatric hospital, whose voice narrates the opening sequence describing the nuclear catastrophe to come, and whose first shot includes clearly hypermasculine attributes: she is presented working out in her cell, sweating in an undershirt which reveals her bulging muscles. The body's fragmentation (the camera does not show Sarah's face but only her left shoulder) and the close-up of her biceps evoke the extreme close-ups of body parts which often introduce hypermasculine action heroes, for instance in the opening scenes of *Rambo: First Blood, Part II* (George Cosmatos, 1985) and *The Terminator*. Sarah Connor is thus masculinised not only through her mastery of weapons (she handles many guns throughout the film and even keeps an impressive cache in the middle of the desert), but also through the transformation of her body. The film's promotion insisted on Hamilton's months of training, notably in traditionally masculine fields, prior to the shooting: running, cycling and swimming, but also weight-lifting, judo and heavy-duty military training with an Israeli commando.[28] Unlike Ripley, whose body retains its femininity at the end of *Aliens*, Sarah is marked as unfeminine by the masculinisation of her very body, as underlined by her description in *New York* magazine:

> the power body – the arms and shoulders packed with muscle, the straight thick waist, the boy's hips, no ass, the bosom so small it doesn't require a bra ... the arms have rivers of veins rising above the bulging muscle.[29]

The two references to muscle and the absence of waist, hips, buttocks or bosom paint her almost as a biological male. Sarah adheres entirely to the codes of warrior masculinity, as emphasised by her costume and demeanour, so that she is ready to kill an innocent computer scientist and his family in her rage. She even orders his wife to get down on her knees and calls her a 'bitch', using the most common degrading sexist insult, thereby positioning herself as the dominant, that is, masculine, subject. Ripley, and Sarah Connor even more so, can thus be seen as hypermasculine women who project a masculine ideology of domination through violence. These action heroines were indeed sharply criticised by feminist critics, who saw them as merely reproducing male attitudes in a woman's body, without any subversive effect; for Jeanine Basinger, '[p]utting women in traditional male action roles, without changing their psychology, is just cinematic cross-dressing'.[30]

The importance of being female

However, Ripley and Sarah are precisely *not* men, and *Aliens* as well as *Terminator 2* actually attend to female concerns insofar as they adopt their action heroines' points of view and develop specifically female themes. Unlike the first instalment, *Aliens* focuses from the beginning on Ripley's past and her traumatising experience, so that she becomes the centre of the narration. As Krämer underlines it, 'the film is effectively the story of a woman who suffers from a trauma which she can only overcome by restaging it in real life'.[31] Furthermore, Ripley's trauma is presented to the audience in the form of a dream, giving us access to her inner thoughts and feelings. Upon learning that she spent 57 years drifting in space, Ripley seems to have a panic attack: her breathing overwhelms the soundtrack, covering the words of the Company official, and the camera centres on her face. Suddenly she convulses, as an alien tries to come out of her stomach, and it is only when she wakes up screaming that we realise it was only a dream. Yet because the dream sequence is filmed in continuity with the film's diegetic reality, the dream is not only given emotional importance, aiding the audience's identification with Ripley, but also narrative weight, as if it were part of this reality. Indeed, the nightmare is a clear echo of Kane's memorable death in *Alien*, but also foreshadows the Company's plot to bring back an alien via Ripley's impregnated body, a theme that will be furthered in the third and fourth films of the franchise.

Similarly, *Terminator 2* opens with Sarah's premonitory vision of the future after Judgment Day, described by her in a voice-over that is validated as truthful by the preceding intertitles giving the date and location of the action. Sarah Connor is therefore presented as the omniscient narrator of the action, and her vision acquires 'objective' legitimacy: the lengthy pre-credit sequence set in 'Los Angeles 2029 AD' appears not as a product of her imagination filmed in subjective camera, but as the likely future of humanity within the film's narrative economy. The duration of the scene (over two minutes long) and the erasure of the source of the image, in effect, posit Sarah's point of view as that of the camera's, so that the nightmarish future she foretells, like a Cassandra whom nobody believes, is presented as 'real' to the viewers and will be borne out by the rest of the film (as well as the franchise). Sarah and Ripley are thus introduced as truthtellers with whom the audience should side against the ignorant men of the medical establishment or the Company, whose patriarchal power over better-informed women is unfounded.

Furthermore, both *Aliens* and *Terminator 2* develop the theme of motherhood as an essential element of their heroines' feminine identities. In *Aliens*, Ripley is the only one who can relate to Newt, the little girl found on the abandoned planet: actually, as the only female civilian on the team, she is immediately called on by the Marines to take care of her.[32] Her interaction with Newt highlights her maternal tenderness, as she soothes and pets her, but also her protectiveness, when for instance she asks the lieutenant who wants information from the girl to 'leave her alone', bringing her hot chocolate and gently wiping her face instead. Ripley's behaviour alternates between warmth towards Newt and aggression against potential threats to her adoptive daughter. In fact, it is to deliver Newt that Ripley transforms into a hypermasculine warrior willing to confront the alien queen. The film thus seems to oppose two types of maternity, one 'conscious, chosen and controlled', embodied by Ripley's adoption of Newt, the other 'uncontrollable and monstrous',[33] embodied by the innumerable viscous alien eggs covering the floor and walls of the queen's chamber. However, the confrontation with the alien brings Ripley into very close contact with 'the amoral, primeval mother',[34] highlighting the proximity between the two mothers who understand each other precisely at this *primeval* level, as each seeks to protect her progeny: when Ripley points her flame thrower towards the eggs after having burned one of them, the queen understands the threat and has her alien guards move away from the exit, in effect exchanging Newt and Ripley's safety for her offsprings' lives. It is only because Ripley breaks her 'promise' and decides to set the eggs on fire anyway that the queen goes after her and Newt: the alien's attack is indeed motivated by revenge and by the same aggressive maternal instinct which led Ripley to enter her nest. The portrayal of the Alien queen as a 'monstrous feminine' maternal figure tends to contaminate Ripley: this proximity will in fact be at the heart of the two sequels, *Alien*[3] (David Fincher, 1992) and especially *Alien Resurrection* (Jean-Pierre Jeunet, 1997).

As in the *Alien* saga, the theme of motherhood pervades *Terminator 2*, but the tender side of maternity has all but disappeared. Sarah Connor is first and foremost a mother intent on protecting her son in every way possible, as David Ansen emphasised in his review for *Newsweek*: 'Hamilton's sinewy Sarah, a fanatical matriarchal warrior, is a wonderfully gaga heroine, as ferocious as a lioness protecting her cub, and twice as butch as Sigourney Weaver in *Aliens*.'[35] Ansen insists on her masculine traits, making of Connor a warrior more than a mother, so that in the end she is discredited as 'fanatical' and 'gaga'. Indeed, Connor appears devoid of traditional feminine characteristics, so that the film tends to present her as a bad mother, concerned only with her son's physical well-being rather than his emotional happiness. Her lack of tenderness and emotional intelligence is apparent in the scene which follows her escape from the psychiatric hospital with her son John and the Terminator: when she asks him how he is and opens her arms, John rushes to her in search of affection but is disappointed when she starts palpating him frenetically to make sure he has not been wounded. John's disappointment with and rejection of his mother highlight Sarah's inability to behave as a 'normal' feminine mother would, expressing feelings and emotions. Sarah is depicted as lacking in femininity, as underlined by the end of the scene, which contrasts Sarah's cold and stern expression with John's tears, as well as with the Terminator's concerned reaction to those same tears: several reaction shots of his perplexed expression in the rearview mirror insist on his concern for John, as opposed to Sarah, who turns away from her son.

Moreover, at the beginning of the scene mentioned above, Sarah yells at John for risking his life to rescue her, asserting that '[she] can take care of [her]self', so that her fierce independence is linked by the film to her lack of emotions, and hence seen in an increasingly negative light. Indeed, her unilateral decision to kill Dyson, the computer scientist who will develop Skynet, is presented as terribly mistaken, thus calling into question her judgement and rationality, especially since she herself breaks down and is unable to carry out her plan. Consequently, her status as heroine is seriously compromised, which also challenges her female point of view, as emphasised by the contrast between her cold and cynical voice-over about Dyson ('It's not every day that you find out you're responsible for three billion deaths. He took it pretty well') and the image, focused on Dyson's distressed expression as he mumbles: 'I feel like I'm gonna throw up.' Set apart from the others by the staging (she is sitting on a kitchen counter while Dyson, his wife, the Terminator and John are all sitting together at the same table) and emotionally detached, smoking her cigarette in the background and out of focus, Sarah is set at a distance by the film, so that her response to Dyson, a feminist diatribe against 'fucking men like you [who] built the hydrogen bomb', is debunked as extreme and unwarranted, the black and wounded Dyson appearing more like a victim than an oppressor. In addition, the harsh light and grey geometrical background contribute to dehumanising the overly aggressive Sarah, further discrediting her simplistic speech which denounces men as destructive while praising women as life-giving ('You don't know what it's like to really create something, to create a life. All you know how to create is death and destruction'), ironic words given her own lack of compassion. Sarah Connor can thus be considered as a caricature of the 'women's libber' or 'bra burner', those Second Wave feminists who supposedly rejected femininity to become 'butch' (like Connor and Ripley, neither of whom wear bras) and constantly vituperated against men, making everyone ill-at-ease: during Sarah's speech, John covers his face and finally interrupts her, asking her to be more 'constructive', that is, less rigidly intolerant and counterproductive. From then on, Sarah is, in fact, sidelined: her last voice-over before the conclusion occurs a few minutes later and announces the end of her status as omniscient narrator, since she no longer knows what the future holds ('the future, always so clear to me, had become like a black highway at night'). The last third of the film does not use her voice-over and favours the Terminator's point of view, so that she is replaced in the narration as well as in the diegesis by the Terminator, who outshines her both as a warrior and a parent, and is the film's true hero.[36]

Thus, not only do *Aliens* and *Terminator 2* justify their action heroines' use of violence by insisting on their maternal instinct – as Thomas Doherty puts it: 'Newt gives Ripley a culturally permissible way for a woman to fight and kill, not for her own advancement but for her children'[37] – but they also present them as bad mothers. The repeated birthing nightmare in *Aliens* and the special connection between the alien and Ripley (made explicit in *Alien Resurrection*, where Ripley has been bioengineered into an alien host) taint her attempt at motherhood with a monstrous quality. A deleted scene in the *Aliens* Special Edition in which Ripley learns that her daughter died childless before her return from her mission, sobbing 'I promised I would be home for her birthday', even implies that Ripley has failed as a biological parent, as Gallardo and Smith underline: the scene

> rewrites [Ripley] as a mother, and a bad one at that, an example of the 'soft' Carter era women misled by feminists and the idea of the New Woman into a career that led directly to her failure to keep her parental promise.[38]

Sidelining Women

Both Ripley and Connor are presented as unstable, with the second being even more discredited than the first, since she compares unfavourably with a Terminator in terms of reliability but also, ironically, in terms of emotional sensitivity. Sarah's portrayal as a brutal and unfeeling mother disconnected from femininity and unproductively hateful towards men thus echoes the criticism directed against Second Wave feminism by the mass media[39] and some postfeminist writers such as Naomi Wolf in *Fire with Fire* or Rene Denfeld in *The New Victorians*,[40] who rejected the previous generation's feminism as an outdated sexually repressive 'victim feminism' that denigrated female (hetero)sexual pleasure, feminine glamour and any other form of overtures to men. Indeed, the 1980s and especially the 1990s saw the emergence of a new buzzword in the media, 'postfeminism', an ambiguous and hotly contested term since the prefix 'post', as Stéphanie Genz and Benjamin Brabon demonstrate, can be read both as celebrating feminist achievements or emphasising what Yvonne Tasker and Diane Negra call 'the pastness of feminism'.[41] The move to postfeminism and the ambiguities it implies are apparent in *Starship Troopers* and *Ghosts of Mars*, which both feature several women of action as prominent characters – Diz (Dina Meyer) and Carmen (Denise Richards) in *Starship Troopers* – or main protagonist – Lt Melanie Ballard (Natasha Henstridge) in *Ghosts of Mars*.

The makers of *Starship Troopers* took heed of the social changes of the 1990s, especially the integration of women as combat soldiers, by positing from the very beginning of the film a gender-integrated military. The film opens with an army recruitment advertisement whose first image is that of a soldier in uniform and helmet standing at attention among hundreds of other undiscernibly male and female soldiers, and who is identified as female only because of her voice. *Starship Troopers* depicts the army as a gender-neutral environment where men and women fight, die and even shower together, in a memorable scene developing on the locker room scene in *RoboCop* analysed at the beginning of this chapter. As in *RoboCop*, the camera pans from naked male bodies to naked female ones without making any distinction, for more than a minute. In *Starship Troopers*' army of the future, women are equal to men and are even portrayed as more capable than men, who are repeatedly presented as stupid: Johnny (Casper

Van Dien) is humiliatingly compared to his extremely intelligent girlfriend Carmen on numerous occasions, first when they receive their math scores (after she gets 97 per cent, his 35 per cent score is publicly displayed for the whole high school to mock), then when they join the army: she gets into flight academy while he is drafted into the infantry, so that he has to salute her when they meet before going to war, and she outranks him at the end of the film (she is a captain, he is a lieutenant). More generally, men tend to display an overconfidence matched only by their ineptitude, resulting in catastrophically bloody mistakes, so that the hawkish male sky marshal who led the failed invasion of the supposedly inferior arachnids' planet is replaced with a female sky marshal intent on learning more about the 'bugs'. However, onscreen, almost all of the older authority figures are men, be it Johnny's drill instructor Zim (Clancy Brown) or Rasczak (Michael Ironside), his philosophy teacher turned lieutenant; in fact, Johnny only serves under other men and nominates Diz as squad leader only after his male friend Ace turns down the promotion.

In comparison, *Ghosts of Mars* stands out as being one of the only science fiction films that envisions the future as matriarchal, as specified by one of the opening intertitles presenting Martian society. Martian matriarchy is presented not as exotic or odd, but as perfectly natural, seen by John Carpenter as a 'logical' consequence of the lack of resources and the consequent need to control births on Mars.[42] The opening scene shows a board meeting headed by a woman dressed in a grey suit and attended by other women in grey, as well as by a few men. The meeting seems perfectly ordinary, even mundane: the costumes are drab while the setting, which features leather chairs in a concrete box of a meeting room, is particularly minimalistic. *Ghosts of Mars* thus seems to realise the goals of Second Wave feminism insofar as female power is in place and is a given: female authority is never questioned because it is female but because it is a form of authority, both by women – Lt Melanie Ballard asks for a lawyer before her hearing, and by men – Desolation Williams (Ice Cube) complains about being held down by 'the Woman' instead of the (white) Man.

All the figures of authority in the film are women, played by well-known mature actresses, producing intertextual homage: to blaxploitation in the case of Pam Grier, who plays the decisive Commander Helena Braddock, to westerns (e.g. *Shenandoah*, 1965) in the case of Rosemary Forsyth, the Inquisitor heading the board meeting, and to science fiction in the case of Joanna Cassidy (best-known for her role in *Blade Runner*), the scientist who let the ghosts of Mars loose and alone understands what is happening – the exception being Natasha Henstridge, who was actually cast at the last minute to replace the older, edgier and better-known Courtney Love. Moreover, as members of the Martian police force, Commander Helena Braddock and Lt Melanie Ballard repeatedly demonstrate assertiveness in their decision making and unquestionable leadership abilities, with absolutely no reference being made to motherhood: they are professionals doing their job. During the squad's investigation in Shining Canyon, the Commander systematically leads the way as well as the interrogation of the prisoners they meet, and, upon her death, is replaced without a hitch by her second-in-command. Melanie indeed meets every challenge to her authority with vigour and cunning. When forced by his accomplices to open Williams' cell, she waits for them to enter and locks them all in, then negotiates with Williams for them to submit to her command and twists his huge brother's arm when he refuses to obey; later, she orders the train to stop and convinces her partners to turn back in order to eradicate the mob of ghoulish miners once and for all by setting off a nuclear bomb. In addition, Melanie is the one who displays most of the fighting skills throughout the film, whether it be shooting, martial arts or hand-to-hand combat: she is the only character given a prolonged fight scene with an individual ghoul and is constantly sought out by the leader of the possessed miners, Big Daddy Mars. Furthermore, the power of narration also belongs to women: the film begins with a woman asking another to describe what happened, so that the story is told as a series of embedded flashbacks as Melanie recounts what she has seen and what others have told her. The entire story is, in effect, narrated by Melanie, with her voice and point of view therefore controlling the narration, as the film resorts to internal focalisation from her perspective except when she recounts what someone else has told her. Moreover, like *Aliens* and *Terminator 2*, *Ghosts of Mars* establishes the female narrator as the privileged site of identification by giving the audience access to her mental images, first to her drug-induced reverie, then to her possession-induced visions. Melanie is indeed the only character to experience and reject possession by the ghosts of Mars, an experience that makes her stronger and sharper by giving her insight into the evil spirit, marking her as a trustworthy narrator and necessary mediator between the audience and the supernatural forces which are the main focus of the film.

However, the most graphically brutal death of the film is the beheading of Commander Helena Braddock, who disappears early on to reappear as a severed head on a spike in extreme close-up, the only character to receive such gory attention in death. This sadistic treatment could be seen as a rejection of Second Wave feminism as embodied by Pam Grier and her earlier roles in 1970s blaxploitation films (although Pam Grier blaxploitation films were amply criticised as objectifying women). In addition, this death comes as punishment for Helena's inappropriate conduct at the beginning of the film, when she takes advantage of her higher rank to try and seduce Melanie, tainting both her lesbianism[43] and contempt for men (she wishes she had been given a 'good strong woman' as part of her team) with the smear of sexual harassment. In fact, what Carpenter presents in his interview as a form of 'equality' (power corrupts all, women as well as men)[44] reads in this scene as a way of attacking women in power and female solidarity against men, while it also diverts attention away from the more persistent sexual harassment of Melanie by Jericho (Jason Statham), which appears retrospectively as harmless flirting when Melanie eventually gives in to his advances. In contrast to the Commander's more uncompromising brand of feminism, Melanie is much more open to men, and her explicit refusal of the former's overtures as well as her active vindication of heterosexuality (she tells Helena, 'I'm as straight as they come', which is confirmed when she acts on her sexual desire and kisses Jericho full on the mouth) position her more as a representative of postfeminism. Indeed, Melanie is much more glamorous than Helena, Ripley or Sarah Connor, as she is played by a former model whose blond hair and large breasts are discretely but nonetheless effectively put forward by the lighting and costumes. She is also shown as 'in touch' with her (hetero)sexual needs and has no problems working with men; while her pairings with the rookie policewoman (Clea Duvall) lead to catastrophe (for instance when the rookie kills a possessed woman, thus liberating a ghost that infects Melanie), she is more comfortable with men, trusting Jericho's judgement on numerous occasions then teaming up with Desolation Williams until the end of the film.

Ghosts of Mars and *Starship Troopers* reflect the influence of 1990s postfeminist culture and its promotion of glamorous and confident 'asskicking' female figures like Buffy the Vampire Slayer, moving away from Second Wave feminism towards 'Girl Power', as underlined by *Starship Trooper*'s high-school setting and choice of young and sexy actresses from high-school TV series (Dina Meyer appeared in *Beverly Hills 90210*, Denise Richards in *Melrose Place*). While both women are presented as strong and confident – Diz is captain of the mixed high-school football team and later unflinchingly challenges her drill instructor to a fight, while Carmen's assertiveness with her male flight instructor inverts the pattern set by *Top Gun* – they are also glamorised by the film, in the prom dance scene, for instance, where Diz appears wearing a low-cut shimmering blue dress and Carmen a tight pink dress enhancing her large breasts. The two women embrace (hetero)sexuality and even take the lead: Carmen invites Johnny to her absent father's place after the dance, while Diz jumps on top of him when he eventually accepts her advances. However, Carmen especially is constantly objectified and set at a distance by the film, so that Verhoeven's surprise at the level of animosity triggered by the character in the audience previews (many hated her and wanted her to die for being 'a flirt' and 'liking two guys'[45]) is, well... surprising, given the way she is treated by the camerawork and the editing.

Pointedly, Carmen is always shown *after* other characters, incorporated in the scene through an eyeline match and a male point-of-view shot emphasising her status as desired object. She appears for the first time in the film after several two-shots of Johnny (always in the foreground) and Diz (always in the background), when Johnny looks at her with desire to check the portrait he has just drawn of her. Carmen is constantly being looked at, and the point of view adopted by the film is never hers: when she exits the frame, the camera does not follow her but usually remains on the male protagonist, that is, Johnny Rico. Although *Starship Troopers* features strong women, it actually centres on Rico, who is the emotional and narrative focus of the film, appearing in every scene for the first 30 minutes, the only character whose parents are presented onscreen before being killed, and whose overcoming of initial setbacks and sorrows makes him the film's true hero. In fact, the audience is given access to Johnny's emotions often to the detriment of Carmen, who is held responsible for his suffering; the 'Dear Johnny letter' scene focuses only on Rico's reaction, while the scene when Rico is whipped in boot camp is immediately followed by a dissolve to Carmen's ship. The editing constantly links Rico's difficulties to Carmen, contrasting his failures with her success, so that she is presented as a cold career woman with whom it is difficult to empathise, since the audience is never given access to her point of view, motives or emotions.

Starship Troopers and *Ghosts of Mars* thus exemplify the glamorisation and sexualisation of action heroines as a response to the demands of postfeminism and the criticism of Second Wave feminism. The two films also offered two distinct directions to be taken by their successors. While Lt Melanie Ballard could be said to have paved the way for a horrific strand of science fiction centred on sexy action heroines, like the *Resident Evil* and *Underworld* franchises, *Starship Troopers* is an early instance of the shift in focus away from women carried out under the guise of postfeminism and its trumpeting of female success.

Back to the Sidelines

In the end, if we consider the bulk of mainstream science fiction production, the action heroines of the 1990s and the cult figures of Ripley and Connor seem to have had a very limited legacy in the 2000s and early 2010s. This general sidelining of women could be seen as an instance of the remasculinisation of America after 9/11 denounced by Susan Faludi in *The Terror Dream*,[46] yet I would argue that it is more the pervasiveness of postfeminism in popular culture and the idea that women now have achieved equality that has in fact resulted in an erasure of feminism, as well as the marginalisation of women's issues and presence as a whole. As Ann Braithwaite explains, 'feminism is "written in" precisely so it can be "written out"'.[47] Along these principles, recent science fiction blockbusters include women in power but, as I shall demonstrate, sideline them from the action, acknowledging the gains of feminism while hollowing them out.

Women of power as antagonists

Many science fiction films introduce women in positions of power very early on, whether it be governmental positions or the high echelons of business. However, these women are often antagonists who must be bypassed or eliminated. Thus, *Terminator 3* cast a Terminatrix as fearsome opponent, while both *The Day the Earth Stood Still* (Scott Derrickson, 2008) and *Elysium* (Neil Blomkamp, 2013) feature hard-edged and warmongering Secretaries of Defense whose actions are reminiscent of the controversies surrounding the decisions and personalities of Madeleine Albright and Hillary Clinton. Interestingly, both *Terminator 3* and *Elysium* link these women's power to specifically female attributes. *Terminator 3* immediately underlines that femaleness does not equal vulnerability but is a source of power: when the Terminatrix appears naked among mannequins in a Beverly Hills clothes shop, the film playfully alludes to Kristanna Loken's career as a fashion model, so that her naked body is a site of power rather than vulnerability – the very name of the character combines the physical strength of the Terminator and the sexual power of the dominatrix. As Charles-Antoine Courcoux underscores, the Terminatrix embodies from the outset 'the archetype of the sexually and financially independent woman' with her sexy leather outfit, sports car and enhanced breasts.[48] Female victimhood is rejected, as symbolised by the murder of the woman who offers to call 911, having misconstrued the Terminatrix's nakedness as the result of sexual assault. The Terminatrix does not need her help, but wants her car: she is no victim but rather a powerful female machine able to take what she wants, magnified by low-angle fixed close-ups and the editing of the soundtrack, which juxtaposes her desire ('I like this car') and its fulfilment, the roar of the sports car engine. Furthermore, the Terminatrix uses her female attributes to gain power over men, as exemplified when she enhances her breasts for the policeman who stops her for speeding. Indeed, the scene humorously plays with gender codes, since the Terminatrix's answer, 'I like your gun', could be read as an enticing sexual innuendo intended to appease a dominant male, but expresses in fact her indomitable will and the policeman's impending death. The Terminatrix's castrating power is most explicitly developed in her fight scene against the

Figure 3.2 The castrating Terminatrix in *Terminator 3*

Terminator in the toilets of the Skynet headquarters. His efforts at destroying her, by crushing a urinal on her head for instance, are fruitless, and she defeats him by grabbing him by the crotch and ramming him through walls, then wrapping her legs around him and decapitating him with her high heels (Figure 3.2). Even though the film plays with the social construction of gender, the Terminatrix is always presented as a woman, never changing genders, contrary to the T1000 antagonist of *Terminator 2* for instance, and is repeatedly opposed to a male cyborg in a robotic version of the battle of the sexes.

Similarly, *Elysium* locates power in the female attributes of a woman of steel. Defense Secretary Delacourt (Jodie Foster) appears first as a loving matriarch bestowing presents on her grandchildren, and defends her merciless approach to illegal immigrants trying to enter Elysium by invoking the need to protect Elysium's children. In fact, she denigrates the President in charge as a weak man who cannot take hard decisions precisely because he does not have children, whereas she embodies the omnipotent phallic mother. Again, female power is seen in negative terms as castrating: faced with resistance to her ruthless tactics, Delacourt decides to take over and stage a coup. Thus, both *Terminator 3* and *Elysium*, released more than ten years apart, deny feminist demands for more women at the top by featuring women who *are* in power and by presenting them as iron-hearted antagonists who are unwilling to share power but seek rather to take it away from men and eliminate the latter. In fact, these powerful women's negative portrayal as castrating tyrants who lack empathy is enhanced by a contrast with supporting female characters of inferior status and power – Kate Brewster (Claire Danes) in *Terminator 3* and Frey (Alice Braga) in *Elysium* – who, as doctors and veterinarians, embody care and compassion, using their skills not for themselves but to help the male heroes, and who are therefore presented in a positive light.

Indeed, the powerful female antagonists have appropriated male power for themselves by taking control of technology, thus calling into question 'men's monopoly on technology as a source of their power'.[49] Both the Terminatrix and Delacourt are fully knowledgeable and operational in the latest information and communication technologies, which allows them to take charge of operations and implement their battle plans, manoeuvring sophisticated machines. The Terminatrix is equipped with 'nanotechnological transjectors' that enable her to control numerous vehicles in the lengthy chase scene, while Delacourt commands a sophisticated military operations room where she can track and destroy any movement on Earth or Elysium via huge satellite screens. In effect, the Terminatrix as well as Delacourt use information and communication technologies to take control of masculine public spheres, headed by a male president in *Elysium* and peopled almost exclusively with male figures of authority in *Terminator 3*, be it Robert Brewster, Kate Brewster's father who oversees the Skynet project, or the numerous police*men* who periodically attempt to come to the rescue. Furthermore, they disrupt 'meanings and values that identify masculinity with machines and technological competence'[50] by displaying a feminised mastery of technology: Delacourt communicates through a shiny white earpiece that matches in shape and colour her opal square earrings, while the Terminatrix connects to the police network with her long and slender index finger, a scene that gracefully reworks Robocop's plugging into the police database with a metal spike coming out of his clenched fist in *RoboCop*. Technology is embedded in their femininity, so that *Terminator 3* and *Elysium* could be seen as postfeminist reinterpretations of Donna Haraway's famous conclusion to her 'Cyborg Manifesto': 'I would rather be a cyborg than a goddess',[51] since the Terminatrix and Delacourt are cyborgs *and* goddesses. While Haraway saw the cyborg as 'a bad girl'[52] able to go beyond dualistic nature/culture and male/female oppositions, in *Terminator 3* and *Elysium* technology actually enhances the characters' assigned gender (e.g., the breast enhancement scene), as well as allowing them to seize power, but on an *individual* basis, reiterating the postfeminist rhetoric that 'women can do whatever they please, provided they have sufficient will or enthusiasm'.[53]

The Terminatrix and Delacourt embody the idea that women can succeed in masculine worlds, but they are held up as negative exemplars, representing a hyperconnected and privileged elite who behave as cruelly as the evil male CEOs of 1980s science fiction films discussed in Chapter 2. *Terminator 3* and *Elysium* thus combine class resentment with the fear of women taking power, perhaps to channel resentment against the technologically savvy and educated elite of Silicon Valley and beyond, expressing the anxieties of those on the other side of the digital divide.[54] This resentment is expressed through a feminisation of information and communication technologies,[55] as both films contrast the women's fluid but remote control of technology through data with the male heroes' more hands-on manipulation of concrete machines. The Terminatrix can, indeed, operate machines remotely, as underlined by the many close-ups of her determined stare during the chase scene, while the Terminator, more often filmed in medium or full shots showing his body, has to hold on to a moving crane and then jump onto her truck to confront her directly. The film emphasises the Terminator's physical trials as he is methodically destroyed by the Terminatrix, who remains largely unscathed, repairing her damaged gun arm by mentally selecting another weapon while the Terminator has to repair himself manually by cutting out one of his burnt fuel cells – in general, the film includes far more digital images from the Terminatrix's brain than from the Terminator's. Similarly, Delacourt operates military weapons indirectly, by giving orders according to the information she sees on screens, and never pushes a button, while Max (Matt Damon), who assembles military weapons in a factory, succeeds in manually unblocking a jammed door only to be fatally sprayed with toxic chemicals. In contrast to difficult and physical industrial labour, new information and communication technologies are denigrated as smart resources used by a physically weak elite – the information vital to Delacourt's planned coup is actually stored in an arrogant CEO's brain. ICTs are therefore treacherous, since they can be (mis)used by anyone, including women, in effect revalidating manual and technical work as the locus of 'true' and reliable masculinity.[56]

Supporting scientists

In general, their overdeveloped intellectual abilities hamper brainy women from participating in physical action, going back to 'a common sf evolutionary division of labour' in 1950s Hollywood science fiction, where men are 'virile soldiers capable of using advanced weapons' while women are the 'brain giving out instructions'.[57] Films like *I, Robot* (Alex Proyas, 2004) and the remakes of *The Day the Earth Stood Still* and of *Planet of the Apes* (Tim Burton, 2001) again support the postfeminist illusion that women are now in power by presenting their female characters as members of the establishment and of a certain intellectual and economic elite from which the male protagonists are excluded. In *The Day the Earth Stood Still*, Dr Benson (Jennifer Connelly) is introduced in her professional environment, lecturing in astrobiology at Princeton. The first post-credits shot shows her in close-up as she addresses her class in front of a high-tech screen in a scientific jargon incomprehensible to the layperson. Her position of knowledge and authority is further confirmed when she is selected by the government to take part in their crisis response team as a UFO approaches Earth at great speed. Similarly, Dr Calvin (Bridget Moynahan), the chief psychologist at USRobotics who is called on by the CEO himself to help Detective Spooner (Will Smith) in his investigation, has to re-explain in 'English' what she does and how the robots work to the less knowledgeable detective. However, both characters are the only prominent women in otherwise male-dominated work environments; the other characters in the crisis response team being airlifted to see the UFO in *The Day the Earth Stood Still* are all male, while in *I, Robot* the corridors of USR are mainly peopled by male staff and its CEO is, of course, a man.

Dr Benson and Dr Calvin are thus examples of what Holly Hassel has called 'babe scientists', beautiful scientists whose 'function is to reveal complex plot devices, usually scientific in origin' but who are sidelined during the course of the action, unable to vanquish the threat because of 'their over-reliance on science' and weakness compared to 'the brute physical force, quick reflexes, powerful muscles and combat skills'[58] of the male protagonists. The scene in *I, Robot* when Dr Calvin and Detective Spooner discover the unique robot Sonny sets up early on this process of sidelining. While Dr Calvin seems, at first, to be the rational one, keeping her calm and asserting her authority when she orders Sonny to deactivate and picks up Spooner's service weapon, Spooner's apparent overreaction is justified when Sonny disobeys the command and grabs the gun from Calvin, pointing it at Spooner unheeding of Calvin's increasingly frantic orders. Dr Calvin is then literally pushed out of the action by Spooner, who tackles her while shooting at Sonny, and reappears more than 30 seconds later running after Spooner. In this scene, Dr Calvin is dissociated from the action by her inability to maintain her authority and hold a gun. These two aspects will be the targets of the film's humour later on. In a first instance, she shouts orders at an army of robots who all respond in the same way, so that she is unable to pick out Sonny from the crowd, while Spooner does so in a matter of seconds thanks to his trustworthy gun. In a second instance, she awkwardly shoots, with her eyes closed, an aggressive robot standing right behind Spooner, nearly shooting the detective rather than the machine.

The Day the Earth Stood Still is even less generous to its supposed heroine, since it disqualifies her both as an action heroine and a scientist. Indeed, the remake adapted to contemporary expectations by 'pumping up the action', giving the alien Klaatu (Keanu Reeves) supernatural powers – he can telepathically control machines and people, causing electrocutions, car and helicopter crashes, and finally a huge plague of metallic insects – which the original (*The Day the Earth Stood Still*, Robert Wise, 1951) assigned solely to Gort, Klaatu's powerful robot, which could also be activated by a woman. The power of technology is thus transferred directly into the hands of the male hero in the remake, as if his masculinity were the source of his power. Dr Benson's only active role seems to be to chauffeur Klaatu about town. For lack of better ideas, she finally drives him to see the wiser and better qualified Nobel prize-winning Professor Barnhardt (after all, she is only a doctor) who is, of course, a man (played by an institution, John Cleese). The whole scene at Professor Barnhardt's house completely marginalises Dr Benson: she can only watch while the two men finish each other's equations on the blackboard and discuss the future of humanity. In fact, in the second half of the film, following Barnhardt's advice ('Change his mind, not with reason but with yourself'), Benson abandons any attempt at scientific enquiry or reasoning to become what a woman truly is at heart: a mother, not a scientist. It is indeed after watching the tearful reunion between Benson and her son that Klaatu is moved to save humanity, but he quotes *Barnhardt's* argument (it is only on the brink of destruction that civilisations change): 'Your professor was right. At the precipice, we change.'

The female scientist is likewise downgraded in Tim Burton's 2001 remake of *Planet of the Apes* (1968), which not only furthers an essentialist vision of women as female animals but also highlights the role female supporting characters play in consolidating the male protagonists' hegemonic masculinity. In the original, Zira (Kim Hunter) is a scientist who defends Taylor (Charlton Heston) out of scientific curiosity and conviction, standing up repeatedly to ape patriarchy, whereas in the remake, Ari (Helena Bonham Carter) has become a mere activist, a senator's daughter who behaves more like a spoiled child than a woman of conviction. For instance, the scene when she breaks into the human trader's den focuses on her grotesque and mannered antics as she jumps from one liana to another, speaking in histrionic tones. In the end, she achieves nothing since she only manages to release a few humans by buying them as slaves. Furthermore, the remake insists on Ari's immediate attraction to the hero, fleshing out the supposed sexual tension between Zira and Taylor expressed by the kiss at the end of the original, thus setting up a strange love triangle between Leo, the human male hero (Mark Wahlberg), Ari the female ape and Daena (Estella Warren), the beautiful blonde replacing Nova whose name is actually never uttered in the film. The two women are always shot in parallel, both constantly looking at the male hero 'either significantly or winsomely',[59] embodying in their rivalry the conflict between the humans and the apes. In this way, the two female characters are reduced to their biological difference, both as females and as representatives of their species: when Leo stops what Roger Ebert sees as 'the squabbling among his fugitive group of *men* and apes' by yelling: 'Shut up! That goes for all species!', he is in fact addressing the two *women*, highlighting their belonging to a species and imposing male authority over bickering females.

Indeed, whereas the 1968 *Planet of the Apes* commented ironically on Taylor's domineering and arrogant masculinity,[60] for instance through his nostalgic reminiscence of his past philandering while alone in a cage with the mute Nova, or in the scene where his conceited vision of himself ruling the planet ('If this is the best they've got here, in six months we'll be running this planet') is immediately followed by a long shot of him hiding from the apes in a corn field with all the other supposedly inferior humans, the remake shamelessly asserts Leo's power and superiority over all, male and female, human and ape. Leo is, for instance, immediately singled out as his worthy adversary by Thade, the brutal leader of the apes, and is constantly shot in medium-close-ups, leading a group who trail behind him in the background (Figure 3.3). Leo's hegemonic masculinity is further vindicated through the point of view of the female Ari, who contrasts her suitor Thade's brutish alpha male behaviour with Leo's 'sensitive' nature: 'I knew it, you're sensitive', she tells him when he acknowledges his fellow humans' violence toward apes and men. Thade's brutality towards Ari in the scene where he brands her with a hot iron is, for instance, immediately followed by a fade-in on Leo alone on a horse, making of Leo a meritorious leader and validating Leo's less violent, more

Figure 3.3 Leo leads the way in *Planet of the Apes*

sensitive, but no less hegemonic masculinity. Not only is Leo presented as eminently desirable (in contrast with Zira's reluctance to receive Taylor's kiss in the original, Ari relishes Leo's, and Daena rushes to kiss him fully on the mouth), he is also cast as the saviour of the human race, a Messiah who leads an army composed mainly of men and defeats the superior apes, whereas Ari and Daena are deprived of any agency. Unlike Judith who succeeded in slaying Holophernes after seducing him, Ari is found out and crushed by Thade after bravely walking into his tent, while Daena refuses to talk to 'her people' and become their spokesperson, convincing Leo instead of leading them to freedom.

As we have seen, the physical abilities of female characters tend to be disqualified in twenty-first-century mainstream science fiction blockbusters: female supporting characters are included not to drive the action but to vindicate the male heroes' masculinity or hypermasculinity. Female supporting characters are repositioned as 'bearers of the look', as in the 1980s, but their gaze often expresses desire rather than, or in addition to, compassion. Films like *Planet of the Apes* and *I, Robot* include female points of view to enhance the desirability of the hypermasculine body, mediating its display so that hypermasculinity becomes acceptable and even desirable. Rather than highlighting the heroes' sexual impotence and the limits of hypermasculinity,[61] *Planet of the Apes* and *I, Robot* combine hypermasculinity with sensitivity by including tender, or even sensual, scenes of physical contact, such as the scene in *I, Robot* when Dr Calvin examines Spooner's arm, shoulder and torso after realising that he was implanted with robotic prostheses. The scene is particularly interesting as it is both sensual (Dr Calvin is stunned at the sight of the half-naked Spooner and clearly mediates, through a point-of-view shot, the gaze of the audience on Will Smith's beautifully sculpted muscular frame) and medical: she palpates his body muscle by muscle, rib by rib, until she reaches his human body and he pulls away. Her admiration for the robotic work done to restore his body can, of course, be read as mediating desire for Will Smith's body, but also underlines his vulnerability, the frailty of his human body as well as his emotions. Indeed, this scene of physical contact is immediately followed by Spooner's revelation of the traumatic accident that transformed him into a cyborg and caused the death of a little girl, an outpouring that underlines his emotional sensitivity through close-ups of his eyes full of tears and reaction shots of the sorrowful Dr Calvin. Dr Calvin's desiring female point of view thus vindicates Spooner's muscular, forceful and often violent hypermasculinity, while her compassion underlines his fundamental humanity. By bringing out the emotional side of hypermasculine heroes, female supporting characters therefore contribute to recasting hypermasculinity as an acceptable model of masculinity, while by underlining their human values and emotions they naturalise the hegemony of male heroes who become humanity's natural leaders and its best representatives.

Despite the emergence of active female sidekicks in the 1980s and the rise of action heroines in the 1990s, feminist critics' hopes for strong female heroes have been dashed in the past two decades: Sarah Connor, for instance, is dead in the third and fourth instalments of the *Terminator* franchise, while Ripley disappears completely from the last *Alien* film, which focuses solely on the monsters (*Alien vs Predator*, Paul W. S. Anderson, 2004). The last few years have seen the role of women dwindle to almost nothing in Hollywood science fiction movies, as evidenced in the *RoboCop* remake (José Padilha, 2014) where Lewis is played by a man, or in the prequels to *Planet of the Apes* (*Rise of the Planet of the Apes*, Rupert Wyatt, 2011 and *Dawn of the Planet of the Apes*, Matt Reeves, 2014) where women play minor characters who never appear onscreen without their male companions. Women are hardly ever cast as the central protagonist,[62] even though female heroes have recently appeared in the sci-fi horror subgenre (such as the *Underworld* (2003–16) and *Resident Evil* (2002–16) series), in teen fantasy cycles like *The Hunger Games* (2012–15) or *Divergent* (2014–16), and in such TV series as *Battlestar Galactica* (2004–9) or *Terminator: The Sarah Connor Chronicles* (2008–9). Generally, science fiction films continue to see humanity as male, seeking to define not what it means to be human but what it means to be a man. Female supporting characters are thus included not so much for what they have to say about *women* (in our postfeminist world, women are no longer the issue), but for what they have to say about *men*. In this respect, the inclusion of women does succeed in some ways in destabilising male hegemony. Some films do present a future where power belongs to women (*Ghosts of Mars*, *Elysium*), while the female sidekicks of the 1980s bring to light the sexual impotence of hypermasculine heroes, and female antagonists of the 2000s underline the weaknesses of the male establishment. However, most often, female supporting characters only provide a locus of difference from which hegemonic masculinity can be remodelled and, in the end, validated. In the end, the inclusion of women tends to erase male violence and domination, as well as the persistence of unequal gender relations, as if, on the whole, Hollywood were unable to imagine a future with a different gender order.

4

'White Folks Ain't Planning for Us to be Here'

Adilifu Nama humorously notes in his introduction to *Black Space*, an insightful overview of black presence in science fiction cinema, that most people reacted to his book project by quipping that it was going to be a very short book.[1] Indeed, notwithstanding a few exceptions like *The World, the Flesh and the Devil* (Ranald MacDougall, 1959) and *The Brother from Another Planet* (John Sayles, 1984), African Americans were cast as minor characters (when they were present at all) in science fiction films up to the early 1990s. As I noted in Chapters 1 and 2, African Americans were often demonised in 1980s dystopias as criminals bent on destroying white civilisation (as in *RoboCop*, *Escape from New York* and *Total Recall*) or included as ineffectual members of the police or the army, like the spurned police captain of *RoboCop*, the weary detective of *The Terminator* and the brutalised soldiers of *Predator*. The publicity orchestrated by the 1988 Bush campaign around Willie Horton, a convicted murderer who had stabbed a man and raped his fiancée during a weekend furlough, in order to undermine the Democratic candidate Michael Dukakis, confirmed the weight of negative stereotypes against black males and the divisiveness of the race issue.

Indeed, the 1980s witnessed a backlash against the civil rights and especially affirmative action measures taken in favour of African

Americans, with the Supreme Court, for instance, making decisions that jeopardised minority set-aside programmes and non-discrimination in the workplace (*City of Richmond v. J.A. Croson Co.*, 1989 and *Ward's Cove Packing Co. v. Atonio*, 1989).[2] Race relations hit a particularly low point in the early 1990s with the 1992 Los Angeles riots that erupted after four white LAPD officers charged with beating an African-American motorist, Rodney King, were found not guilty by an all-white jury, despite a widely circulated film documenting their brutality. As Ed Guerrero noted in 1993, 'the 1990s saw a renewed sense of racial oppression and sinking social expectations', with drugs or AIDS seen by many in the black community as white conspiracies to eliminate blacks.[3] However, following the recovery from the recession of the early 1990s, African Americans made economic gains – black poverty declined from 31.9 per cent of all blacks to 22 per cent in 2000, while black median household income increased by 27 per cent from 1990 to 2000 (from $24,000 to $30,400), compared to 10 per cent for whites (from $40,100 to $44,200)[4] – as well as advances in local politics, with African-American mayors being elected with a minority of black voters in cities such as New York, Seattle, Denver and Minneapolis. Despite important inequalities (exemplified by the big gap remaining between black and white incomes), the 1990s also saw greater integration in the workplace, as well as an increase in mixed neighbourhoods and interracial marriages.[5] The integration of blacks seemed complete with the election – and subsequent re-election – of Barack Obama in 2008, which led many commentators to speak of a 'post-racial America' where 'race no longer matters or influences individual opportunities and life chances'.[6] Indeed, the rise in African-American income and graduation rates, the growth of a black middle- and upper-class, as well as the success of a number of African Americans like Tiger Woods or Antron Brown in predominantly white fields, all tend to support the post-racial thesis. Yet observers such as Eduardo Bonilla-Silva argue that President Obama has not done much on the race front, while a new segment of 'aristocratic Blacks', which he calls 'neo-mulattoes', has emerged, distancing itself from the black community to espouse white power.[7] According to Bonilla-Silva, this has brought about a '"multicultural White supremacy" regime' which has hegemonically included some minority members in leadership positions without challenging the dominant order,[8] while the problems faced by the majority of blacks continue to be explained by the 'culture of poverty' thesis that informed the deeply criticised 1965 Moynihan report,[9] perpetuating the negative stereotyping of black males as irresponsible fathers living outside lawful, respectable society.

This chapter thus seeks to examine how the science fiction genre has responded both to the growing integration of blacks in American society and to the persisting stereotypes that continue to plague the community and especially black men. Capitalising on the success of biracial buddy films like *48 Hours* and its sequel *Another 48 Hours* (Walter Hill, 1982 and 1990, with Nick Nolte and Eddie Murphy) and the *Lethal Weapon* franchise (Richard Donner, 1987, 1989, 1992 and 1998, with Mel Gibson and Danny Glover), producers and filmmakers started casting African Americans in prominent narrative positions in science fiction films as early as the 1990s. The *Predator* sequel (*Predator 2*, Stephen Hopkins, 1990) replaced Arnold Schwarzenegger with Danny Glover as its main protagonist, while *Demolition Man* (Marco Brambilla, 1993) top-billed Wesley Snipes, its charismatic antagonist, alongside Sylvester Stallone. The last-mentioned two films are especially interesting insofar as they incorporate a racially specific point of view to offer a critical commentary on the demonisation of blacks in the 1980s, calling into question the white hegemonic order and its manipulation of black violence. Underpinned by the threat of race riots, the films thematise the stereotype of the black man as Other, presenting his point of view on a flawed white society. *Predator 2* and *Demolition Man* paved the way for more racially diverse science fiction films, where black male characters are fully integrated into a multiracial team and even spearhead the survival of humanity, as in *Independence Day* (Roland Emmerich, 1995) and *The Matrix* trilogy (Lilly and Lana Wachowski, 1999 and 2003), at the cost perhaps of perpetuating a 'multicultural White supremacy regime'. Eventually, Will Smith's success in *Independence Day* and a host of science fiction buddy films ensured the rise of the first black science fiction star in the 2000s, as proven by the success of *I, Robot* (Alex Proyas, 2004) and *I Am Legend* (Francis Lawrence, 2007) – followed by the less successful Will Smith production *After Earth* (M. Night Shyamalan, 2013). These films address the question of a post-racial America and offer a model of masculinity that counterbalances the negative stereotyping of black males embedded in the 'culture of poverty' arguments, yet they favour an upper-middle-class version of black masculinity that tends to erase the problems of the poor.

Taking up on Richard Pryor's comment following the release of *Logan's Run* (Michael Anderson, 1976), 'I just saw Logan's run and ain't no niggas in it! I said, well white folks ain't planning for us to be here!', this chapter thus not only examines what the future looks like *with* African Americans but whether black men can actually embody the human race and replace white people as the 'human norm'.[10] Furthermore, if the black man becomes the norm, can he challenge the white order by offering an alternative model of masculinity, or does the decentring of the white man enable the recentring of hegemonic masculinity, only painted black?

Demons with a Purpose

In response to the typecasting of African Americans in 1980s science fiction films, *Predator 2* and *Demolition Man* address the stereotypes of the ineffectual black cop and of the black man as Other to offer a commentary that challenges white supremacy. The two films indeed feature racial Others who take advantage of a dysfunctional white society, highlighting the failures of the white order and its fraught racial relations. Following Todd Boyd's analysis of LA-based gangsta rap, I want to show how the Predator (Kevin Peter Hall), an alien being come to hunt in an imploding contemporary Los Angeles, and Simon Phoenix (Wesley Snipes), a 1990s psychopathic criminal turned loose in a pacified futuristic Los Angeles, are figures of excess that '[do] much more than simply fulfil the societal stereotypes of the threatening male Black. Instead, [they] den[y] the White supremacist denigration embodied in the stereotype and reverse the impact to become a true purveyor of unadulterated Black rage.'[11] By presenting the point of view of America's demons, the Predator and Phoenix provide the cognitive estrangement sought by science fiction and underline at the same time the alienness-as-alienation of blacks living under white rule.

Blacks as alien bodies

As Ed Guerrero and Adilifu Nama both suggest, science fiction films often use black characters to signify difference – what is alien to, and repressed by, the dominant white order.[12] Hence Nama's very critical assessment of the characters of the Predator and Simon Phoenix, who offer 'powerful spectacles of alien difference'.[13] These two characters can indeed be seen as embodiments of racial difference, as signified by the Predator's repulsive face and fluorescent blood and Phoenix's dyed blond hair and eyes of a different colour. These alien bodies are all the more unsettling because they are hybrids, bringing together signifiers from altogether different 'races'. The final act of *Predator 2* discloses the Predator's pink-speckled white flesh, contrasting it with the dreadlocks that connected him to the Jamaican gang members. He is both linked to the black body (through the dreadlocks and the fact that he is played by a black actor[14]) and distinguished from it, as in the shot when, dangling from a building, his white long-fingered hand grips the black hero's arm in close-up, so that the opposition in colour, contrast and texture is made clearly visible. As Nama underlines, Phoenix is also caught between two identities, a 'racial duality'[15] emphasised by close-ups of his eyes, one blue, one brown and his bleached blond hair, negating any claim to black nationalism and their 'black is beautiful' motto.

In both films, black masculinity is presented as exotic, arousing the fascination of the audience by its willingness to flout the rules of white 'civilization'. Indeed, the Predator and Simon Phoenix can be seen as contemporary avatars of the 'Black Buck'[16] in their primitive brutality and defiance of the white order. The opening images of *Predator 2* insist on the primitiveness of its antagonist: the film opens with a high-pitched animal screech on a black screen that dissolves into an aerial travelling shot of a forest of palms and pines that ends on a wide-angle shot of the Los Angeles cityscape, making a clear link between the South American jungle of the first film and the urban jungle of the second. Subsequently, the Predator's arrival is systematically announced by African drumming playing on the soundtrack. In addition, the Predator, who wields sophisticated versions of primitive weapons, such as metallic nets or extendable spears, hangs, skins and decapitates his victims, leaving blood everywhere, in an echo of the equally bloody voodoo practices of the Jamaican gang he is first thought to belong to. The racial stereotyping of the alien Predator as a brutal, primitive and inherently *different* creature comes into sharp focus when contrasted with a preceding example of a black alien creature, the protagonist of *The Brother from Another Planet*. Neither exotic nor primitive, this alien 'brother' (Joe Morton) looks exactly like a human except for his three-toed feet, and is so in tune with contemporary human society that he can fix all of its machines instantly.[17]

Indeed, *Predator 2* and *Demolition Man* participate in the objectification of the black body as exotic. Simon Phoenix's powerful black body is displayed and enhanced by the staging and camerawork, as in the scene of his parole hearing, where his bright white plastic prison uniform attracts the light, contrasting with the grey setting and guards' uniforms. Wheeled in to face the prison warden, Phoenix sits at the centre of the frame, with the headless bodies of two guards standing behind him, in an almost perfectly symmetrical composition jarred only by the close-up of his two differently coloured eyes. He is then stretched to a standing position on a metal plank, so that he dominates all the other characters, filmed in low-angle shots (Figure 4.1). This hearing can be opposed to John Spartan's (Sylvester Stallone), where the hero sits limply, head bent down. Filmed in high-angle shots and sidelined to the left-hand side of the frame, the belittled Spartan responds mournfully to the standing policewoman who has to bend over to talk to him. By contrast, Phoenix is able to liberate himself

Figure 4.1 Low-angle shot of Simon Phoenix in *Demolition Man*

and overcome the guards in a striking display of martial arts and witty one-liners, so that the theatrical spectacle of the black man affirms in fact his superiority and control over others, in particular the imprisoning white society. This is epitomised in his catchphrase: 'Simon Says.' When Phoenix reappears, after his escape, on the surveillance screen of the police force, it is to openly defy the white American order, refusing to submit to the demands of the police and parodying the national anthem, to the amazed horror of an ineffectual *white* police force. By reprising a children's game as a way of giving orders and singing the national anthem in a distorted voice, Simon Phoenix exposes the signifiers of American innocence as means of control and subjugation. By introducing racial otherness, *Predator 2* and *Demolition Man* point to the confining limits of white society, where only a thickly accented, marijuana-smoking, gang-leading Jamaican voodoo priest can see and face the Predator for what he is, a creature 'from the other side', and a bare-armed black man in colourful clothing is eyed suspiciously, in *Demolition Man*, by fully covered white people when he walks into a museum, despite being the only visitor with a purpose. Phoenix, in effect, 'restores the use value of the guns [exhibited as ancient artefacts in the 2032 San Angeles Museum of History] by blowing away the white guards and police', a scene analysed by Linda Mizejewski as both displaying 'primitive blackness' but also offering a subversive challenge against 'white uptight museum culture'.[18]

Dysfunctional white societies

Simon Phoenix and the Predator thus exemplify 'the monster in the horror, sci-fi, and fantasy genres' as defined by Ed Guerrero, representing 'the incessant return of those repressed fears and problems that society cannot articulate and cope with openly, for example race, immigration, and the unchecked growth of nonwhite populations'.[19] In *Predator 2* and *Demolition Man*, racial issues are brought to the fore through the shadow of race riots. The opening soundtrack of *Predator 2* mixes African drumming, the snarl of the Predator, reporters' voices, Spanish voices, screams and gunfire to suggest a chaotic city dominated by minority groups. This is confirmed by a lengthy sequence staging a confrontation between a trigger-happy

Columbian gang led by El Scorpio, a wild-looking, long-haired, gold-toothed Latino gang member caricature and an ethnically mixed police force who are overwhelmed and abandoned by the white authorities. The mayor has left Los Angeles for his summer residence in Lake Tahoe, and the police captain only appears on site at the end of the shoot-out, 14 minutes into the film, to yell at his officers who 'fight for their lives' while he stays in 'the Palace' downtown, 'pushing pencils and kissing ass', as Detective Harrigan (Danny Glover) reminds him. The inefficiency and corruption of white authorities is also emphasised in *Demolition Man*, where Simon Phoenix forces all city services out of his territory at the beginning of the film, and is then brought back into service by the white mayor of 2032 San Angeles, an aspect I'll come back to below.

Furthermore, both films are set in Los Angeles, a city historically associated with racial tensions and race riots. *Predator 2* continuously stresses the heat that plagues the city – underlined first by a reporter mentioning a heat wave in the film's introductory sequence, confirmed by the numerous red spots on the Predator's heat-sensitive thermal vision, and reaffirmed by the sweat visibly pouring down the characters' faces – a way of evoking the Watts riots during the summer heat of August 1965. Los Angeles continued to be plagued by gang violence and police brutality, which came to public attention in the late 1980s/early 1990s, with the release in 1988 of NWA's album *Straight Outta Compton*[20] and its hit single 'Fuck Tha Police' denouncing the racism and violence of the LAPD. Released in 1990, *Predator 2* fuelled the public perception of Los Angeles as an urban jungle simmering with racial tensions that eventually exploded in April 1992 after the verdict clearing the four white LAPD officers charged with beating Rodney King. The verdict led to the worst riots in recent US history, with African-American and Latino rioters looting and burning down the neighbourhood of South Central for four days, resulting in 55 dead, 2,300 injured, 800 buildings burned down and $1 billion in property damage.[21] The images circulated by the media coverage of the riots are clearly evoked in *Demolition Man*, which opens on an aerial shot taken from a helicopter flying over the Hollywood sign in flames to reveal a panoramic night view of a city dotted with fires, with a soundtrack of police sirens and gunshots.

The two films thus establish a connection between minority violence and a white American society that continually seeks 'regeneration through violence'.[22] *Demolition Man* repeatedly draws a parallel between Simon Phoenix and John Spartan, aka 'Demolition Man', two archenemies who do not hesitate to use violence to reach their goals. Spartan is, indeed, held responsible for the deaths of hostages held by Simon Phoenix, and they are both sentenced to cryogenic deep-freeze at the same time: Phoenix's sarcastic taunt at Spartan, 'We are going to spend a lot of quality time together!', holds true for much of the film, as they each doggedly seek the other out for revenge.[23] The parallel is played up even more explicitly in the pacified futuristic San Angeles, where both Spartan and Phoenix are immediately fined several times upon their release for using foul language and are repeatedly described in the same terms by the San Angeles police, who see them as old-fashioned maniacs – an extremely wary police captain even declares that '[John Spartan] comes from a dissimilar method of law enforcement. I'm not sure he's any different than Simon Phoenix himself.'

Black violence parallels white violence and is even manipulated and exploited by whites. In *Predator 2*, the white FBI agents want to capture the Predator in order to appropriate his sophisticated weaponry and launch 'a new era of scientific technology', as the excited head of the FBI team, Keyes (Gary Busey) explains to the sceptical Harrigan. The scene in the FBI bunker opposes the cold rationalistic approach of white FBI agents to the more instinctive and emotional approach of the black detective: their scientific jargon contrasts with his emotional outbursts, while the screens that fill the bunker as well as the silver suits worn by the agents stand out in a film designed overall to have the dusty tobacco look of a western.[24] As in the first two *Alien* films, the capitalistic callous white male rationalism of the government takes no heed of minority opposition based on emotional instinct: the hubristic Keyes ignores Harrigan's instinctual fear but ends up underestimating his practiced opponent. In *Demolition Man*, it is the dictatorial white mayor of San Angeles, Dr Raymond Cocteau (Nigel Hawthorne) who organises Phoenix's escape so that he will kill the leader of the underground resistance to his regime, Edgar Friendly. White manipulation is underscored in the scene where, having taken the guns from the museum, Phoenix is unable to kill Cocteau, who redirects the latter's aggression towards his own intended target. In fact, the mayor trained and brainwashed Phoenix during his cryogenic rehabilitation so that he would become a hardened assassin, and is even willing to bargain with him, giving him back his crew and a territory to run in exchange for the murder of Edgar Friendly. In this way, *Demolition Man* briefly highlights the 'ongoing complicity of the American state apparatus in supporting the international narcotics trade to further the ends of elite interests' exposed by James Nadell in his analysis of *Boyz n the Hood*,[25] thus confirming the widespread belief among the African-American community in the early 1990s that 'the easy accessibility of drugs in poor black communities was part of a government conspiracy'.[26]

Black violence as an assertion of power

Predator 2 and *Demolition Man* point to the responsibility of white authorities in promoting black violence, but both films also underline that black violence cannot be appropriated. Indeed, as mentioned earlier, the FBI underestimate their prey in *Predator 2*, relying on human technology that is no match for the Predator, who senses their presence and switches his vision sensors so that he can see their flashlights and attack them. The Predator is not easily subjugated, nor is the black detective he considers his only worthy opponent. Here, I go against Nama's analysis of the Predator in *Predator 2*, whom he sees mainly as an urban vigilante targeting black and brown criminals,[27] minimising the importance of Detective Harrigan as the film's hero and the Predator's main adversary. Indeed, Harrigan is the first individual to be singled out by the Predator, who snarls with interest when he witnesses his daring attack against the Columbian gang. Harrigan is also the one who finally manages to kill the alien, disavowing the stereotype of the ineffectual black cop so present in 1980s science fiction, as well as countering the long-standing tradition perpetuated by *Predator* where black supporting characters are 'most likely to be maimed, to die, or to be killed outright in service of the plot'.[28] Furthermore, the fact that the Predator picks out choice opponents and spares those considered harmless (a child and a pregnant woman[29]) emphasises his ethics, giving him a certain moral dignity that qualifies his primitiveness and brutality, especially since the end of the film includes him in a band of warriors with long-standing traditions and a sophisticated habitat. The protracted confrontation between the Predator and Harrigan can thus be compared to a duel that ennobles both characters, distancing them from unworthy whites whom they dominate physically (Kevin Peter Hall and Danny Glover are both extremely tall) and morally. Unlike Dutch (Arnold Schwarzenegger) in *Predator*, Harrigan indeed has to overcome the constant rebukes and scorn of his white superiors and FBI competitors, until the end, which stands in sharp contrast with the first film. Whereas the end of *Predator* expresses gratitude and admiration towards the lone-standing, mud-covered Dutch, who is rescued by a helicopter to the sound of military brass music and admired by the tearful woman he saved and his awed superior in reaction shots, the FBI helicopter at the end of *Predator 2* does not land to rescue Harrigan but to chastise him, as an agent runs towards him, pushes him and yells at him for failing to capture the Predator alive: 'What the fuck happened in there? Damn it! We came so close!' The dust covering Harrigan's body does not signal his oneness with his environment in a new dawn, as it does for Dutch at the end of *Predator*, but on the contrary marks him out, as his ghostly figure emerges in the black of night, lit up by the helicopter's searchlight like a wanted criminal. His final sentence, 'Don't worry asshole, you'll get another chance', uttered with a smile as he holds up the pistol given to him by the chief alien, can, then, be read as a gesture of defiance against a white order that acknowledges neither his feats nor the knowledge he has gained from his battle experience against the Predator.

The arrival of Glover to replace Schwarzenegger makes *Predator 2* especially interesting in terms of race, first because it features a black hero and gives Glover the opportunity to widen the range of black masculinities offered on Hollywood screens in the late 1980s and early 1990s. Glover moves away from the respectable *pater familias*/white hero helper of *Lethal Weapon* to a more combative and outspoken tough cop protagonist, a lone warrior able to fight on his own without the help of white authorities. Secondly, choosing Glover to replace Schwarzenegger, who could not do the sequel because of his commitment to *Terminator 2*,[30] turns the film into what could be considered a black film, where the action is driven solely by black characters. These characters share a special bond in their awareness of another world, as expressed by the recurring phrase 'shit happens', uttered first by a Jamaican gang member when performing a voodoo ritual on a Latino rival, recorded and repeated by the Predator at Harrigan as he holds onto his arm, and finally reiterated by Harrigan to the Predator upon their final contact. This expression of African-American oral tradition emphasises the circularity of racial signifiers in the film, as the characters constantly borrow from each other's vocabulary and weaponry. Finally, by presenting several types of black men and a new Danny Glover, the film challenges the dichotomy between the socially and economically integrated 'immaculate black man'[31] and the Black Buck so common in Hollywood images, presenting instead a range of black masculinities that deconstruct the recurrent association between LA-based black males and gangs operated by the mainstream media.

Yet the FBI-hunted Predator, the Jamaican gang members and especially Simon Phoenix can be read as embodiments of the 'defiant lower-class black ultramasculinity' promoted by gangsta rap at the time. Indeed, Phoenix's exhilaration at striking fear in all those he meets, underscored by the beatbox sound cues accompanying his martial arts moves[32] in his first confrontation against the San Angeles police, echo gangsta rap's celebration of menacing black males, so that the negative stereotype embodied by Simon Phoenix, that of the all-threatening drug-dealing black criminal, can also be read as a 'purveyor of unadulterated Black rage'.[33] This rage is expressed against white society through repeated assault and looting, especially against institutional forms of white authority, be it the police, the mayor or the museum. Phoenix's gleeful violence against the predominantly white San Angeles police force after the museum robbery recalls Dr Dre's song about the Rodney King riots, 'The Day the Niggaz Took Over' (*The Chronic*, 1992), encouraging blacks to shoot and loot. For that is exactly what Phoenix does throughout *Demolition Man* with the explicit aim of 'taking over', as represented visually in the arresting image of Phoenix sitting in the mayor's chair with his back to the audience, placed in the foreground of a darkly lit expressionist composition, while the mayor and his assistant appear in the background, separated from Phoenix and the audience by the horizontal line of the mayor's desk. In this scene, the audience shares Phoenix's point of view as well as his sardonic satisfaction at having turned the tables on a despicable mayor who meekly accepts to release Phoenix's fellow inmates and even cede the whole of the west coast, including the symbolic preserve of the rich, Malibu, to an empowered member of the underclass. Through the character of Simon Phoenix, *Demolition Man* offers a carnavalesque reversal of power, where a weakened and feminised white society in robes is rocked by a raging Black Buck.

Indeed, *Demolition Man* presents a satirical vision of a 'pussy-whipped' (Phoenix's words) white society unable to meet the challenge presented by the black man's phallic hypermasculinity, symbolised by Phoenix's enthusiastic grabbing of the biggest gun in the museum, with which he almost blows Spartan away. The message is clear: dominant white society has to 'man up' to be able to face the challenge, which is underlined by the casting of Stallone as its champion. The violent black foe is thus a means of promoting the remasculinisation of white society at the expense of women,[34] as is made clear at the end of the film, when John Spartan, Edgar Friendly (Denis Leary) and the police captain (all white men), surrounded by a circle of white and Latino men, discuss the city's future, rejecting any feminine influence – Lenina Huxley (Sandra Bullock) is excluded from the group and even thanks Spartan for knocking her out of the final battle with Phoenix, while Friendly chastises the eunuch-like mayor's assistant for his dyed hair and costume, inviting everyone to get 'shitfaced' and have a 'blast'.

Nama concludes that

> the symbolic message of *Demolition Man* is clear. Southern California race relations will require that black militancy be eliminated and that a moderate white alternative or certainly more 'friendly' representative of the socially marginalized and economically displaced is put in place to negotiate the shifting fault lines and centers of racial politics and power in Los Angeles.[35]

Demolition Man can, in effect, be read as a whitewashed, happy-ending revision of the Rodney King riots, where white police brutality is justified against hardened maniacal black criminals and the rioters are sympathetic, harmless whites (and a few Latino subordinates) in search of fun and food. Yet Nama fails to note that Phoenix is, despite the ending of the film, the most memorable character of the film. While Edgar Friendly is highly forgettable, being given hardly any screen time, Phoenix is played by the already renowned Wesley Snipes, who shared top billing with Stallone and was praised by critics for his 'vibrant energy'[36] and 'delicious badness'[37] – even Donald Bogle acknowledges his fascination with Snipes' 'vigor' and 'giddy malevolen[ce]'.[38] While *Demolition Man* and *Predator 2* could be seen at first sight as perpetuating the negative stereotype of black men as exotic savages prone to violence, they also present a black point of view on a flawed white society which has nurtured this violence, trying to appropriate it to its own ends. In both films, black violence can be seen as a form of resistance and an assertion of power by the disenfranchised over a 'civilisation' always defined as white.

Integrated Members of Multiracial Teams

The confrontational mode of *Predator 2* and *Demolition Man* could still be found in *Strange Days* (Kathryn Bigelow, 1995), which restages the Rodney King riots, and *Virtuosity* (Brett Leonard, 1995), where the confrontation is reversed in terms of race, with Denzel Washington playing a police officer and Russell Crowe a criminal maniac. However, it quickly gave way during the more prosperous and integrated 1990s to the celebration of interracial alliances within multicultural teams, notably in the hugely popular *Independence Day* and *The Matrix* trilogy.

Promoting virile masculinity through interracial alliance

Independence Day insists on the diverse ethnic origins of the survivors who gather around the President of the United States to fight extra-terrestrials hidden in identical machines, thus contrasting human diversity with alien sameness. The film clearly references 1950s science fiction classics like *The War of the Worlds* (1953) and *The Day the Earth Stood Still* (1951) – the latter is actually shown on TV within the narrative – but it replaces 1950s anticommunist and nuclear paranoia with the celebration of human diversity, especially that of the American people. The shots of the crowd show blacks and whites, rich and poor, gathered together opposite the metallic saucers, so that the definition of humanity no longer rests on the foundational American individualism but on ethnic diversity and multicultural cooperation. The first human scene, at the Search for Extraterrestrial Intelligence Institute, celebrates from the outset the harmonious cooperation between different minority groups: the young Asian who first receives the extra-terrestrial signal immediately alerts his white boss (whose Woody Allen-like intonation and anxiety suggest that he is Jewish), who then turns to his African-American and female aides.

The film further expands on this idea of a diverse and plural America in a long expository sequence presenting a panel of Americans from different social and ethnic origins. Each two-minute scene clearly marks out the socio-ethnic backgrounds of the main characters: there is the young WASP (White Anglo-Saxon Protestant) president in Washington DC (Bill Pullman), the nerdy Jewish genius in New York (Jeff Goldblum) and the down-and-out hick living in a caravan in the middle of the Californian desert with his three Chicano children (Randy Quaid). All these characters are developed in parallel, before gathering on a military base to launch a common attack on the aliens. Only Captain Steven Hiller (Will Smith) appears later, marking him out as the star of the film, and his racial background is de-emphasised: the film shows him living in a racially mixed suburban home with green lawns and a dog, presenting him as a gentrified African American. Conveniently sidestepping the contemporary problems faced by the majority of African Americans, many of whom still belong to the working class and underclass, the film nostalgically invokes the multi-ethnic platoons of 1940s–50s war films to rebuild the *e pluribus unum* ('out of many, one') motto of the United States – but as a male middle-class *unum*.

Indeed, according to Michael Rogin, one of the objectives of *Independence Day* is to 'resurrect the New Deal-Great Society coalition of Jew, Black and public-spirited WASP'[39] that was threatened during the 1990s by extremist views, including Louis Farrakhan's widely publicised anti-Semitism. Steve's remark to David during their space flight together, 'We're going to work on our communication', is thus especially relevant in a context of tensions between the Jewish and black communities, which prominent intellectuals from both sides sought to soothe, like Michael Lerner, a progressive rabbi and editor of *Tikkun Magazine*, and Cornel West, a well-known African-American academic and activist, in their book of conversations revealingly entitled *Jews and Blacks: Let the Healing Begin*.[40] *Independence Day* stereotypically insists on the complementarity between Jewish intellect and African-American bodily strength and dexterity, through the typecasting of Jeff Goldblum, known for his roles as scientist in *The Fly* and *Jurassic Park* (Steven Spielberg, 1993), and of Will Smith, the athletic young rapper turned star after the success of *The Fresh Prince of Bel Air* (1990–6) and *Bad Boys* (Michael Bay, 1995). In keeping with ethnic stereotypes, David (Jeff Goldblum) is a computer whiz who wears huge glasses, while Steve (Will Smith) is a pilot whose muscular body is exhibited as soon as he appears onscreen, bare-chested, and then again when he drags an alien across the desert by the strength of his muscular shoulders and bulging biceps. The gift exchange mentioned by Rogin, when a black laboratory assistant gives a Torah to David's father who in return gives two cigars to Steve, seals the renewed alliance between middle-class Jews and blacks, but also emphasises the dichotomy between mind (Jewish spirituality) and body (the phallic cigars).

However, Rogin notes that 'nostalgia for the Jewish-black alliance takes the place in this film of equal opportunity for those post-1960s multicultural groups, Latinos, Asians, women and gays … Not all ethnic, racial and sexual identities will get equal billing'.[41] For example, Asians disappear from the film entirely after the brief introductory scene mentioned earlier, while Russell Casse's Chicano children and claim of having been abducted by aliens

> link the illegal aliens of American politics … to the space aliens of American film … The alien-Casse liaison fills the gap of the missing Chicana mother. Russell's Chicano children are the products of one alien miscegenation, and his breakdown is the product of the other.[42]

Mostly though, the black/Jewish rapprochement operates to the detriment of women. The celebration of the muscular African-American hero is used in *Independence Day* to remasculinise the less-obviously virile Jew in order to rebuild a strong nation where women are relegated to their proper place. David's masculinisation begins when he finds a solution to bring down the aliens (by transmitting a computer virus to the alien machines) and explains it to a sceptical audience. He is first presented in a position of weakness, in a series of shot/reverse shots that place him next to his ex-wife and in front of two other women, and oppose him to a doubtful and exclusively male group of military, political and scientific authorities. As David talks, however, a tracking shot eliminates his ex-wife to focus solely on him, while the reverse shots now show the other men's growing admiration. David becomes more and more confident, straightening up to reveal muscular pectorals under a white vest and banging the board with his fist to strengthen his argument. Against the authorities' lingering doubts, Steve then enters the discussion to support David's idea. After some cross-cutting and further discussion, the camera finally unites the two men in a single shot which shows David standing erect with his hands on his hips. His friendship with Steve is sealed through virile daring, as underscored by the musical crescendo of horns and drums and the cocky dialogue: 'Do you really think you can fly that thing?' David asks, to which Steve replies: 'Do you really think you can do all that bullshit you just said?'

Independence Day kills off or silences all of its female characters, especially the career women. The President's wife, on a business trip during the attack, apologises for not having been there with him ('I'm so sorry that I didn't come home when you asked me to') before dying, punished for her transgression. She literally disappears from the screen even in death, since the camera focuses on the President's face during their last embrace, and her tragic fate is signified by her husband's distraught expression upon leaving her hospital room. David's ex-wife, Connie (Margaret Colin), is also blamed for her ambition that led her to leave her loving genius husband to become the White House Press Secretary, and finally gives up her professional ambition and independence to devote herself to him. In fact, the last third of the film, which occurs on the Fourth of July, celebrates a victory that is strictly male, with women being relegated to supporting roles in both senses of the word. Connie sheds her career woman suit and heels to adopt the same clothes as David, slacks and a loose checked shirt, and anxiously awaits his return for the last 30 minutes of the film. Women are reduced to silence; Jasmine (Vivica A. Fox) does not utter a single word during her own wedding to Steve, while David and Connie join hands, a close-up of David's hand on top highlighting *his* wedding ring.

The very last scene of the film confirms that humanity's victory is tantamount to the reassertion of patriarchy and works as a condensed version of *Independence Day*'s ideological project, that of building a new friendship between a Jew and an African American that will confirm the former's masculinity while sidelining women. Steve pats David's shoulder as they reappear together, striding confidently through the desert, dressed in military gear and holding cigars, while their wives run towards them and David demonstrates his newly found virility by lifting Connie from the ground. The two women stand silently by their side as they are rejoined by the white figures of authority, the President and his military advisors, who validate the men's courage, including them in the sphere of white patriarchal power.

The primacy of whiteness?

Indeed, as we can see in this last scene, as soon as the white president enters the screen, he becomes the primary focus of the camera. Despite its promotion of ethnic diversity, *Independence Day* is centred on an unmarked white man, positioned as the leader of the fight against the aliens and as humanity's best exemplar. The conflation of the two is most apparent in the scene where he delivers his rallying speech. As he makes his way through the crowd to reach an elevated spot, both member and leader of the group, he becomes a central focus point, a process underlined by the numerous reaction shots of the gathering audience, the prolonged zoom-ins on him standing alone (10, then 15 seconds) and the length of his speech (more than one minute) in an otherwise very fast-paced film. Moreover, the camera zooms in on him precisely when he repeats the word 'mankind', singling him out as its leader, spokesman and embodiment. Just as nations of 'others', like Iraq and Japan, are portrayed in the film as happy followers of American leadership,[43] minorities are, in fact, auxiliaries at the service of a structural white domination, as revealed by the President's central position in most of *Independence Day*'s scenes and shots. In the end, the victory of humanity in *Independence Day* is the result of American ethnic cooperation under the leadership of white patriarchy.

The white man thus remains the best representative of humanity, even in a context of multicultural cooperation, as evidenced in *The Matrix*, which reprises the familiar motif of the white saviour. Although I find Christopher Sharrett's analysis of the film as 'the *locus classicus* of neo-conservative apocalypticism' that 'uses a well-worn and incomprehensible messiah narrative to carry a jumble of special effects'[44] dismissively simplistic, *The Matrix* does resort to obvious and hackneyed Christian symbolism in its portrayal of its hero, Mr Anderson (Keanu Reeves), renamed Neo or 'the One'. Neo is indeed reborn after waking up in the matrix's core, naked as a baby, where he is plunged into its water and then lifted out, arms outstretched, left with stigmata (the holes in his neck and arm) upon his awakening before becoming the saviour of humanity, his immanence revealed when he merges with Agent Smith.

Moreover, even if Keanu Reeves, a Canadian citizen born in Lebanon of a British mother and a Chinese-Hawaiian father, can be seen as 'a postnational poster boy',[45] he was mostly perceived, according to R.L. Rutsky, as a 'middle-class white boy',[46] especially at the time of the film's release, less than ten years after his rise to fame thanks to his role as dumb metalhead in the Bill and Ted movies.[47] The film itself enhances the character's whiteness – Reeves appears much paler than in *Point Break* (Kathryn Bigelow, 1991) where he plays a surfer, but also than in *Devil's Advocate* (Taylor Hackford, 1997) where he portrays a lawyer – and this paleness is even commented on within the film, in Neo's first scene, when a red-haired and rosy-skinned visitor asks if everything is alright since he 'looks even whiter than usual'. Neo's face does seem whiter than usual, with a luminous quality to it as if it had been overexposed. It is brought out by the contrast with his dark clothes and his pairing with Laurence Fishburne. Moreover, Neo is regularly associated with white backgrounds, like the empty computer program where anything can be downloaded. This digital whiteness even seems to spring from his own pale face, since his first visit is triggered by a tight close-up of his face followed by a zoom-out into bright whiteness, as if his face had triggered the fade to white. His second visit reprises

Masculinity in Contemporary Science Fiction Cinema

Figure 4.2 The possibilities of whiteness in *The Matrix*

this effect of white on white, with a medium close shot of Neo's face against the luminous white background. This time, Neo takes advantage of the possibilities of whiteness, ordering infinite rows of weapons that fill the white screen (Figure 4.2). The superimposition of his white face on white backgrounds represents Neo's face as a blank page where anything is possible. Indeed, the effect is repeated after Neo has saved Morpheus and Trinity and is revealed to be the One. The exclamation of a fellow crew member, 'I knew it, he's the One', is immediately followed by a low-angle shot of Neo's face against the white sky of the matrix. These luminous white backgrounds contrast with the greenish hue of the matrix, as well as with the grey tones of the rebels' battleship. White backgrounds function as an opening of possibilities, in contrast with the many fades to black charting Neo's progression. Like the bright and empty screens he appears on, Neo is a blank page on which the future of humanity will be written. Again, it is the white man who ensures the survival of humanity, his whiteness pitted against the grey of the machines and the black and green code. At the end of *The Matrix*, the camera zooms into the code before a fade-out signals the end of the matrix, while light reappears through Neo's white face, announcing a bright new world liberated from the machines, 'where anything is possible'.

However, *The Matrix* and its sequels consistently offer a strong critique of dominant white society by pitting a black leader and his ethnically diverse followers against a malevolent matrix colour-coded as white, which Tani Dianca Sanchez links to Patricia Hill Collins's concept of 'matrices of domination',[48] 'extensive systems of control maintained by elite white men', i.e. the Agents, who are 'allegories' of a system which is 'completely indifferent to human welfare'.[49] Indeed, the matrix is painted as a homogenised environment where everyone (the Agents as well as the inhabitants) is white. This is made apparent in the program reproducing the matrix for Neo's sake, where everyone is white, dressed in black and white, with the exception of a beautiful blonde in a red dress, who is immediately replaced by an Agent. Everyone looks alike, and the humans are all interchangeable, since they can be replaced by an Agent at any moment. As Morpheus explains to Neo, 'The matrix is a system, and that system is our enemy ... These people are part of that system and that makes them our enemy.' The matrix is clearly equated with an oppressive white society whose Agents try to infiltrate and destroy minority movements, just like the FBI infiltrated the different protest movements of the 1960s and 1970s. Morpheus is, indeed, brutally arrested by the police; first battered by Agent Smith, he is then punched to the ground and hit by encircling helmeted police, a scene reminiscent of police brutality during the Civil Rights Movement or the Rodney King riots. The next scene shows Morpheus handcuffed to a chair, tortured by an Agent who compares the human species to a virus or a disease and expresses disgust at their stink, words that could easily evoke racism against blacks. The film clearly takes the side of the rebels or so-called terrorists, presenting Morpheus as a charismatic leader vilified by white society, evoking the Black Panthers[50] (also referenced by the sunglasses and black leather costumes) or even Jesse Jackson.

Indeed, to fight the white matrix, Morpheus assembles what could be called, in reference to Jesse Jackson's political organisation, a 'rainbow coalition'. Apart from Neo, the rebel crew includes two women, three blacks, a Hispanic, a teenage white boy and one white man, Cypher, who is revealed to be a traitor working for the Agents and a white supremacist rejecting interethnic cooperation. Cypher can no longer bear Morpheus's authority and gives him over to the Agents, before killing the minority members of the crew, first the two blacks, then the Hispanic and one of the two women. He betrays his comrades in order to reintegrate the system and become a member of its dominant class: in the matrix, he calls himself Mr Reagan and demands to be 'someone important ... like an actor'. Beyond the ironic nod to Ronald Reagan, the scene also implicitly denounces white men's exclusive control of power.

As Tani Dianca Sanchez brilliantly shows, *The Matrix* uses black history and ideology to challenge whiteness, increasingly disrupting whiteness and its norms in its sequels, *The Matrix Reloaded* and *The Matrix: Revolutions*.[51] Indeed, most of the important new characters are black, like Niobe (Jada Pinkett-Smith), Link (Harold Perrineau) and Commander Lock (Harry Lennix). Ximena Gallardo even notes that *The Matrix* trilogy casts 'every black actor in a heroic role while antagonists, villainous or otherwise, are represented by white actors'.[52] Black characters are placed in positions of power and agency, with Morpheus and Lock both vying for leadership in Zion, one a powerful orator, the other a strategic mastermind, echoing the rise of African Americans in politics and the army in the 1990s (for example, Colin Powell became the first African-American Secretary of State in 2001 followed immediately, in 2005, by the second, Condoleezza Rice). Even black female characters have agency, as exemplified by the Oracle (Gloria Foster) and especially Niobe, whose skills and decisions trump Morpheus's in the third instalment of the franchise. Above all, the two sequels centre on the preservation of Zion, in reference to the Rastafari belief that Ethiopia is Zion, the original birthplace of humankind. Zion is portrayed as a multicultural haven in opposition to the matrix, so that the sequels differ in their overall production design with darker sets and fewer 'outdoor' scenes shot in 'daylight', especially in the third film, which takes place mostly underground. The sequels oppose the human authenticity of Zion to the artificiality of the matrix, contrasting the warm colours and textures of the characters' costumes in Zion (coloured wool and patterned silk) with the black leather worn in the matrix. As Sanchez underlines, this opposition is especially striking during the dance sequence in *The Matrix: Reloaded*, where the drumbeats, bared bodies and golden hue given by the torches in a cave of earth and stone contrast with the electronic music, constraining costumes and neon of the clubs in the matrix. The dance sequence thus 'exudes the essence of a diverse, creative humanity',[53] suggesting 'not a sexuality out of control' but a life-giving communal strength.

Nevertheless, Sanchez downplays the emphasis placed in all three films on Neo's role as humanity's saviour, worshipped by the Zion community and some of the most prominent black characters, as well as his being the main focus of the narrative. Although Sanchez insists that the last images of the trilogy are not of Neo, the white man, but of the Oracle, a black woman, and her dependents, an Asian man and a young Indian girl,[54] they are nonetheless *about* him, since the characters are discussing his fate and the last image of a beautiful sunset has been designed by the little girl in his honour. As Krin Gabbard argues, the main purpose of the Oracle and of Morpheus throughout the trilogy has been to establish that Neo is the One,[55] so that Neo remains the representative of humanity, the one targeted by the Agents who deride *him* specifically as 'only human'. Blackness still serves to help and support white masculinity, although the latter is presented as weak and uncertain until the end (an aspect I'll come back to in Chapter 5), unlike the successful remasculinisation operated in *Independence Day* by Captain Hiller.

Will Smith, Lone Black Hero

Despite the centrality of the white president in *Independence Day*, it is indeed the Will Smith character who 'comes out on top', according to Amy Taubin in her review.[56] The film launched the actor's prolific career in the science fiction genre, with ten films to his credit: *Independence Day*, *Men in Black* (Barry Sonnenfeld, 1997), *Wild Wild West* (Sonnenfeld, 1999), *Men in Black II* (Sonnenfeld, 2002), *I, Robot* (2004), *I Am Legend* (2007), *Hancock* (Peter Berg, 2008), *Men in Black 3* (Sonnenfeld, 2012) and *After Earth* (Shyamalan, 2013). From comic black buddy teamed with a white partner, Smith has moved on to being the central hero of more serious science fiction dramas that address the question of race through a critique of whiteness, most visibly in *I, Robot* and *I Am Legend*. His films offer a positive image of black masculinity through the trappings of the middle or even upper class, so that they tend in the end to reinscribe it in the hegemonic capitalistic patriarchal mould, as evidenced most blatantly in *After Earth*.

A critique of whiteness

I, Robot and *I Am Legend* exemplify Richard Dyer's chapter on 'white death' developing 'the idea of whites as both themselves dead and as bringers of death'.[57] The robots of *I, Robot* and the zombies of *I Am Legend* are, in effect, embodiments of 'extreme whiteness' or what Bakke calls 'hyperwhites',[58] since they are 'hue white' rather than 'skin white'.[59] The beginning of *I, Robot* thus contrasts the warm colours of downtown Chicago teeming with people of different colours and old-fashioned coloured robots (for example, the blue FedEx delivery robot or the orange garbage collectors) with the advertisements for the new NS-5s, translucent white robots who appear in a fade to white against a luminous white background. The warmth of a human environment is encapsulated by the hero's grandmother's apartment, with its wooden floors, golden lights and table laid with a big breakfast including sweet potato pie, and stands in stark contrast to the crime scene at USRobotics that follows, where Spooner (Will Smith), dressed in black leather, seems out of place in an entirely white environment. He has been sent to investigate the death of Dr Lanning, an old white scientist, who appears before him in a hologram, his ghost-like presence emphasised by his pale skin, white laboratory coat and white beard against white steps in the background. Whiteness is here associated with the absence of colour and substance, that is to say the absence of life, as underlined by the camera, which follows the disappearing hologram to focus on the translucent transmitter in the middle of broken glass and tilts up to show the actual dead body of the old man, all in the same tracking shot, making a clear link between translucent technology, whiteness as absence of colour, destruction and death (Figure 4.3).

Moreover, the scene ends on a long shot showing the massive white columns that support the USR headquarters, followed by a pan to a low-angle shot of a huge robot overlooking the premises on a tense musical soundtrack that makes the robot, and more generally white USR technology, seem menacing to diminutive yet colourful humans. White technology is presented as oppressive and is rejected throughout the film by the black hero, who insists on doing everything manually so as not to be controlled by white forces: his black music, therefore, cannot be played by a

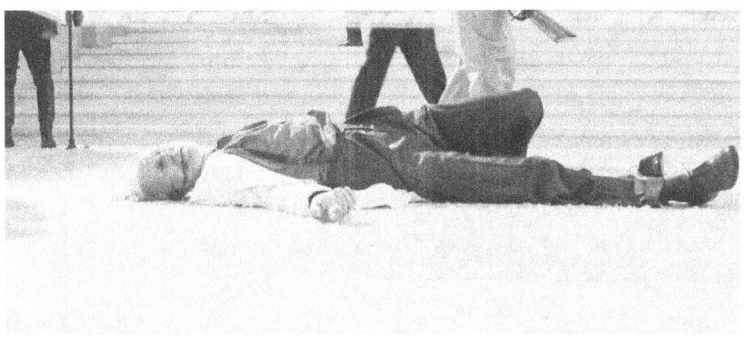

Figure 4.3 Whiteness as death in *I, Robot*

white woman unable to operate his CD player, while he is the only human able to roam freely after the NS5 take-over thanks to his old-fashioned manually driven motorcycle. Indeed, as in *Virtuosity* and *The Matrix*, white technology imposes a reign of terror through an artificial intelligence represented as 'an uncontrollable white Freudian Id feeding on humanity's death wish'.[60] Here, it is the female VIKI, a disembodied luminous white face, who controls and directs the equally luminous NS5s to form infantry squares, impose a curfew and eliminate the legitimate police force, in a clear echo of fascist regimes bent on containing the population and suppressing dissent. As Sean Brayton has argued, *I, Robot* 'explores whiteness through a trope of inhumanity and terror',[61] drawing a parallel between political terror regimes and what bell hooks describes as 'the way whiteness makes its presence felt in black life, most often as terrorising imposition, a power that wounds, hurts, tortures'.[62]

Whiteness is therefore a 'representation of terror'[63] that is political in *I, Robot* but also aesthetic, especially in *I Am Legend*. The robots of *I, Robot*, and even more so the zombies of *I Am Legend* are indeed fast, agile and very strong, in line with the evolution of zombies in contemporary horror movies analysed by David Roche, which 'are played up as figures of terror rather than figures of horror'.[64] Like the remake of *Dawn of the Dead* (Zack Snyder, 2004), *I Am Legend* increases the zombies' 'danger factor',[65] leaving little time for contemplation, contrasting with the representation of the undead members of the Family in *The Omega Man*, the 1971 adaptation of Richard Matheson's original novel[66] and one of the inspirations for the 2007 film.[67] Indeed, the members of the Family move slowly, one of the symptoms of 'third stage zombification' being torpor, and in the 1971 scene where they prepare to execute Dr Neville (Charlton Heston), they remove their hoods so that the hero (and the audience) can fully see their horrifying marks. On the contrary, the CGI zombies (aka darkseekers) of *I Am Legend* are only glimpsed at as they zip out of the dark to leap at the hero, attacking him from all sides.

Indeed, *I Am Legend* presents all whites as potential threats and 'bearers of death', including the apparently harmless and immobile white mannequins, in a clear echo of *The World, the Flesh and the Devil*, a much earlier example of last *black* man on earth, starring and produced by Harry Belafonte in the midst of the Civil Rights Movement. Like Ralph (Harry Belafonte), who first befriends a white mannequin only to resent its perpetual smile as sneering condescension ('You've laughed at me once too often') and then throws it out of the window, Neville (Will Smith) is horrified at finding Fred, the mannequin he rents DVDs from, standing far from the DVD shop at the end of a road bridge. Whites cannot be trusted (a feeling emphasised by the fact that the mannequin is played by an actor and therefore appears almost alive[68]), since this move is a trap to capture Neville, who ends up hanging upside down from the road lights, awaiting his lynching by the darkseekers. To develop Sean Brayton's analysis, the darkseekers can thus be read as figures of white supremacy instilling terror in all those not of their race, creatures of white biotechnology gone awry – the devastating KV virus was designed by one of the few speaking white characters in the film, Dr Alice Krippin (Emma Thompson) – and infected racists refusing the cure offered by the black Dr Neville.[69]

Furthermore, whereas the white zombies of *I Am Legend* and the white robots of *I, Robot* all look alike, living and moving in packs where they are undifferentiated, the black man's bodily difference is seen as positive, since the hero's cyborg strength enables him to defeat VIKI in *I, Robot*, while he is immune to the virus in *I Am Legend* and able to 'ghost', that is to say suppress his fear and its scent, in *After Earth*. In Gretchen Bakke's words, the black hero enables the world to return 'to a version of "normalcy" that explicitly excludes white men, their consumer cultures and their sterile logics'.[70] Indeed, while the infected are all white, the visible survivors in *I Am Legend* are mostly non-white – Neville is joined by the Hispanic Anna (Alice Braga), while one of the soldiers who open the gates of the refuge at the end of the film is also black – and it is the hero's black blood that will enable the human race to regenerate.[71] In this respect, both *I Am Legend* and *I, Robot*, which includes many African Americans in minor roles, herald a multiracial future. As such, they can be seen as responses to Richard Pryor's scathing remark about the all-white futuristic world of *Logan's Run*.

Black humanity: an alternative vision of masculinity?

As in *Virtuosity*, *Strange Days* and *The Matrix*, blackness is positioned in *I Am Legend* and especially *I, Robot* as 'on the side of the Human and the Real'.[72] Gallardo thus underlines that the black hero has become the new representative of humanity, carrying out science fiction's avowed aim of defining the human. Yet the black hero remains male, so that the science fiction films of Will Smith participate in defining *masculinity* rather than humanity. Do these films adhere to the white middle-class hegemonic model of masculinity or can they offer an alternative vision?

In his surprisingly short analysis of Will Smith's science fiction films, Adilifu Nama declares that Will Smith allowed 'a more central, defiant and charismatic version of black cool to enter the SF film genre'.[73] While Smith is often seen as emblematising the 'cool pose',[74] I want to examine his evolution towards a more emotional and responsible model of masculinity within *I, Robot*, in *I Am Legend* and (less so) in *After Earth*. *I, Robot* emphasises Will Smith's 'coolness', defined by Majors and Billson as 'poise under pressure and the ability to maintain detachment, even during tense encounters',[75] most heavily at the beginning of the film. His black leather costume and skull cap clearly invoke such figures of defiant cool as Shaft, the blaxploitation icon, and rappers like Ice Cube. The cool pose is a way to express blackness and stand tall in front of more powerful upper-class whites, as exemplified in Spooner's confrontation with USR's white CEO (Bruce Greenwood). Throughout this important interview, Spooner maintains detachment by using humour, especially sarcasm, to destabilise his mighty interviewee, so that the two men are presented as equals by the camera, their faces level in a shot/reverse shot dialogue that enhances Will Smith's bulky shoulders against the CEO's slighter frame.

Yet because it stresses what Gallardo terms the 'self-loathing' felt by a black human 'painfully infiltrated by white technology', *I, Robot* spells out what is at the core of white cyborg films – rather than contrasting with them,[76] emphasising the limits and vulnerability of the cyborg hero analysed in Chapter 1. Signifiers of blackness, especially music, open up space for emotion and vulnerability from the outset of the film, which begins with Stevie Wonder's 'Superstition'. If the song can be seen, in Sean Brayton's words, as situating Will Smith in a 'safe' role, with Spooner listening to Motown rather than gangsta rap,[77] it also suggests a more sensitive model of masculinity, since, according to Kobena Mercer, 'black male musicians like Stevie Wonder or Marvin Gaye undercut the braggadocio to make critiques of conventional models of black masculinity'.[78] As in *The World, the Flesh and the Devil*, where Ralph relieves his loneliness by improvising a blues song when trapped in the coal mine, *I, Robot* and *I Am Legend* both use music, and especially song, to soothe their protagonist's pain, as he hums along to Bob Marley or Stevie Wonder. Thus, the shower scene in *I, Robot*, which, for many viewers, emphasises Smith's muscularity and attractiveness,[79] also insists on Spooner's vulnerability, since the full shot of his body can be explained by the character's paranoia (according to Smith, Spooner suffers from survivor's guilt, which leads him to leave all doors open[80]), while the zoom-in on his bent head suggests emotional anguish, underscored more specifically by his humming the line 'seven years of bad luck' from 'Superstition'.

Smith's 'safe' brand of blackness can be criticised as being sanitised for white viewers, but it also offers an emotional model of masculinity. This is put forward in *I, Robot* in the scene where Spooner tells the story of his traumatic accident and the death of a little girl to Dr Calvin (Bridget Moynahan).[81] As we have seen at the end of Chapter 3, this scene highlights the hero's emotional sensitivity through the compassionate gaze of the cold female scientist, contrasting the tears that well up in his eyes with her medical approach to his half-robotic body. The black hero's emotional vulnerability is further developed in *I Am Legend*, contrasting sharply with

'White Folks Ain't Planning for Us to be Here'

The Omega Man while drawing on *The World, the Flesh and the Devil* in the type of masculinity it presents. Indeed, *I Am Legend*'s Dr Neville is constantly associated with figures of vulnerability, be it the deer he never manages to shoot or the young dog he cowers with in his bathtub as the darkseekers roam the streets. He expresses a range of emotions from despair to rage that contrast with Neville's self-control and 'crusty good humour'[82] in *The Omega Man*, while his emotional outbursts and desperate shouting recall Ralph's forlorn calls and loneliness in *The World, the Flesh and the Devil*. Unlike *Omega*'s Neville, he does not hunt down the darkseekers, as stressed by Will Smith in the DVD extras: 'Neville is not trying to fight these things; he's not a superhero. The last thing he wants to do is have to interact with these things.'[83] Furthermore, *I Am Legend* includes many flashbacks of Neville with his wife and child, including his tearful goodbye to his daughter as she boards an evacuation helicopter – the back story of his failed attempt to protect his family, which the film repeatedly evokes through flashbacks, insists on his loss and failure to carry out his role of manly protector. As Claire Sisco King notes, these flashbacks present the hero as a traumatised victim and underline the 'disruption of his masculine subject position' as he fails to perform hegemonic masculinity both as a public figure of authority and as a father.[84] In contrast with the white manly toughness, arrogance and heroic bravado displayed by the bachelor Neville in *The Omega Man*, *I Am Legend* and *I, Robot* (and even *After Earth*) allow their heroes to express emotions, often including a scene where the protagonist cries because of the loss of a child, and emphasise his inclusion in a nuclear family (the trio formed by Spooner, Calvin and the child-like Sonny forms a family of sorts at the end of *I, Robot*). The characters played by Smith have gradually abandoned 'the cool pose' to reveal their emotional engagement and take on the responsibilities of fatherhood, as they move up the social ladder. In the process, Smith's star persona has shifted from rapper to father, as underscored by the casting of the actor's own biological children, Willow and Jaden as, respectively, Marley in *I Am Legend* and Kitai in *After Earth*.

However, the films fall short of presenting a real challenge to white hegemonic masculinity. First of all, Will Smith portrays heroes who are either left alone (on a stranded ship in *After Earth*) or are paired with white or

Masculinity in Contemporary Science Fiction Cinema

light-skinned women (*I, Robot* and *I Am Legend*). There is no interracial sex or even kissing, reinstating on the sly the taboo of miscegenation, which was openly broken in *The Omega Man* and explicitly addressed in *The World, the Flesh and the Devil*. While the hero is included within strictly African-American families (his grandmother in *I, Robot*, and his wife and child in *I Am Legend* and *After Earth*), there is no mention of a wider black community, contrary to *The Brother from Another Planet*, *Strange Days* or *The Matrix*, for instance, so that Will Smith's films perpetuate the strategy for containing blacks exposed by Ed Guerrero in 1993, that is to say:

> the industry practice of giving an African American top billing in a film in which he or she is completely isolated from other blacks or any reference to the black world. Black culture is embodied in the black star's persona, surrounded and appropriated by a white context and narrative for the entertainment of the dominant or crossover audience.[85]

Indeed, in spite of a few references to black culture (through costume, music and minor characters), the heroes played by Smith inhabit very white and upper-class worlds, far removed from lower-class African-American neighbourhoods, not to mention the ghettoes. In contrast with the warm colours of Harlem in *The Brother from Another Planet* or of Zion in *The Matrix*, *I, Robot*'s production design is dominated by the gleaming USR tower staffed with white employees and white robots, while *I Am Legend* focuses on white upper-class areas of Manhattan, showing, for instance, Neville driving through the Financial District, playing golf from the Intrepid into the New York skyline or fishing on the white steps of the Sackler Wing in the Metropolitan Museum of Art (Figure 4.4). Neville goes nowhere near Upper Manhattan or the Bronx, and Spooner visits his grandmother's apartment once, never to return, so that in the end, as Tani Dianca Sanchez underlines, the films tend to present white futuristic cities, 'the emphasis [being] on males working within a white systemic order. They correct problems within the system but not the system itself.'[86]

Indeed, the heroes of *I, Robot* and *I Am Legend* do not seek to overthrow the system, as Morpheus does in *The Matrix*, but focus on correcting its flaws to bring back the old (white) order, crushing those who stand in

'White Folks Ain't Planning for Us to be Here'

Figure 4.4 Neville fishing on the steps of the Sackler wing in *I Am Legend*

the way. Smith's black protagonist is deprived of his full transformative potential in *I, Robot*, since it is Sonny who leads the final rebellion at the end of the film. According to Sean Brayton, Sonny, the only white robot with a conscience, can, in effect, be read as a 'post-racist' white subject 'that aspires to racial reconciliation',[87] thus blunting the critique of whiteness and white technology as a fundamentally oppressive system, especially since the robots are presented as slaves throughout the first half of the film, while Spooner is the 'essentially racist'[88] one – the tables are turned on the historically oppressed and the issue of white responsibility is sidestepped. The terror spread by whites is also attenuated in *I Am Legend* by the contemporary aesthetics governing the representation of zombies discussed by David Roche.[89] The white zombies have become ephemeral threats deprived of any agency or social organisation (Neville sadly remarks that 'social de-evolution appears complete'), in contrast with *The Omega Man*'s highly organised Family, a fanatical sect that seeks to return to a pre-modern era without printed books or machines and threatens all those who are different from them.[90] The science fiction films starring Will Smith can therefore be seen as participating in the post-racial ideology that was validated by the rise of Barack Obama to the highest office in the land.[91] As Janani Subramanian argues, his heroes, especially Neville in *I Am Legend* and Commander Cypher Raige in *After Earth*, partake of a post-racial meritocracy where race no longer matters: 'Neville's Washington Park townhouse and his former prestigious position as government scientist associate him with an upper-middle class urbanity that distances him from any kind of historical connection to the black community'.[92] The heroes played by Smith belong, indeed, to the segment of 'aristocratic Blacks' or 'neo-mulattoes' criticised by Eduardo Bonilla-Sanchez.[93] The films never explicitly mention the issue of race, and Smith himself is repeatedly seen as 'transcending race' by industry officials and viewers alike,[94] so that his heroes not only emblematise the possibility of individual success in a 'colour-blind' American society,[95] but participate in promoting what Subramanian calls a 'colorless American nationalism',[96] since they always serve the state.

Indeed, the heroes portrayed by Will Smith systematically serve in the police or army, which are presented as all-male preserves. As Brayton argues in his article on *I Am Legend*, 'since the black hero stands in for the state, giving the appearance of diversity and multicultural tolerance, *Legend* is able to indulge in a conservative utopia that privileges both militarism and masculinity'.[97] Thus his heroes tend to revalidate patriarchal masculinity at the expense of women, who are repeatedly sidelined (as seen in Chapter 3) and even openly targeted by the films. Dr Calvin is the butt of most of Spooner's jokes, while the virtual yet clearly female VIKI is held responsible for the robots' fascist turn in *I, Robot*.[98] Similarly, in *I Am Legend*, 'the promotion of Neville's manliness relies on an active displacement of women through most of the film'.[99] Brayton gives the example of Dr Alice Krippin (Emma Thompson) who, again, is both sidelined within the narrative and blamed for the deadly virus (the 'Krippin Virus' actually bears her name), yet the same goes for Anna, who appears very late in the film, a pious 'angel in the house' who saves the hero in a flash of light and is then confined to his house,[100] cooking and listening, until the last two minutes of the film, when she drives to safety singing his praises and celebrating his name. The film's, as well as Neville's, insistence that he can 'fix this', that this 'Ground Zero' is 'his site' thus participates in the post-9/11 heroic remasculinisation of America,[101] which will be discussed in the next chapter. Despite his emotional outbursts, Neville still displays all the hallmarks of virile hegemonic masculinity, dismissing Anna's vision of a refuge as a utopian dream, then displaying his superior skills with firearms in the final confrontation with the darkseekers. Neville's athleticism, as well as his weapons and driving skills, present 'a stalwart masculinity'[102] that is this time closer to the Neville played by Charlton Heston in *The Omega Man* than Harry Belafonte in *The World, the Flesh and the Devil*. This is evidenced by the first scene, which reprises *Omega*'s opening sequence, Neville driving a sports car at full speed in an empty city, signifying from the outset his connection with the white upper class.

The revalidation of patriarchal masculinity is most blatant in *After Earth*, where women are completely marginalised (the sister is dead while the mother remains at home), so that the film can focus entirely on the relationship between father and son. *After Earth*, in effect, charts the initiation of Kitai Raige (Jaden Smith) by his father Cypher Raige (Will Smith) into hegemonic masculinity and the domination of others (Earth's natural environment and the evil alien Ursas) through an ethos of self-control and the rejection of emotions, especially fear (which is what betrays humans to the Ursas). Derided by the critics[103] and shunned by audiences in the United States,[104] the film seems to glorify a father tragically unable to express any emotion (Smith gives an unusually wooden performance), who thanks his son for saving his life by giving him a military salute. The gesture, which is repeated twice and is central to the film, signals Kitai's entry into adult manhood first and foremost as a soldier, thus perpetuating and encouraging a model of black masculinity founded on repressed emotions and soldierly behaviour, a model specifically denounced by bell hooks: '[black men] are taught to believe that a real male is fearless, insensitive, egocentric, and invulnerable' and should 'block out all emotions.'[105] *After Earth* helps inscribe black masculinity in the hegemonic order, especially through its insistence on fatherly responsibilities and patriarchal mentoring. It counters the negative stereotype of black males as absent fathers by abiding the long-standing call for the black man's return as head of the family urged both by the white establishment (still influenced by the controversial conclusions of the 1965 Moynihan report), and part of the black community (as evidenced by Louis Farrakhan's 1995 Million Man March, which encouraged black men to 'clean up their lives and rebuild their neighbourhoods'). More generally, by emphasising the heroes' agency at the micro level (that of the nuclear family) as well as at the macro level (the future of the nation), Will Smith's science fiction films reclaim the masculine attributes that sociologists like Robert Staples have argued were historically denied to black male slaves, such as authority and familial responsibility,[106] and assert the black man's role in building and preserving the nation. In effect, the science fiction films starring Will Smith turn a *subordinated* masculinity into a *hegemonic* masculinity by conforming to the mainstream dominant model, that of the middle-class *pater familias* who adheres to the structures of power and maintains his own power through the subordination of women. The black man is welcomed into the fold by becoming an upper-class patriarchal capitalist. Only in that way, it seems, can the black male become Man, humanity's last hope and its best representative.

Science fiction has come a long way since the release of the entirely white *Logan's Run*. From alien Others in a civilisation defined as white, African Americans have become humanity's saviours as well as its exemplars against Others coded as white, challenging to some extent Richard Dyer's analysis of unmarked whiteness as human norm.[107] Moreover, all the science fiction films analysed in this chapter offer a critical analysis of whiteness as lifeless and destructive: whites are now the ones being othered and dehumanised, providing a new form of science fictional estrangement. However, this attempt at racial estrangement fails to offer a new gender order and an alternative model of masculinity, despite the efforts of *The Matrix* trilogy to include active women and the display of an emotional sensitive masculinity in *Predator 2*, *I, Robot* and *I Am Legend*. Indeed, the black body tends to be used as a remasculinising force, working to the benefit of white characters in the 1990s, and to the benefit of black characters in the 2000s, including them in white capitalistic patriarchy. The science fiction films of Will Smith have, in effect, turned a historically subordinated masculinity into a hegemonic one by mimicking white hegemonic masculinity, its suppression of 'feminine' influences and its subordination of women. They also consistently present an upper-class version of black masculinity that ignores the problems of the majority of African Americans still living in poverty. In the end, an intersectional analysis of the increasing presence of black men in science fiction films, combining race, gender and class, shows that black presence does challenge white hegemony, by othering whites, but not hegemonic masculinity, since black heroes, especially those played by Will Smith, tend to integrate into the system and assimilate its values whereby empowerment comes from material success and the domination of others.[108] Finally, Will Smith seems very lonely at the top, without any female or African-American peers, while science fiction continues in many ways to favour whiteness, presenting aesthetically white worlds dominated by gleaming technology and peopled almost exclusively by whites, from *Gattaca* (Andrew Niccol, 1997), *AI* (Steven Spielberg, 2001) and *Minority Report* (Spielberg, 2002) to, more recently, *Inception* (Christopher Nolan, 2010), *Her* (Spike Jonze, 2013), *Interstellar* (Nolan, 2014), *Terminator Genisys* (Alan Taylor, 2015) and *Arrival* (Denis Villeneuve, 2016).

5

Redefining Masculinity in Times of 'Crisis'

In *American Masculinity under Clinton*, Brenton J. Malin emphasises the 'crisis of masculinity' discourses that dominated the 1990s in the media, academia and society at large.[1] This crisis was often lamented, for instance by Robert Bly and his 'mythopoetic men's movement', which vowed to help men find 'the deep masculine' they had lost by drumming, crying and bonding in forest retreats.[2] The decade indeed saw the rise of many men's movements seeking to heal men's crisis by enjoining them to behave better and fulfil their family obligations, like the evangelical Promise Keepers founded in 1990 by Bill McCartney,[3] or the Million Man March organised in 1995 by the leader of Nation of Islam Louis Farrakhan. Although these movements were decried by many as conservative and anti-feminist,[4] they can be seen retrospectively as a form of therapy and a promise of change for men suffering from an identity crisis, as Nancy Cohen explains:

> Each of the men's movements called on men to engage in rituals of personal transformation as a step to a new way of being a man – in relationship to other men, to women and children, and in American culture and society.[5]

Masculinity in Contemporary Science Fiction Cinema

We can see in Cohen's description how masculinity was being redefined in the 1990s, away from hypermasculinity and its emphasis on physical strength and invulnerability, towards emotional intelligence and exchange with others.

This change in the definition and representation of masculinity appears quite strikingly in 1990s Hollywood science fiction films, which generally focused more on the mind than on the body, especially films on the nefarious influence of information technology and/or virtual reality such as *Strange Days* (Kathryn Bigelow, 1995), *Johnny Mnemonic* (Robert Longo, 1995), *Dark City* (Alex Proyas, 1998) and *The Matrix* (Lilly and Lana Wachowski, 1999). These films feature heroes whose physique is markedly different from the hypermasculine heroes of the 1980s, and who appear passive and weak. Hounded by patriarchal figures, the male protagonists all experience identity crises and are presented as men in distress who need rescuing by stronger female partners.

Yet, as Brendon J. Malin and many others have underlined, the 'crisis of masculinity' discourse is a recurrent one,[6] and was reactivated in the United States after the attacks of 11 September 2001 (9/11), when 'there was a rush to defend and bolster an American manhood compromised and belittled by the attacks', whereas in the media, women were either absent or represented as damsels in distress.[7] While many authors stress the return to traditional gender roles and the restoration of hegemonic masculinity based on control of and superiority over women after 9/11, the discourse of crisis can again be seen as a vehicle for transformation, as evidenced in some post-apocalyptic films released since. Indeed, while the trauma of 9/11 led to the return of heroic hypermasculinity in the host of superhero films that followed,[8] saturating the youth segment of the market,[9] a series of science fiction films addressed issues faced by older men by focusing on the challenges of fatherhood. Post-apocalyptic fatherhood films, including *War of the Worlds* (Steven Spielberg, 2005), *The Road* (John Hillcoat, 2009), *Interstellar* (Christopher Nolan, 2014) and even *Terminator Genisys* (Alan Taylor, 2015), feature nurturing males obsessed with the material but also emotional well-being of their children in worlds facing destruction, so that the films present a model of masculinity that engages with emotions and takes others into account. Thus, this chapter not only examines how the models of masculinity showcased by science fiction film have changed since the 1990s, with an emphasis on emotional sensitivity and interaction with others, but also endeavours to determine whether or not discourses of crisis can challenge hegemonic masculinity, or at least redefine it.

Away from Hypermasculinity

Passive heroes

The 'crisis of masculinity' of the 1990s produced a different model of masculinity onscreen in terms of physique, with slimmer, less muscular heroes. The protagonists of *Johnny Mnemonic*, *Strange Days*, *Dark City* and *The Matrix* are a far cry from the hypermasculine cyborgs of the 1980s. The films showcase feminised heroes who are often presented as passive objects to be gazed upon, subverting the codes of the traditionally active male hero. *Dark City* thus presents its main protagonist, John Murdoch (Rufus Sewell), by zooming in through the round window of a bathroom where he lies asleep in a bath, feminised by the reference to Sleeping Beauty, the iconography of the bathing scene and the voyeurism of the camera. Contrary to the nude scenes of hypermasculine science fiction films like *Universal Soldier* analysed in Chapter 1, the protagonist's nakedness does not serve to display the toned muscularity of a bodybuilt hero (he is shown mostly from behind), but underscores his weakness and vulnerability, as he gets out of the bathtub confused, afraid and disoriented, almost slipping on the wet floor of the dimly lit bathroom. Similarly, *Johnny Mnemonic*'s opening scene shows the hero (Keanu Reeves) waking up, as did *Total Recall*, but, unlike Schwarzenegger who immediately sits up so that the camera can highlight his pectorals in a medium-close shot, Reeves appears sprawled out in bed in a bird's-eye shot that objectifies him, contrasting his flat white chest with the blue satin sheets (Figure 5.1). The following shots are close-ups emphasising the features of his face, as well as the curves of his shoulders and neck rather than his pectorals, which remain off-screen.

In *The Matrix*, the hero, Neo (also played by Keanu Reeves), likewise first appears asleep. The first shot shows a beautiful face, which the

Masculinity in Contemporary Science Fiction Cinema

Figure 5.1 Johnny sprawled in bed in *Johnny Mnemonic*

spectator is invited to contemplate through the use of a very slow track-in and a trip-hop soundtrack creating a dreamy, meditative atmosphere. The next tracking shot follows in close-up the curve of his neck, first presented blurred and then in focus, to sensual effect. In both *Johnny Mnemonic* and *The Matrix*, Reeves gives himself up passively to the camera, without seeking to offset his objectification by an active pose, contrary to the traditional representations of masculinity analysed by Steve Neale or Richard Dyer.[10] Rather than flexing his muscles, Reeves displays a more feminine type of beauty with his white skin, regular features and graceful movements that are highlighted throughout *The Matrix* trilogy. In fact, on the release of *The Matrix* his beauty was commented on by all critics, mostly derisively. *Variety* mocked him as boring 'eye candy',[11] while Janet Maslin sniggered that 'Keanu Reeves makes a strikingly chic Prada model of an action hero'.[12] Charles Taylor, one of the few critics to defend Reeves, provides an interesting explanation for the general sarcasm directed at the actor:

> Reeves is one of the few contemporary male stars whose presence acknowledges that people are out there in the dark looking at him ... his slight languidness encourages looking. That willingness to be looked at evokes ... a homosexual panic.[13]

Reeves, indeed, transgresses the taboo of passive male objectification, adopting the position traditionally assigned by Hollywood to women and famously described by Laura Mulvey as 'to-be-looked-at-ness',[14] a clearly unsettling experience for many reviewers. The way Keanu Reeves is filmed, especially in the first half of *The Matrix*, insisting on his physical beauty and passivity, undermines the male hero's hegemonic masculinity, as it incorporates feminine elements, subverting the dichotomy between masculine and feminine.

In many late 1990s science fiction films, the male heroes passively take orders, insults and beatings while being compared to girls. Neo is compared first to Alice when he is told to 'follow the white rabbit', and then to Dorothy from *The Wizard of Oz* by a crew member who tells him: 'Buckle your seatbelt Dorothy, because Kansas is going bye-bye'; in *Strange Days*, Lenny (Ralph Fiennes) is mocked by his rival's thugs for getting beaten up by a woman: 'We tried to find a smaller woman to beat the shit out of you.' In fact, Lenny is repeatedly beaten up without being able to fight back and is saved every time by a woman, like Johnny in *Johnny Mnemonic*, as we shall see. The heroes of the 1990s tend to be physically weak and are shown again and again in passive positions, either sitting or lying down. As Roz Kaveney notes, there are many moments of stillness and vulnerability in *Strange Days*,[15] which climax, so to speak, in the scene where Lenny receives a tape of himself sleeping on his couch, filmed by the same killer who filmed, raped and killed his friend Iris. Lenny is extremely vulnerable: lying down and unconscious, he is subjected to the same sadistic and objectifying male gaze that killed Iris and he does not wake up when the killer puts a knife to his throat.

The image of the hero forcibly laid down to be maimed or penetrated is recurrent, whether it be Johnny tied to an operating table so that his information-loaded head can be cut off in *Johnny Mnemonic*, Murdoch spread-eagled in the Strangers' headquarters to be injected with their collective memory in *Dark City*, or Neo undressed and stretched on a table by two Agents who insert a repulsive insect in his navel in *The Matrix*. These pale and lean bodies are repeatedly invaded, painful experiences that leave the male protagonists weakened: Johnny almost collapses in the bathroom after being 'hit' with 320 GB of sensitive information, while, once detached from the matrix, the perforated limp body of Neo has to be rehabilitated by needles planted in his inert body. Often, these sexually charged assaults on the heroes' integrity occur under the watchful scrutiny of other males, as exemplified by the video of Lenny (filmed by a male killer) and the reaction shots of the crew watching Neo train in *The Matrix*, where, apart from Morpheus, Trinity and Cypher the traitor, the crew appear mainly as logistical support and internal spectators for Neo's feats.

The heroes indeed need constant support as their bodies fail them, as evidenced by Neo's atrophied muscles in *The Matrix*, his impotence in *Matrix Revolutions*, Johnny's repeated collapsing in *Johnny Mnemonic* and Lenny's fainting at the end of *Strange Days*. The films are punctuated by moments of black-out, where the male heroes are completely unable to operate. Furthermore, these black-outs are not linked to physical injuries caused by bullet wounds, for example, but stem from mental breakdowns due to information or emotional overload. The 1990s mark a radical departure from 1980s hypermasculine science fiction by their promotion of the mind over the body. Nicola Rehling offers an interesting analysis of *The Matrix* and *Strange Days* as cyberfantasies that 'offer the fantasy of the ultimate Cartesian trip at a time when the body is the site of identity critiques',[16] in tune with what Anne Balsamo has perceived as a white male 'desire to return to the neutrality of the body'.[17] Yet this emphasis on the mind also distances the heroes from an essentialised vision of masculinity anchored in the physicality of the body in action. In fact, 1990s science fiction heroes are decidedly *not* physical and move very little. The beginning of *Strange Days* offers a revealing *trompe l'oeil*: the film opens with a highly kinetic action sequence shot from the point of view of an active protagonist who shoots, runs, jumps and finally dies, at which moment the film cuts to the real hero of the film, Lenny, passively watching the actions of others on disc. In fact, only Neo in *The Matrix* displays true fighting skills, after intensive training onscreen, and yet dominates the Agents thanks to his mental ability to stop bullets, which drop to the ground. In both *Johnny Mnemonic* and *The Matrix*, Keanu Reeves measures his movements, sometimes to the point of stiffness, as in the scene where he meets his scientist clients in *Johnny Mnemonic*. Threatened by three guns pointed at him, Reeves stops still in the doorframe, lifts his briefcase to deliver a supposedly witty one-liner ('Double cheese, anchovies?'), then extends his hand and makes one step forward, baring down his gestures and words to an expressive minimum: 'Question. You don't look like the kind of people I usually work for.' The same economy of movements can be found in *Dark City*, where Murdoch defeats his enemies, the Strangers, with his stare, sending telepathic shock waves while standing absolutely still, unperturbed either by the disintegration of the building surrounding him or by his slow floating rise above the city in outer space.

The dangers of hegemonic masculinity

The male protagonists' limited actions (they tend to act defensively and seldom kill) point to their more general difficulty at performing hegemonic masculinity. For instance, they are unable to operate outdoors and tend to prefer the safety of private spaces. Lenny spends most of his time indoors and depends on his friend Mace (Angela Bassett) to drive him around after his car has been impounded; Murdoch is confined to the eponymous dark city, vainly searching for Shell Beach and finding refuge only at his wife's or his uncle's apartments; Neo and Johnny are so dependent on technology that they cannot be autonomous agents, as evidenced by Johnny's anguished cries for a computer when stranded in Newark's wastelands. Nineteen-nineties cyber films generally focus on dark indoor spaces, as opposed to the more expansive landscapes of other science fiction films: the heroes are constrained by space rather than buoyed by it, generating a sense of entrapment and suffocation. Open spaces are sites of danger and chaos: in *Strange Days*, Los Angeles is ablaze, a theatre of war where the police have gone mad, shooting unarmed civilians in the open;[18] in *Johnny Mnemonic*, Johnny arrives late to his meeting because of massive demonstrations in the streets of Beijing and is later ambushed in a vacant lot in the free city of Newark; in *Dark City*, Murdoch is trapped in an ever-changing city where phallic towers rise out of nowhere and collide, crushing anyone caught in between.

The chaos and confusion that rule the films' spatial landscapes reflect the inner state of the heroes, who do not know who they are. The films all insist on the instability of identity, based on treacherous memories. The people in the matrix, including the ordinary office worker Mr Anderson, live fake lives in a constructed environment designed to 'blind them from the truth' of their bondage to the machines in *The Matrix*, while in *Dark City*, the Strangers seek to find the essence of the soul by repeatedly erasing old memories and implanting new ones, overhauling people's identities completely from one day to the next. In *Strange Days*, Lenny is mired in old memories, which he compulsively watches in the vain hope of reliving a disappeared past 'by proxy', since, as Steven Shaviro underlines, 'the gulf between who he was then, and who he is now, is all too painfully, even pathetically, evident'.[19] Johnny had his memory erased to have more brain storage and thus earn more in *Johnny Mnemonic*, so that he does not even know his own last name. Yet Johnny realises that fancy hotels and ironed shirts cannot replace childhood memories, and seeks to retrieve those memories at any cost, suggesting that normative male identity is not only deceptive but ultimately disappointing. In virtual reality, all identities are constructed, a fact that is deeply unsettling to the heroes of *The Matrix* and *Dark City*.[20] Their status as normative white males is called into question from the very beginning: formerly a loving husband, Murdoch wakes up as a serial killer of prostitutes, while program writer Thomas Anderson, after almost being fired, tries to flee the well-regulated business world of the matrix by stepping out of the window of his company tower, only to be arrested by the police. In all four films, the heroes ultimately realise that their identity as moneymaking controlling hegemonic white males (even Lenny sees himself during most of *Strange Days* as the protector of his ex-girlfriend Faith) was a sham, leading them into angst, 'that uneasiness that results from the individual's awareness that he could possibly be different than he is currently'.[21] Thus, the heroes' confusion and difficulty in performing hegemonic masculinity lead them to reject a model felt as oppressive and to consider alternatives more open to dialogue with others.

Indeed, the heroes continually seek to escape from patriarchal society and its representatives, be it the Agents of the matrix, the alien Strangers of *Dark City*, the police force in *Strange Days* or the Yakuza in *Johnny Mnemonic*. *The Matrix* and *Dark City* both open under the close watch of patriarchy, symbolised by the police torch (the eye of the police) in the former and embodied in Dr Schreber's (Kiefer Sutherland) voice-over in the latter. The point of view is thus at first patriarchal and immediately demeaning of women: the police think they can 'handle one little girl' when talking about Trinity at the beginning of *The Matrix*, while the Strangers have wantonly killed a woman in *Dark City* to test the hero's reaction and ultimately capture his soul. However, patriarchal society is revealed as manipulative and inept, assigning false identities based on false assumptions. The films lead the spectator to question the voice of patriarchy: Trinity will not be easily 'handled', while Murdoch and the detective in charge of the case quickly realise that he had nothing to do with the prostitutes' murders. Patriarchy should not be trusted and should even be feared, as all four films underscore by pitting their heroes against violent and powerful all-male groups headed by domineering male patriarchs. Old white men often embody a duplicitous patriarchy that has betrayed the human race, like Dr Schreber and the Strangers in *Dark City*, the Architect in *The Matrix Reloaded*, or Johnny's manipulative agent in *Johnny Mnemonic* – their extreme whiteness marks their hegemony as deathly and unnatural.[22] The sensitive heroes hence seek refuge from a cold and calculating patriarchy with more protective women, and end up overthrowing the system, except, surprisingly (and disappointingly), in *Strange Days*. Indeed, the potentially liberating riot against a violent police force triggered by Mace's beating at the end of the film is stopped by the old white police commissioner, who suddenly appears in the middle of the crowd as a *deus ex machina*, magnified by low-angle shots, and restores order. As John P. Garry argues, by having the commissioner benevolently look down at Mace and call an ambulance for her before helping her walk to a police car, this scene not only offers a centrist compromise at odds with the more revolutionary promise held out by the film, but also, via the rehabilitation of the police, reinstates patriarchy as a not so new social order where 'white male authority tower[s] over dependent non-whites and women'.[23]

However, an interesting aspect of both *Strange Days* and *The Matrix* is the way the two are built on a specular system that conveys their opposition to patriarchy by opposing the hero to a hegemonic alter ego.[24] *Strange Days* pairs up its hero with a stronger and better built double, Max (Tom Sizemore), a more hegemonic version of Lenny ultimately revealed as psychotic. Max's first appearance highlights first the similarities between the

Figure 5.2 Max holds a gun to Lenny's head in *Strange Days*

two men, but also the hierarchy of power that Max seeks to impose on Lenny. When Max surprises Lenny during one of his deals and pretends to arrest him, the two men are presented as belonging to the same world: both have long hair and leather jackets, in contrast with the clean-cut lawyer in a light grey suit who feels nervous and out-of-place in the seedy LA underworld, and flees immediately when ordered by Max: 'Beat it, fuckwad.' Max is holding a gun to Lenny's head and clearly enjoys the power it gives him – this is his idea of a funny joke (Figure 5.2). With his dishevelled hair and worn jacket, Max thus appears as a rougher, tougher version of Lenny, and the conversation at the bar that follows insists on his desire for masculine hegemony, at the expense of the weaker, feminised Lenny. Indeed, Max continually makes fun of Lenny, disparaging him implicitly for not being a real man; Max calls Lenny a pimp because of the expensive and colourful ties he wears, feminising his concern for appearance as vain whereas real men like Max do not care about what they wear, as the dialogue suggests: 'This tie cost more than your entire wardrobe', says Lenny, to which Max replies: 'That's not saying much.' Furthermore, Max is repulsed by Lenny's sensitivity and emotional heartbreak over his break-up with Faith (Juliette Lewis), constantly denigrating Lenny's emotions with words expressing disgust and even aggression: 'I hate to see you pining away, it makes me want to vomit', and later: 'Use the F-word around Lenny, it triggers a maudlin display, and you got to tranquilize him.' His hostility towards anything feminine can be read in the pun around the F-word, which associates Faith with fuck, suggesting both that Faith 'fucked' Lenny over and should be 'fucked' for it.

Moreover, while Lenny and Max are both ex-policemen who now spend their time in the night bars of Los Angeles, Max remains on the side of patriarchy and the law, since he works for the rich music producer Gant (Michael Wincott) as a private investigator assigned with tailing Faith, who is now Gant's girlfriend. Max therefore carries a gun and is in a position of control over Faith and Lenny, who cannot approach her without getting beaten up by Gant's thugs. Max even acts as a sort of stand-in for Lenny, who asks him to 'watch her for [him]' – both men spend their time watching Faith. The film constantly underlines the importance of the gaze, opening with a shot of Lenny's eye – throughout the film, there are many extreme close-ups of his eyes, usually watching Faith – and comments on the disturbing pleasures of voyeurism through the invention of SQUID, a device which enables viewers to see and experience another person's memories and physical sensations. Many critics have underscored the parallels between SQUID and the objectifying cinematic gaze,[25] especially in the controversial rape scene filmed from the point of view of the killer rapist, Max, who, in Nicola Rehling's words, 'literalizes the sadistic Mulveyan gaze'.[26] Max's obsession with the gaze, filming for instance his masked reflection in the mirror when breaking into Iris's apartment, then again without a mask when he makes love to Faith, thus highlights and calls into question Lenny's obsession with looking at women. The last clip Lenny watches (of Max having sex with Faith) recalls the first video of Faith that Lenny watches at the beginning of the film, where she undresses for him and he looks at them in the mirror, holding her half-naked in his arms. In the clip, she insists on the power of his gaze: that is what she loves in him ('I love your eyes, I love the way they see'). The triple *mise en abyme* of the gaze in both videos, with the characters being watched in the mirror, on SQUID disc and on film, not only equates the spectator with the SQUID recorder/viewer, but also presents Max as Lenny's sadistic and psychotic alter ego, who amplifies the pleasure of voyeurism through male control and domination, handcuffing and strangling his female partners, sometimes to death. Lenny's bewildered recognition of Max in the mirror in the final tape is also a recognition of himself, which is emphasised by the shot where Lenny turns around to see himself in the mirror, wedged in between a brain-dead Gant and Max pointing his gun at him. As Christina Lane remarks, this 'mirror stage' forces Lenny to 'confront his similarity between these two violent, pathological men' and 'see those qualities of the murderer (the need to dominate, the moral shadiness, the colonisation of others' experiences) in himself'.[27] This recognition enables him to finally sever the homosocial bond woven through SQUID around Faith and concentrate solely on Mace, offering 'a progressive theme about the reformation of aggressive masculinity',[28] since Lenny overcomes the powerful lure of the gaze and moves beyond his own fantasies, finally taking heed of the emotions and desires of the female Other.

A critique of hegemonic masculinity through a structural opposition between doubles can also be found in *The Matrix* trilogy, where Neo is repeatedly confronted with his hyper-normative alter ego Mr Smith, who insists on calling him Mr Anderson, drawing attention to their common identity as white males. Nicola Rehling underlines that 'as Thomas Anderson in corporate America, Neo looks little different from the agents, who are represented by an overdetermined image of straight white masculinity'.[29] This resemblance is underscored when Smith interrogates Neo in a white-walled room, each sitting opposite the other in a white shirt and tie. Smith accuses Neo of leading a double life, inside and outside of normative patriarchy, trying to convince him to help him maintain the system by finding Morpheus, the rebel non-white. Yet what Smith calls their 'connection' in *The Matrix Reloaded* continues beyond the corporate world with each trying to remake the other in his image throughout the trilogy: Neo dives into Smith to break him apart at the end of the first film, while Smith plunges his hand to morph Neo into another copy of himself in the second and third films. In the end, as Kord and Krimmer note, 'since Smith is defined as his negative, self-erasure is the only way to defeat him'.[30] Like Lenny in *Strange Days*,[31] then, Neo spurns the hegemonic alliance offered by Smith, rejecting the homosocial bond and male solidarity at the heart of patriarchy in favour of a relationship with a woman and the defence of rebel minorities.

Seeking refuge with strong women

Hollywood science fiction films of the 1990s tend to distance their heroes from a hegemonic identity, that of the normative white male, portraying it not only as 'depthless and sterile',[32] but also as eminently threatening. In *The Matrix* trilogy, *Strange Days* and *Johnny Mnemonic*, the heroes end up siding with the rebels, initiated by powerful women to the 'real' embodied by African Americans,[33] 'the real world' being both the space of resistance to the lure of white capitalism and the lived experience of oppression as opposed to virtual reality. In these films, physical and political action rests with female characters, action heroines who appear both feminine and masculine, further undermining the hegemonic gender norms and the traditional dichotomy between active masculinity and passive femininity. Unlike Ripley in *Aliens* or Sarah Connor in *Terminator 2*, Trinity (Carrie-Ann Moss) in *The Matrix* trilogy, Mace (Angela Bassett) in *Strange Days* and Jane (Dina Meyer) in *Johnny Mnemonic* do not reproduce the characteristics of male action heroes, nor do they appear stereotypically feminine. In fact, the first appearances of these female protagonists highlight their sensuality through an emphasis on their lips and voice: Trinity opens *The Matrix* with her soft and measured voice, while the first shot of Mace is an extreme close-up of her lips answering the phone in a sensuously deep voice. Yet Mace's fetishised femininity is immediately counterbalanced by a vertical tracking shot from her high heels to an elegant but dark and covering pant suit. The fetishistic shots of the women, emphasising for instance Trinity's buttocks in tight-fitting leather or Jane's rouged lips, are immediately followed by action feats which further their eroticisation: Jane overpowers a practiced bodyguard in one fast martial move, while Trinity escapes the police in a spectacular action sequence at the beginning of *The Matrix*.

In all three films, the male heroes are weaker than their female partners. In *The Matrix*, Neo is submitted early on to women's authority, ordered about by Trinity and threatened by Switch (Belinda McClory), the other female crew member, a masculine woman with hard features and cropped hair who points a gun at him and commands him to undress, addressing him scornfully as a 'coppertop' still plugged into the matrix. This scene in the limousine repeats and inverts the rape-like torture inflicted by the Agents, this time with a woman in charge: Trinity again takes off Neo's shirt to extract the bug inserted by the Agents. Neo thus loses control over his body, which is first manipulated by the Agents and then disinfected by women who overpower him physically and narratively. In fact, Trinity leads the way for most of the film, demonstrating in the opening sequence a number of physical feats which Neo will then have to learn or will not be able to replicate (her final dive into a very small window). This leads Pat Mellencamp to conclude that 'it will take the entire film before Neo gets up to his woman's speed, fighting skills, awareness and black-leather fashion'.[34] In *Strange Days* and *Johnny Mnemonic*, the male heroes are left even further behind: unable to fight, they are repeatedly saved by the female protagonists. As trained bodyguards, Jane and Mace indeed display efficient fighting skills, throwing knives, punches and kicks to rescue males in distress. Moreover, contrary to the heroes, they are able to operate and master the spaces around them, leading the men smoothly through the chaotic landscapes described above: Jane hides Johnny in the Low-tech slum and then navigates the sewers and wastelands of Newark, while Mace drives a sophisticated limousine around violent Los Angeles, escaping from a police chase by driving it straight into the water and pulling Lenny out of the car.

Thus the line between femininity and masculinity is blurred through the feminisation of passive male heroes and the relative masculinisation of active female characters. This blurring is especially apparent in *The Matrix*, where the androgynous Trinity and Neo look very similar, as underlined during the attack on the Agents' headquarters. Indeed, they are presented almost as duplicates in the first freeze frame, which ironically follows the Agents' call to 'Freeze!' Matching from head to toe in their black pants, belts and long coats, their dark sunglasses and slick black hair combed back, the pair's movements are perfectly synchronised, their heads turning at the exact same moment before each darts to one side. The film then cuts from one to the other as they perform the same moves, such as a cartwheel filmed in slow motion and amplified by their long coats, before freezing on them again as they stand next to each other in the elevator at the end of the carefully choreographed battle. Even more interesting is the tonal similarity between Neo and Trinity's skin colour, which goes against the

Hollywood convention according to which the hero's skin should be darker than the woman's.[35] This is highlighted in shots where their faces are shown right next to each other, as in the nightclub scene at the beginning of the film and the final kiss. In the latter, their two faces are positioned symmetrically, both in profile, so that the light shines on them in the same way, the centre of their faces in the shadows while the corners of the shot (Neo's forehead and Trinity's chest) are lit, the two faces merging in the same shaded and pearly white, in a shot which erases sexual difference.

Lenny's paleness is also underscored in *Strange Days*, where he never goes out in the sunlight. The only time he is shown in the sun is in his memory disc with Faith, and even then his skin colour is not much darker than hers, which contributes to his feminisation. Whiteness, in the film, tends to be associated with passivity and display, in opposition to blackness, which embodies action. *Strange Days* opposes the extremely feminised body of Faith, whose very white body is constantly on display throughout the film[36] – she is shown semi-naked in several scenes and otherwise wears very revealing outfits – and the more androgynous black body of Mace, who remains fully clothed in black pants and jacket for most of the film. Even when her body is shown (for instance, her muscular arms), it is to emphasise her potential for action. Yet Mace combines masculine and feminine elements until the end, as underlined when she arrives at the party of the millennium in a very short, sexy black dress. In her careful analysis of the white male gaze on racial bodies in *Strange Days*, Hélène Charlery notices how Lenny's objectifying male gaze at Mace – he looks at her bottom and compliments her on her dress – is immediately undercut by Mace's strapping her gun in a holster around her thigh. This shot contrasts with the vulnerability of Faith and especially Iris in similarly focused shots of women's crotches filled by the male gaze or the male penis. To quote Charlery, 'in Mace's case, the gun has come to fill that space',[37] lodging the phallus safely in between a black woman's legs and pointing to her status as phallic woman.

In *Strange Days*, *Johnny Mnemonic* and *The Matrix*, women compensate for the lack of political and bodily identity of passive white males. They represent a challenge to white patriarchal power, which they push the heroes to escape and then defy. In *The Matrix*, Trinity first appears in an underground club and is recognised with surprise by Neo as a famous hacker whom he thought was male. Her reply, 'most guys do', points to his subjection to corporate white patriarchal ideology. In *Johnny Mnemonic*, Jane saves Johnny from eradication by white patriarchal capitalism and drives him to donate the life-saving cure in his head to the Low-tech led by J-Bone (Ice-T). In one of the last shots of the film, the white protagonist is framed by the dreadlocked African-American rebel leader and his female bodyguard/lover as they watch the evil pharmaceutical company's headquarters burn down: the white hero has been given meaning and purpose by politically conscious others. In fact, contrary to *The Matrix*'s conclusion, which gives the final liberating speech to Neo the white saviour, the final words of *Johnny Mnemonic* are given to J-Bone, who offers a more forceful call to arms against white patriarchy: 'It's payback time', and declares the white Aryan assassin's corpse to be 'garbage' to be thrown into the river. In *Strange Days*, as Christina Lane points out, Mace is given political weight and a strong critical voice by being closely bound to the Jeriko One subplot. She appears for the first time in full shots as intercuts in the Jeriko One video which Max and Lenny are watching, and seems to be the only one to understand the seriousness of LA's racial situation, shushing Lenny, who greets her joyfully, and listening unconvinced to Max's postmodern 'end of history' rant, which takes no account of the racial oppression denounced by Jeriko a few seconds earlier. Her reaction shots, as well as 'the visibility of her African-American body in the frame', provide a critical perspective on the supposedly universal yet white male 'objective view on history'.[38] Moreover, Jeriko's murder is seen through the eyes of Mace, who tries SQUID for the first (and only) time to watch that specific disc. This moment is the film's turning point: it marks a shift away from the focus on voyeurism and female objectification associated with Iris and Faith, towards political and physical action contesting the white patriarchal order.

In the three films, the female protagonists thus pull the heroes into 'the real', that of African-American rebellion against white patriarchy, but also that of 'real' action rather than virtual reality. Female partners offer a more grounded and more politically engaged alternative to the pleasures offered by technology, enabling the heroes to leave the maternal and smothering womb of virtual reality, whether it be the cocoons of the matrix or the engulfing SQUID. In *The Matrix* and *Strange Days*, the technologies of virtual reality tend to be feminised, even eroticised, providing release and pleasure to passive males. Nicola Rehling talks, for instance, of Neo 'gasp[ing] orgasmically'[39] when he jacks into the matrix for the first time, while SQUID is used almost exclusively by men mainly to gaze at women or feel like them, and the pleasure it provides is all too evident in the reaction shots of their faces, be it Lenny watching Faith roller-skating in a bikini, the grey-suited client who experiences bliss as an 18-year-old girl taking a shower or even the amputee DJ, whose pleasure at running on a beach 'enables the most traditional male hetero fantasy',[40] looking at a girl running in her bikini. Claudia Springer's analysis of 'the pleasures of the interface' thus still holds true in the science fiction of the late 1990s, where 'the act of interfacing with a computer matrix [is still] represented as a masturbatory fantasy expressed in terms of entering something, but lacking the presence of another human being or mind'.[41]

Yet the female characters force the male heroes to take into account 'the presence of another human being', leading them away from the solipsistic masturbatory pleasures of the interface into a relationship which acknowledges the desires of others. The late 1990s science fiction films under discussion all develop a (heterosexual) relationship that shows female desire and includes a kiss (or an embrace in *Johnny Mnemonic*) as a climax, unlike post-2001 science fiction films, where kisses have nearly disappeared. Even though kisses can be seen, as John Garry argues in his article on *Strange Days*, as participating in a centrist movement re-establishing heterosexual monogamy and displacing political resolution with an individual romantic resolution,[42] they can also be the symbols of an alliance between men and women, between the hegemonic centre and a more critical minority voice. Kolker thus describes the interracial kiss between Lenny and Mace at the end of *Strange Days* as a 'small utopian moment',[43] utopian in that it breaks the taboo of miscegenation still upheld by many Hollywood films (for instance in the Will Smith films analysed in Chapter 4), but also in that it acknowledges and satisfies *female* desire. Indeed, the female characters are presented as desiring subjects, especially in final scenes where they become the bearers of the look. The final frame of *Johnny Mnemonic* shows Jane in profile looking amorously at Johnny, while even *Dark City* ends with Murdoch's amnesiac wife inviting him to follow her to Shell beach. In *Strange Days*, Mace is given several long point-of-view shots expressing her desire for Lenny as he walks away, to which he finally responds, 'recognis[ing] her unrequited desire instead of wallowing in his own'.[44] Similarly in *The Matrix*, Neo is positioned as the one being looked at and desired, reclining on a chair, while Trinity stands above him, watching him anxiously. She is the one who kisses him, bending over his dead body, the camera focusing on her mouth and eyes in extreme close-up. Moreover, as she resuscitates Neo, Trinity's power to give life outside the matrix makes her, in a way, the sole real agent within the narrative logic of *The Matrix*, leading Christopher Williams to argue that she is the real heroine of the film, 'who has made all worlds subject to herself'.[45]

The presence of active female characters thus destabilises gender norms, highlighting the passivity of weaker, more static and feminised males in *Dark City*, *Johnny Mnemonic*, *Strange Days* and *The Matrix*. With the exception of *Dark City*, these films tend to locate action with women and draw attention to female desire, decentring the white male as sole locus of agency. However, the narratives of the four films revolve around a white male hero, who is still seen as the best representative of all of humanity, as underlined by James Cameron *à propos* Lenny in *Strange Days*: 'I always had in mind the fate of this one guy, Lenny Nero, and his ability to find what's right, and what's wrong. If one person can elevate themselves or redeem themselves then, by extrapolation we all can.'[46] The 'one person who can elevate themselves' continues to be male then, even if the need for elevation suggests weaknesses in the white male's dominant position, as underscored in the questioning of hegemonic masculinity found throughout 1990s Hollywood science fiction[47] and its challenge to patriarchy.

The Turn to Fatherhood

Nineteen-nineties science fiction can also be seen as challenging patriarchy in its refusal to appeal to the figure of the father, despite the success of *Terminator 2: Judgment Day*, where the antagonist Terminator of the first film comes back as a good father intent on protecting the teenage John

Connor at all cost. The film was seen by many, including Susan Jeffords in *Hard Bodies*, as encapsulating the idea that men could and would change thanks to fathering in the early 1990s.[48] The absence of fathers in 1990s science fiction is all the more surprising as many successful films in other genres of the decade highlighted the transformative potential of fathering after the late 1980s box office success of *Three Men and a Baby* (1987) and *Look Who's Talking* (1989). Examples include the romantic comedies *Father of the Bride* (1991, followed by part II in 1995), *Sleepless in Seattle* (1993), *Mrs Doubtfire* (1993), *The American President* (1995) and *One Fine Day* (1996), the male melodramas *A River Runs Through It* (1992), *My Life* (1993), *Legends of the Fall* (1994) and *A Perfect World* (1997), and the action films *True Lies* (1994), *Ransom* (1996), *Con Air* (1997), in addition to the *Die Hard* and *Lethal Weapon* franchises. Furthermore, this emphasis on fathers and fatherhood was widespread in a public discourse centred on family values and the problem of absent fathers under the Bush and Clinton Administrations alike. During his 1992 presidential campaign, George H. Bush denounced 'deadbeat dads',[49] while Vice-President Dan Quayle, in a speech at the Commonwealth Club of California on 19 May 1992, condemned the sitcom *Murphy Brown* for having a single mother as heroine and mocking the role of men in procreation. Bill Clinton also lamented the breakdown of the 'traditional' family with mother and father, referring to the model offered by 1950s sitcoms.[50] Whether conservative or liberal, many strands of US society took up the issue of fatherhood, with movements like the religious Promise Keepers and the African-American Million Man March urging men to accept their responsibilities as heads of families. The 1990s saw many books come out on the primary role of fathers and the devastating consequences of their absence, like *Absent Fathers, Lost Sons: the Search for a Masculine Identity* (1991), *Fatherless America: Confronting our Most Urgent Social Problem* (1995), as well as the more feminist *Slow Motion: Changing Masculinities, Changing Men* (1990) and *Stiffed: The Betrayal of the American Man* (1998).[51]

Apart from a few family-oriented productions like *Last Action Hero* (1993), *Bicentennial Man* (1999) and the *Jurassic Park* franchise, fatherhood was not prominently thematised until the following decade. This shift can perhaps be explained by the 9/11 attacks and their aftermath when, according to Mathias Nilges, 'the inability to rely upon traditional definitions of order, safety, and protection has become ever more apparent'.[52] As Claire Sisco King argues in her analysis of *I Am Legend*, post-9/11 apocalyptic films can be and have been read as responses to the trauma of 9/11, revealing anxieties about performing traditional masculinity. As much as *I Am Legend*'s Dr Neville is desperately anxious to 'fulfill the patriarchal injunction to be a provider', in the end he offers 'a synecdochic figuration of the allegedly emasculated nation that was unable on 9/11 to protect its citizens from the terrorist attacks'.[53] The aftermath of 9/11 did indeed see a rise in apocalyptic narratives depicting the desperate attempts of fathers or fatherly figures to protect their children and thus preserve the future in doomed worlds. Hannah Hamad quotes *The Day After Tomorrow, 2012, Take Shelter, Beasts of the Southern Wild, The Impossible, Signs, War of the Worlds, Skyline, The Mist, The Happening, Knowing, Children of Men, I Am Legend, The Road* and *After Earth*,[54] to which can be added *Interstellar* and *Terminator Genisys*. Many critics, including Hannah Hamad and Mathias Nilges, have argued that these narratives exemplify the return to traditional gender roles that has been the hallmark of post-9/11 America, according to Susan Faludi.[55] Hamad writes that

> apocalyptic events and situations enable common sense appeals to be made for a paternally signified masculine protector protagonist. Drawing these figures as fathers *invariably* validates the recidivist gender discourse they must necessarily embody, however much this is negotiated through an *apparently progressive veneer* of involved fatherhood that enables this formation of post 9/11 manhood to adhere to postfeminism's cultural script of fatherhood as ideal masculinity.[56]

I would like to qualify this statement by drawing on four post-9/11 apocalyptic fatherhood films, *War of the Worlds, The Road, Interstellar* and *Terminator Genisys*. First, I would disagree with the term 'invariably', even though elements of a 'recidivist gender discourse' remain. Secondly, I argue that involved fatherhood in those films is not only an 'apparently progressive veneer', but calls into question male and masculine hegemony by underscoring the transformation and especially the failings of hegemonic masculinity. Furthermore, even though fatherhood is emphasised in the absence of mothers, it can nevertheless be enabling for women through the rise to prominence of productive father-daughter relationships.

Nurturing protectors

Apocalyptic narratives do emphasise the need for protective father figures, with global crises being often closely linked with family crises. The beginning of *War of the Worlds*, for instance, closely intertwines the tensions between Ray Ferrier (Tom Cruise) and his children with the brewing of the alien storm. The film not only makes Wells' story personal by adopting the point of view of one family[57] (contrary to the 1953 adaptation by Byron Haskin, where the point of view is that of a couple), but builds the family as a point of origin, as underlined by Nigel Morris: 'the central family is not merely a point of access for focalisation but appears to originate the cataclysmic events'.[58] Indeed, Ray is confronted by the storm as he runs out in anger after his son, who borrowed his car without permission, the darkened skies being a metaphor for the state of their relationship. His reaction to the multiple lightning bolts, one of childish fascination for what he sees as Fourth of July fireworks, is contrasted with his daughter's fear, which he initially does not take into account until the repetitive lightning forces them both under the table. However, the cataclysmic circumstances will require Ray to move from irresponsible fatherhood to protective fatherhood, so that, as Hannah Hamad notes, 'the transformation of the protagonist's fatherhood [is] co-dependently constituted within the overarching narrative: Ray needs a crisis to stage his paternal rehabilitation'.[59]

The Road also interrelates the apocalypse with a family crisis, as the undetermined apocalyptic event happens during the mother's pregnancy, conditioning the birth of the child as well as the breakdown of the couple.[60] The birth itself is filmed and experienced as a catastrophe, as the woman repeats 'Oh no' and 'I don't want to do this'. Sorrow and anguish dominate the whole scene, with the characters shot in pale light or at night, most often backlit so that everything appears greyish, especially the mother's wan face. The characters' voices are reduced to a murmur on a soundtrack of barely audible long, sustained harmonic notes, until the woman utters a cry of pain, which can also be heard as a cry of anguish as it rings through and overlaps with the next shot of the post-apocalyptic deserted road. The progression of the flashbacks charts the disintegration of the couple: their luminous, harmonious relationship gives way to distress and quarrelling, as the mother is unable to cope with a violent and joyless post-apocalyptic world she no longer wants to live in. The apocalypse leads to the destruction of the couple, since she chooses to leave (i.e., to die) while he chooses to stay and look after their son, his only reason to survive.

In a general context of crisis, fathers reclaim their role as protectors and providers in a literal nurturing sense: they have to protect their children against attackers and provide food and shelter in worlds turned hostile. Food shortage is a major concern in both *The Road* and *Interstellar*, while Ray's first reaction after the alien attack in *War of the Worlds* is to take refuge in his former wife's home to find food and shelter, manically preparing peanut butter sandwiches for his children. These fathers are obsessed with home and its comforts, as in *The Road*, where all the flashbacks are set in the father's former house and where he goes out of his way to find the house where he grew up, remembering the tender gestures of daily life that have disappeared since the apocalypse, such as charting your children's height on the doorframe or smoothing the cushions of the sofa before settling down comfortably. The importance of the house is also underscored in *Interstellar*, since most scenes of the first half are set in a farmhouse, which the father revisits at the end of the film when it has become a museum rebuilt by his daughter to remember the past and honour his sacrifice. In addition to food and shelter, fathers also provide emotional and intellectual sustenance throughout the films. *The Road* shows the father reading to his son, while *Interstellar* insists on the scientific education provided by Cooper (Matthew McConaughey) to his daughter. *War of the Worlds* and *Terminator Genisys* also show fathers creating an emotional bond with their offspring, through music, with Ray singing the only song he knows (about a car) to his daughter to help her fall asleep, and the Terminator (Arnold Schwarzenegger), recast as Sarah Connor's adoptive 'Pops' in *Terminator Genisys*, placing her favourite tape in her old stereo for her to find after her brutal time travelling experience. As stressed in *Interstellar*, men have become 'caregivers', responsible for the well-being and future of their children in inhospitable worlds. This emphasis on nurturing fatherhood distances the men of post-apocalyptic science fiction from the hypermasculinity displayed by 1980s science fiction heroes analysed in Chapter 1.

Stella Bruzzi suggests, in fact, that hypermasculinity and fatherhood are incompatible since

> the father's power resides in keeping his phallus constitutively veiled. The flaunted presence of the male body in action cinema serves to displace the father ... This male body suggests a masculinity that is not only potent but pre-paternal, still bound up in its own narcissism.[61]

This distinction between the flaunted muscular body of the hypermasculine action hero and the 'veiled phallus' of the father is presented explicitly in *Terminator Genisys* in the multiple first appearances of Arnold Schwarzenegger, where it is played for laughs. Indeed, Schwarzenegger's very first appearance reprises to a T his first scene in *The Terminator*: he lands naked, crouched next to a garbage truck, then rises slowly to an erect position, shot in a low-angle close-up of his pectorals and inexpressive face, before walking slowly to contemplate the city lying at his feet, shot fully naked from the back. This nakedness is stressed in his second scene, his encounter with three punks, again a reshoot of *The Terminator*, with the same dialogue mocking the Terminator's nakedness: 'Wash day tomorrow. Nothing clean, right?' The end of this scene provides a humorous twist that highlights the distinction between action hero and father when Schwarzenegger's voice is heard challenging his naked self, 'He won't be needing any clothes', as he starts shooting at him. The two Terminators are starkly contrasted in terms of bodily display, since the first (computer-generated) Terminator is shot naked and mostly in close-up, while the second Terminator (played by Schwarzenegger) appears in a long shot, dressed in dark clothes with his hood up, barely visible in the distance. *Terminator Genisys* thus pays homage to the *Terminator* franchise while at the same time moving away from a hypermasculine model of masculinity: the naked, prepaternal version of the Terminator is eliminated as the bad guy by the fatherly version, which remains fully clothed throughout the film, reconfirming the spectacular shift operated by *Terminator 2*, as well as acknowledging the ageing of the main star (to which I'll return later).

Muscularity and toughness thus tend to be de-emphasised in post-apocalyptic fatherhood films: the heroes are, for instance, rarely shot naked. The main exception, in *The Road*, underscores the father's increasing frailty as he takes his son to bathe in a waterfall, and then, towards the end of the film, much thinner, swims to a wreck in the ocean. The fathers are not invincible – Cooper is knocked out by a fellow astronaut (Matt Damon) on a hostile planet in *Interstellar*. Nor are they fearless – the father openly acknowledges his fear to his son in *The Road*, while Ray looks at himself wildly in the mirror, traumatised by the realisation that he is covered in human ash at the beginning of *War of the Worlds*. The emphasis is, rather, on emotions. The fathers are shown crying several times in *War of the Worlds*, *The Road* and *Interstellar*, as well as hugging and kissing their children, and even the Terminator folds Sarah (Emilia Clarke) in his arms when he reappears at the end of *Terminator Genisys* (Figure 5.3). The four films are even openly melodramatic at times, especially when the fathers are separated from their children, for instance when Ray loses sight of his son Ronnie who joins the army against the aliens in *War of the Worlds*, or

Figure 5.3 The Terminator hugs Sarah in *Terminator Genisys*

when Cooper, trapped in space, tries to tell his former self to stay with his daughter in *Interstellar*. Both scenes create a heightened emotional impact by emphasising the unbridgeable distance opened between father and child – a wall of fire obscures Ronnie's fate in *War of the Worlds*, a wall of books and another dimension separate Cooper from his daughter – and the resulting loneliness of the fathers, alone in infinite landscapes, crying helplessly after their children. The moments are especially melodramatic as these separations are acts of sacrifice: Ray lets go of his son at his behest and to rescue his daughter, Cooper leaves to find a hospitable planet in order to save humanity. The fathers are thus presented as sacrificial heroes, even in *The Road*, where the father stays to keep his son alive despite his wife's decision to commit suicide. After their discussion, a long shot of him alone, as in *War of the Worlds*, underscores his loneliness and despair. Such scenes adopt what Hamad calls a 'melancholic affective register' that is recurrent in postfeminist films about fatherhood and that she sees as giving rise to 'the ubiquitous figure of the widowed single father'.[62]

Legitimating hegemonic masculinity

In fact, as Hamad notes, the focus on nurturing, emotionally sensitive, postfeminist fathers tends to displace women from the narrative: mothers are either dead, sidelined early on or mothers-to-be in *Interstellar*, *War of the Worlds*, *The Road* and *Terminator Genisys,* respectively, giving the Darwinist impression that men are the only ones fit to survive in post-apocalyptic worlds. At the beginning of *War of the Worlds*, Ray's ex-wife, Mary-Ann (Miranda Otto), who has remarried upwards, is thus presented as out of place, an intruder in Ray's masculine working-class space. She is hardly given any long shots and is repeatedly disseverered by the framing, as in her first appearance in a reverse shot of Ray arriving late to their meeting, her back to the camera and left hand on her hip, signifying the woman as 'an unwelcome, censorious presence'.[63] Her disapproving inspection of his house, as she underlines his shortcomings as a father, furthers this idea of an incongruous intrusion, her body cut off by the engine in the middle of the kitchen, fragmented by a close-up of a bottle of soured milk in the fridge or weighed down by high-angle tilts of her pregnancy, as she carries her daughter's suitcase up the stairs and hovers above her teenage son's tiny bed in a messy room too small for two grown children. Even though Ray is presented in those scenes as a bad father, the film's camerawork, as well as Ray's resentment of her intrusion as he asks her to close the door to *his* refrigerator and shuts the door to his bedroom, tend to present Mary-Ann as the one who is out of place. Consequently, as Hamad notes, 'her concerns are silenced as she is removed from the narrative'.[64]

The mother's concerns are also silenced in *The Road*, where her inability to cope with the post-apocalyptic world and her desire to commit suicide as a family are rejected by the father as a form of mental illness ('you sound ... crazy'). Furthermore, the film transfers the woman's depression at giving birth to a child in a world in ruins onto the father, who takes over her tragic status and despondency as she leaves him alone to take care of their son. Their last dialogue focuses on his emotions and despair as he begs her to stay, crying and holding on to her; she hardly speaks, her face remaining wan and inexpressive. Even the pain of her death is appropriated by the father, since we do not see her die (it is assumed that she dies of cold in the freezing night): she fades into the black of the night as his voice-over returns and the camera cuts back to a close-up of his distraught face. The physical pain of dying of cold is given over to the father, feeding *his* emotional pain. Her coldness, emphasised by her expression and by his voice-over ('She was gone, and the coldness of it was her final gift.'), is contrasted with his sorrow, so that the affective charge of the scene lies with his pain. *The Road* thus follows Juliana Schiesari's analysis of the ideology of melancholia, which 'appropriates from women's subjectivity their "real" sense of loss and ... recuperates that loss ... as a privileged form of male expression',[65] as the melodramatic tone of the film applies only to the father, an emotionally damaged male abandoned by his wife who must throw his wedding ring away in order to overcome his loss.

With women out of the way, post-apocalyptic fatherhood films can focus on rebuilding masculinity as the hegemonic norm, most often by resorting to the traditional association between men, physicality and weapons. As Mathias Nilges argues, this was also one of the tropes of post-9/11 America, which promoted heroic working-class masculinity at the expense of women and corporate masculinity, 'reviv[ing] the investment in definitions of labor and masculinity that remain tied to the physically laboring body'.[66] This is particularly the case in *War of the Worlds*, which presents Ray as an emasculated working-class male who rebuilds his masculinity as well as his relationship with his children through physical heroism. Ray first appears lifting heavy containers atop a huge crane, a 'superior vantage point' that, according to Nigel Morris, 'evokes the power of the all-seeing Father that Ray would like to be'.[67] Yet a few seconds later he is down on the ground, reprimanded by his ex-wife and her well-to-do new husband for being late.[68] His working-class origins are repeatedly underlined throughout the beginning of the film, for instance through the presence of a car engine in the middle of his kitchen, and lead to his estrangement from his wealthier children, be it from his son, who reminds him that his stepfather is the one paying for his expensive school, or his daughter who orders hummus for lunch, which Ray has never heard of. However, through the course of the film, Ray performs physical feats that validate his labouring masculinity as protective fatherhood. As Morris demonstrates, he is the only human with 'the balls' to defeat an alien machine, leaving two grenades inside this vagina dentata[69] seeking to devour his daughter. More controversially, Ray also kills another human being, Ogilvy (Tim Robbins), who threatens his safety as well as his daughter's by his frantic desire to fight back against the invaders. This scene is particularly interesting in the way it reframes violence and what is essentially murder as necessary and even 'good', since it is justified by the need to protect one's children, as Gary Arms and Thomas Riley contend: 'Paradoxically, Ray becomes "good" precisely in the horrific decision to take another person's life with his bare hands for the sake of his special obligation to his daughter.'[70] Ray's masculinity is thus normalised and 'hegemonised' through protective fatherhood and by opposition to threatening female figures (his ex-wife and the alien machines), as well as over-aggressive warmongering male figures.

In a similar fashion, the father in *The Road* also turns into a reluctant but efficient killer when his son is threatened. Derided as 'chicken shit' by a cannibal who eyes up his son and outsmarts him, rushing with a knife to the child's throat, the father instinctively fires a precise shot straight into the barbarian's brains, despite never having killed a person in his life. It is as if protective fatherhood triggered instinctual feats of masculinity that are naturalised as part and parcel of being a father, as the hero in *The Road* underscores when he reassures his son, saying: 'I'll kill anyone who touches you, cause that's my job.' In effect, children legitimate the performance of hegemonic masculinity, notably the domination of others and the conquest of territory. They are enablers, helping men retrieve a sense of responsibility but also supposedly lost power and agency. Thus, the physically labouring father of *Interstellar* can abandon his farm and family, rejecting his role as 'caregiver', to fulfil his dream of becoming an explorer and reviving the American frontier spirit, all in the name of saving his children. As Gary Arms and Thomas Riley say about Ray Ferrier in *War of the Worlds*, we relate to the heroic fathers not because they save the world but because they save their children.[71]

Another element in the fathers' consolidation of power and agency is their mastery of weapons, especially when their children's safety is concerned, as we have seen in *The Road*. Fathers are in fact the only ones seen shooting a gun in both *The Road* and *War of the Worlds*, where Ray shoots his gun to frighten the crowd away from his car and pull his children out. Guns are used as an initiation into masculinity: it is, for instance, what grudgingly brings the Terminator, aka 'Pops', and his prospective son-in-law, Kyle Reese (Jai Courtney), to mutual respect and acceptance as they observe each other loading bullets into clips in *Terminator Genisys*, while in *The Road*, the father shows his son how to cock a gun and pull the trigger, handing him the pistol as his final gift, which he should carry at all times. Obeying his father's commandments after the latter's death, the son cocks the gun and slips it in his belt in cowboy fashion, pointing it unsteadily at the first stranger he meets.

Failing at patriarchal reproduction

However, this initiation into masculinity is often tainted with failure, as the fathers fail in their mission towards their sons and the sons refuse to follow their lead. In *War of the Worlds*, for instance, Ray loses the gun after having fired a shot: the loss of such a phallic signifier is symbolic of how hard it is for him to assert his paternal authority throughout the film. This difficulty is highlighted first in the scene where he attempts to play catch with his son in an effort at ritualistic father-son bonding through a traditional

American male activity. Yet his efforts are presented as counterproductive, because they spring from an outdated vision of patriarchal masculinity that he is not able to impose on his son. His brutal response to his son's latent aggressiveness – he calls him Ray instead of Dad and sports a Red Sox baseball cap when his father supports the Yankees, to which Ray reacts by throwing the ball as hard as he can, hurting his son's hand and boasting about his physical prowess – is both inappropriate and ineffective: his son calls him 'an asshole' and turns away from any confrontation, refusing to catch the last ball, which breaks a window. Ray thus alienates himself from his son, his face encased and isolated in deep focus in the hole of the broken window (Figure 5.4). Presented as too authoritarian at the beginning, Ray is later chastised by his son for lacking 'the balls' to fight the aliens, and cannot prevent the latter from joining the army in the fight. Indeed, even if Ray does attack an alien machine to save his daughter, he is no war hero, and the machines die by themselves, infected by bacteria, as in the original novel. The ending also confirms Ray's absence of authority within the family: he returns his daughter to her mother and even though his son calls him Dad and embraces him, Ray is still excluded from the family. He remains isolated, shot twice in the background of a long shot, in deep focus, while the rest of the family, including his inimical in-laws and his

Figure 5.4 Ray isolated by the broken window in *War of the Worlds*

ex-wife's new husband, who tower above on the landing, are gathered in front of the in-laws' beautiful and miraculously intact house, in which Ray is not welcome.[72] Morris sees the ending as 'bathetic': Mary Ann is already pregnant, so there is no return possible to the original nuclear family,[73] which is confirmed by the presence of her new husband.[74] The reprisal of deep focus as an isolating device further suggests that little has changed and that Ray's actions are, on the whole, irrelevant, as the camera cuts to an aerial shot of a city in ruins and the God-like voice-over returns.

Similarly, the son rejects the father's initiation into masculinity in *The Road*, where the son at first refuses to hold the gun properly, holding it out in his palms and away from his body like a strange and frightening object. If he does manage to point the gun at the stranger at the very end of the film, he puts the gun down as soon as the man asks him to, choosing trust rather than violence. The son repeatedly refuses the lessons in hegemonic masculinity that his father tries to teach him, notably in the scene where the father humiliates a black thief by ordering him to undress and leaving him naked to die by the side of the road, in spite of his son's plea for mercy. While the father tries to teach him to be tough and heartless to survive, yelling at him that he's 'gotta learn', the son replies vehemently that he does not want to learn, at least not this lesson in the domination of weaker others. Thus, the father does not fulfil the patriarchal transmission of masculine hegemony from father to son, since he dies at the end, leaving his son in the hands of a loving *mother*, while his teachings about being 'the good guys' are reinterpreted by the boy as lessons in compassion, sharing and trust, as he constantly convinces his father to share their food with those weaker than them – the old man, the black thief – and agrees in the end to join another family, going against his father's distrust of others, with the last word of the film being his meek 'ok'.

In fact, even the stories that the father reads to his son about 'the good guys' and 'carrying the fire' seem futile in a world overrun by cannibals, where reading has become useless. His son cannot read, and his wife does not believe in the protection he offers them wholeheartedly, underlining the futility of trying to be a good man, a protector in a post-apocalyptic world; to his heartfelt promise that '[he] will do anything' to protect them from rape and murder, she pointedly replies, 'Like what?' and decides to kill herself, negating his ability to succeed in this self-appointed mission. In all four films, fathers appear as outdated models of masculinity, relics from the past like the can of Coke that the father shares with his son in *The Road*, 'a Norman Rockwell-esque ritual'[75] akin to the game of catch initiated by Ray in *War of the Worlds*. The production design of *Interstellar*'s first half is also reminiscent of past Americana, especially of the pictures taken by the photographers sent by the Farm Security Administration to document the farmers' hardships during the Great Depression. The huge dust storms that kill the cattle and crops evidently bring to mind the time of the Dust Bowl, while Cooper's urge to fly a space rocket recalls Kennedy's 'New Frontier' and the enthusiasm aroused by the first moon landing. Cooper thus combines two past archetypal models of American masculinity: the sturdy, down-to-earth farmer, as well as the passionate, adventurous astronaut that became a role model for so many American boys of the 1960s and 1970s. However, as Susan Faludi demonstrates in her mournful profiling of the half-forgotten moon-landing astronaut Buzz Aldrin in *Stiffed: The Betrayal of the American Man*,[76] astronauts are no longer revered as heroes embodying the American spirit of adventure and conquest. They belong to the past, like Cooper on his return from his space expedition, whose house has been turned into a museum with no visitors.

The question of outdatedness is most prominent in *Terminator Genisys*, albeit in a more comical mode. The ageing Schwarzenegger was clearly the film's main marketing asset, with the Terminator's lined, scarred face and greying hair in the foreground of every poster. The new tagline in this fifth instalment of the franchise is 'old, not obsolete', which is one of the first lines of dialogue uttered by Pops the Terminator and is reprised by Kyle as a comforting reassurance by the end of the film. Indeed, the film insists on the process of ageing, underscoring the Terminator's fighting difficulties from his first fight against his younger self, where his arthritis makes it harder for him to retaliate and get back up from the ground, to his battles against the mature, Skynet-controlled John Connor (Jason Clark), a slimmer, faster machine that moves around and through him at such speed that the Terminator is unable to fight back and is ejected from the battlefield, derided as 'nothing but a relic from a deleted timeline'. Pops the old Terminator is opposed to younger new cyborg models three times: first, his younger self; secondly, another version of *Terminator 2*'s 'mimetic polyalloy' T1000; and finally John Connor, the newest cyborg technology, a human being infected with machine matter, 'restructured and rebuilt at a cellular level for maximum combat utility'. The Terminator repeatedly highlights his outdated technological status compared to the enhanced abilities of his opponents, declaring for example that, contrary to the T1000, 'as a T800, I lack the mimetic skills to appear as anyone else'. Furthermore, his metallic body prevents him from going in the time machine, so that he has to take 'the long way', waiting 30 years for Sarah and Kyle's arrival. The process of ageing is thus thematised and dramatised in the film, since the two young heroes remain young throughout the film thanks to time travel, while the Terminator, already old at the beginning of the film as Kyle remarks ('he looks ... old'), ages, his hair gone white in the second part of the film.

However, *Terminator Genisys* is an exception in that it is the only film where the surrogate father not only survives, resuscitated as an upgraded version of himself, but is included in a nuclear family, the film ending happily with Pops the Terminator's intrusion in the middle of the kiss between Sarah and Kyle, the three of them in the same shot centred on the Terminator and his wide, machine-like smile; the family of three then drives off into the sunset on a road to a new future. Otherwise, the fathers are excluded from the family unit at the end of *War of the Worlds*, *The Road* and even *Interstellar*. Cooper indeed returns to find his daughter on her deathbed, and is asked to leave so that she can die peacefully, surrounded by her new family. The last-mentioned films raise the question of the relevance of performing heroic masculinity in post-apocalyptic worlds where this model has become outdated. If the fathers succeed in protecting their children, their very heroism sets them apart from the families they have sought to protect and appears almost vain in the face of widespread destruction. Thus, even though the three films end on a reunion or the promise of one, the very last scenes remain mournful in their photography and soundtrack: the colours are subdued, with a final return to grey in *The Road* and *War of the Worlds*, and the three soundtracks feature repetitive melodies in a minor scale, played by a lone horn in *War of the Worlds* and a lone piano in *The Road*, while in *Interstellar* the melody supports the voice-over of Cooper's dying daughter sending him out on a lone mission into space.

This mournful tone, especially in *War of the Worlds* and *The Road*, reflects the fathers' relative failure to complete their sons' initiation into hegemonic masculinity and thus the transformation of the son into the father at the foundation of patriarchy.[77] However, there is a striking evolution from *War of the Worlds*, where the father recuperates, to some extent, his hegemonic masculinity by protecting and saving his helpless daughter at the expense of training his son, to *Interstellar* and *Terminator Genisys*, where the initiation is between father and daughter. *War of the Worlds* can, indeed, be read as a direct response to 9/11, which saw, according to Margaret D. Stetz, 'the return of the comforting myth' that a father's masculinity 'is measured by his capacity to keep daughters safe'.[78] The daughters emblematise vulnerability, like Rachel (Dakota Fanning), who is very young and unable to defend herself, screaming her way through most of the film. By contrast, the daughters in *Interstellar* and *Terminator Genisys* are combative, pursuing the same goals as the fathers who they team up with, so that the films present a successful initiation of *daughters* by their fathers, challenging the foundation of patriarchy.

In fact, *Interstellar* critiques the vanity of the hero who thinks he can save humanity by conquering new worlds with the help of a happy few. His desire for adventure is presented as misplaced, his departure resented by his daughter for most of the film. Moreover, his refusal to take into account feminine emotions leads him to make mistakes that he pays for dearly, whether it be his daughter's anguish when he leaves or Dr Brand's (Anne Hathaway) intuition that her lover's planet is more suitable for humanity than Dr Mann's, which will indeed turn out to be cold and barren, a 'rational' choice that in effect wrecks the mission. In fact, it is not through heroic action that humanity will be saved but through the communication of information between father and daughter and the transformation of the *daughter* into the father. Indeed, Cooper's son is completely sidelined by the film, which makes it clear from the start that it is Murph who most resembles her father and is being initiated by him into his scientific knowledge and wider aspirations. It is she who inherits his power, as the central sequence underscores by crosscutting constantly from Coop's ordeals in space to Murph's understanding of her father's message in her watch. The watch he gives her is highly symbolic, since it is the masculine attribute to master time traditionally passed on from father to son that is here given to a daughter so *she* can decode time and save the world. It is therefore the connection between father and daughter that saves humanity, not the actions of a single man, as the film underscores by mocking Cooper's hubris in thinking that 'Cooper station', where he wakes up to find that humanity has survived, was named after him and not his daughter. She is celebrated in the end as humanity's saviour – even if the film's narration is centred on the father's actions and sacrifice.

Similarly, in *Terminator Genisys*, the emphasis is on the cooperation between father and daughter (with the belated and somewhat useless help of a son-in-law), who are able to eliminate younger and stronger opponents through teamwork, as in the first duel between the old and new T800, where the young Terminator is slowed down by his older self so that he can be shot down by Sarah Connor, an ironic reversal of *The Terminator*. The final battle against John Connor is again won through teamwork, as underlined by the dialogue: 'You were never strong enough to defeat me', snips John, to which the Terminator replies: 'Not alone.' Sarah and Kyle then appear from opposite ends of the battle ring, each carrying a weapon: Sarah's wielding of a massive gun as she yells 'John' is a twist on Sarah Connor's final rescue of her son in *Terminator 2*, although in both cases it is the Terminator who deals the final blow to their fearsome opponent.

The initiation of daughters thus seems to be more successful than the initiation of sons, but in all cases it is still the fathers who are the central figures of post-apocalyptic films: they are the focus of the narrative and the agents of action. As we have seen, mothers are absent or sidelined, while daughters tend to be of secondary importance in terms of screen time and narrative drive; in *Interstellar* for instance, the daughter's success as an adult is elided by the narrative through long temporal ellipses. White men remain at the centre of the narrative, cast as sacrificial heroes. However, the models of masculinity put forward by post-apocalyptic films redefine the hegemonic norm, especially the films where male parenting is conceived as maternal nurturing, like *The Road* and *Interstellar*. Yet even the films where the protective side of fathers is stressed – *War of the Worlds* and *Terminator*

Genisys – call into question the patriarchal order where father knows best, as opposed to disaster films like *Signs* (M. Night Shyamalan, 2002) or *The Day After Tomorrow* (Roland Emmerich, 2004). I would therefore disagree with Hamad and Nilges,[79] who argue that apocalyptic narratives tend to restore patriarchy and traditional gender norms: in my view, the post-apocalyptic films analysed here actually undermine a hegemonic model of masculinity based on the domination of others by pointing at its outdatedness and highlighting the failure of patriarchal transmission.

Hollywood science fiction films of the 1990s and 2000s accompanied the different 'crises of masculinity' of the Clinton and post-9/11 eras by redefining hegemonic masculinity, moving away from the hypermasculine model of the 1980s based on physical strength and the domination of others, including women and racial minorities. Virtual reality films and post-apocalyptic fatherhood films highlight the physical weaknesses of their protagonists and their emotional anguish, blurring traditional gender norms to include the feminine. Virtual reality films feature passive, feminised heroes being rescued by active female partners who are presented as desiring agents, while post-apocalyptic fatherhood films insist on the necessity for fathers to develop nurturing skills and underscore the special bond between fathers and daughters. The two cycles of films thus go against an essentialised version of masculinity and the gender order: virtual reality films of the 1990s insist on the instability of identity while post-apocalyptic fatherhood films highlight the failures of patriarchal initiation. Indeed, patriarchy is called into question: patriarchal figures are the enemy in the 1990s, pursuing the male protagonists and their female partners to maintain an oppressive status quo, while patriarchal fathers appear ineffectual and outdated in post-apocalyptic films of the 2000s. Distancing itself from the superhero wave, hard science fiction offers a vision of post-feminist masculinity in the lines of what Benjamin Brabon sees as a 'subject position characterised by anxiety, dissatisfaction and inefficacy'[80] that does not participate in the remasculinisation of American society. By stressing the importance of emotional well-being and the connection with others, most importantly women and children, postfeminist science fiction offers a critique of patriarchal hegemonic masculinity that emphasises the vanity and hubris of the male hero who believes he can save the world by himself.

In fact, the pessimistic vision offered by post-apocalyptic films even hints at the responsibility of violent hubristic white males in the destruction of humanity, especially in *The Road* and *Interstellar*. The latter films are especially pointed in their critique of hegemonic masculinity, insisting on the uselessness of the lone hero and the lies on which patriarchy is built. While *Terminator Genysis* is more optimistic about the future of patriarchy, even *War of the Worlds* ends on a pessimistic note that is unusual in Spielberg's filmography. However, if science fiction films of the 1990s and 2000s have definitely participated in the redefinition of hegemonic masculinity, they have not challenged male hegemony: despite the charismatic presence of Laurence Fishburne and Carrie-Ann Moss in *The Matrix* trilogy, white males remain the central figures of the films, with women as supporting characters and hardly any racial minorities, especially in the post-apocalyptic films analysed here[81] (only one black character appears briefly in *The Road*). White males are thus still the representatives of humanity, even if they are dying out.

Afterword

The Gender Politics of Science Fiction Blockbusters

I have chosen in this book to focus largely, though not exclusively, on big-budget, Hollywood-produced science fiction films because of their large audiences and consequently their wider impact on society. Yet this choice was also driven by the feeling that blockbusters are more complex than they seem. Of course, blockbusters tend to be conservative on the whole since they try to appeal to as large an audience as possible, but the aim of the book was also to show the possibilities offered in the cracks of sf blockbusters. Despite their often-disappointing endings, Hollywood science fiction films always include narrative or visual moments that challenge the existing gender order and its hegemonic norms. I am thinking for instance of Ann Lewis's gender-blurring first appearance as she subdues a suspect in helmet and uniform in *RoboCop*, GR44's desperate cries for ice to Veronica before lying down naked on the parking lot of a motel in *Universal Soldier* and the shape-shifting T1000's failed transformation into a model housewife whose unctuous tone sets her stepson (John Connor) thinking that something is wrong in *Terminator 2*.

As I show in Chapter 1, hypermasculine films insist on the vulnerability of their apparently indomitable protagonists while also pointing to the negative effects of hypermasculinity on women as well as men. They offer a critique of hegemonic masculinity that is imposed on men by the rich and powerful, challenging at the same time the capitalist structure of American society. The themes developed by the 1980s dystopias analysed in Chapter 2, especially that of the economic and physical vulnerability of working-class males, have resurfaced with the renewed growth of inequalities in America in the 2000s. Male vulnerability and its link to class are stressed for instance in *Avatar* (James Cameron, 2009), where a wheelchair-bound veteran is hired by a large corporation to exploit a foreign environment, in *Elysium* (Neil Blomkamp, 2013), where an industrial accident leads the blue-collar hero to undergo massive surgery and invade the eponymous haven for the rich and, more recently, in *Self/less* (Tarsem Sing, 2015), where financially strained young men sell their bodies to rich elders so the latter can keep on living forever. Indeed, it comes as no surprise that the 2010s saw the remakes of both *Total Recall* (Len Wiseman, 2012) and *RoboCop* (José Padilha, 2014). Further investigation in science fiction's ability to represent male vulnerability and class resentment is thus called for, given their impact on the 2016 US presidential elections.

The book has also sought to show the alternatives offered by science fiction to hegemonic masculinity. The 1990s witnessed a radical change in body type, with a focus on slimmer, more androgynous and more intellectual male protagonists who share the screen with active women. Yet these films were mostly failures at the box office, with *Dark City* and *Strange Days* making approximately only $5 and $7 million respectively (see Filmography). Even if the latter films have weaknesses, it seems that male emotional sensitivity must be counterbalanced by spectacular action for the films to meet their audience, as further proved by the low earnings of *The Road* ($8 million) compared to the success of *War of the Worlds* ($234 million). Moreover, hypermasculinity seems to be making a comeback in the slew of superhero films that have crowded the screens in the past two decades: physical strength and invulnerability are once again the hallmarks of such characters as Wolverine, Ironman, Batman and Captain America.

Hegemonic masculinity has been challenged more successfully by the rise of black heroes in science fiction blockbusters, especially those of Will Smith. Black men can embody mankind and become the representatives of humanity, calling into question whiteness as the invisible norm. Whites are often the ones being othered and dehumanised, as in *I Am Legend*, thus providing a new form of science fictional estrangement. However, Will Smith science fiction productions have become rarer since *After Earth* (2013) and there is no one to replace him in the genre, as demonstrated by the very short screen time given to his fictional son (played by Jessie Usher) in *Independence Day: Resurgence* (Roland Emmerich, 2016), from which Will Smith himself was conspicuously absent. Furthermore, black heroes tend to be used in conservative ways, featured as middle-class figures of authority that reproduce hegemonic masculinity in terms of class and gender. Nevertheless, there has been progress in Hollywood in terms of race as well as gender, in spite of the reluctance of some in the audience. Indeed, the casting of female leads in the latest releases of illustrious science fiction franchises, like *Mad Max: Fury Road* (George Miller, 2015), *Ghostbusters* (Paul Feig, 2016) and *Rogue One: A Star Wars Story* (Gareth Edwards, 2016) triggered angry or mocking reactions on the part of men's rights activists and masculinists in general,[1] including the candidate Donald Trump,[2] fuelling, for some, a backlash that led to the victory of an unashamedly sexist president in 2016.[3] Have we entered an era where the future predicted by Hollywood is actually more progressive than the present? For once, I hope not.

Notes

Introduction

1. J.P. Telotte, *Science Fiction Film* (Cambridge University Press, 2001), p. 15.
2. Geoff King and Tanya Krzywinska, *Science Fiction Cinema, From Outerspace to Cyberspace* (London: Wallflower, 2000), p. 2.
3. 'In its most radical aspect, science fiction narrates the dissolution of the most fundamental structures of human existence.' Scott Bukatman, *Blade Runner* (London: BFI, 1997), p. 16; '*Blade Runner* and the *Terminator* series not only reflect upon the threats to humanity posed by unchecked technological developments, they raise even more probing questions about the consequences of our definitions of the human.' Forest Pyle, 'Making cyborgs, making humans: of terminators and blade runners', in Jim Collins, Hilary Radner and Ava Preacher Collins (eds), *Film Theory Goes to the Movies* (London: Routledge, 1993), p. 228.
4. For a definition of the genre, see also Vivian Sobchack, *Screening Space: The American Science Fiction Film* (New Brunswick, NJ: Rutgers University Press, 1997).
5. Exceptions include *New Heroes on Screen: Prototypes of Masculinity in Contemporary Science Fiction Cinema* (Huelva: Universidad de Huelva, 2007), which focuses mainly on *Dune* (Lynch, 1984) and *The Matrix* (The Wachowskis, 1999) and Christine Cornea, who devotes a chapter to 'The masculine subject of science fiction in the 1980s blockbuster era' in *Science Fiction Cinema: Between Fantasy and Reality* (Edinburgh: Edinburgh University Press, 2007), pp. 111–44. Scholarship on masculinity sometimes includes chapters on science fiction: for instance, Brian Baker, *Contemporary Masculinities in Fiction, Film and Television* (New York and London: Bloomsbury, 2015), which centres on the theme of mobility; Nicola Rehling, *Extra-ordinary Men: White Heterosexual Masculinity in Contemporary Popular Cinema* (Plymouth: Lexington Books, 2009) on virtual reality films of the 1990s, and Hannah Hamad, *Postfeminism and Paternity in Contemporary US Film* (New York and London: Routledge, 2014) on post-apocalyptic films of the 2000s.
6. Fredric Jameson, *Postmodernism or the Cultural Logic of Late Capitalism* (Durham, NC: Duke University Press, 1991), p. 285.

7. Darko Suvin, *Metamorphoses of Science Fiction: On the Poetics and History of a Literary Genre* (New Haven, CT: Yale University Press, 1979), pp. 4, 6, 7.
8. Ibid., p. 28.
9. Patricia Sexton, *The Feminized Male* (New York: Random House, 1969), p. 15. Quoted in Tim Carrigan, Bob Connell and John Lee, 'Toward a new sociology of masculinity', *Theory and Society* 14/5 (September 1985), p. 562. Emphasis mine.
10. R.W. Connell and James W. Messerschmidt, 'Hegemonic masculinity: rethinking the concept', *Gender and Society* 19/6 (2005), p. 832.
11. Dominic Strinati, *An Introduction to Theories of Popular Culture* (London: Routledge, 2004), p. 152.
12. See, for instance, Jonathan Goldberg, 'Recalling totalities: the mirrored stages of Arnold Schwarzenegger', *Differences: A Journal of Cultural Studies* 4/1 (1992), pp. 190–2.
13. Demetrakis Z. Demetriou, 'Connell's concept of hegemonic masculinity: A critique', *Theory and Society* 30/3 (2001), pp. 337–61.
14. David Buchbinder, *Performance Anxieties: Re-Producing Masculinity* (Crows Nest, NSW: Allen and Unwin, 1998), pp. vii, ix.
15. Suvin, *Metamorphoses of Science Fiction*, p. viii.
16. Ibid., p. 8.
17. Carl Silvio and Tony M. Vinci (eds), *Culture, Identities, and Technology in the Star Wars Films: Essays on the Two Trilogies* (Jefferson, NC: McFarland, 2007); Richard J. Gray and Betty Kaklamanidou, *The 21st Century Superhero: Essays on Gender, Genre and Globalization in Film* (Jefferson, NC: McFarland, 2011); Julian C. Chambliss, William Svitavsky and Thomas Donaldson (eds), *Ages of Heroes, Eras of Men: Superheroes and the American Experience* (Newcastle upon Tyne: Cambridge Scholars Publishing, 2013).
18. A term borrowed from Sally Robinson, *Marked Men: White Masculinity in Crisis* (New York: Columbia University Press, 2000).
19. Connell and Messerschmidt, 'Hegemonic masculinity: rethinking the concept', p. 834.
20. Michael Kimmel, *The History of Men: Essays on the History of American and British Masculinities* (Albany, NY: State University of New York Press, 2005), p. 7.
21. Michael Kimmel, *Manhood in America: A Cultural History* (New York: Free Press, 1996), p. 4.
22. Richard Dyer, *White* (London: Routledge, 1997), pp. 1–2.
23. Connell and Messerschmidt, 'Hegemonic masculinity: rethinking the concept', p. 848.
24. *Alien*, Ridley Scott, 1979; *Aliens*, James Cameron, 1986; *Terminator 2: Judgment Day*, James Cameron, 1991; *Ghosts of Mars*, John Carpenter, 2001.

Chapter 1: Vulnerable Hypermasculinity

1. Susan Faludi, *Backlash: The Undeclared War against American Women* [1991] (New York: Three Rivers Press, 2006).
2. James T. Patterson, *Restless Giant: The United States from Watergate to Bush v. Gore* (Oxford: Oxford University Press, 2005), pp. 136, 138.
3. Susan Jeffords, *Hard Bodies: Masculinity in the Reagan Era* (New Brunswick, NJ: Rutgers University Press, 1994).
4. John Orman, *Comparing Presidential Behavior: Carter, Reagan and the Macho Presidential Style* (New York: Greenwood Press, 1987), p. 18.
5. See the Reagan Library's online archives, which include a series of photographs taken of Reagan at Rancho del Cielo. Available at http://www.reagan.utexas.edu/archives/photographs/ranch.html (accessed 14 March 2013).
6. Robert Dallek, *Ronald Reagan, The Politics of Symbolism* (Cambridge, MA: Harvard University Press, 1999), p. 68.
7. As exemplified by Reagan's inaction and dismissiveness faced with the AIDS epidemic. See for instance the short documentary directed by Scott Calonico, 'When AIDS was funny', VanityFairVideo (2015). Available at http://video.vanityfair.com/watch/the-reagan-administration-s-chilling-response-to-the-aids-crisis (accessed 23 May 2017).
8. Jeffords, *Hard Bodies*, pp. 24–5.
9. 'Hypermasculinity is an exaggerated expression of traits, beliefs, actions and embodiment considered to be masculine ... Enactments of masculinity where aggression and physical strength are accentuated can be seen as hypermasculine.' Donald P. Levy, 'Hypermasculinity', in Michael Flood, Judith Kegan Gardiner, Bob Pease and Keith Pringle (eds), *International Encyclopedia of Men and Masculinity* (London: Routledge, 2007), pp. 325–6.
10. Donald Mosher and Mark Sirkin, 'Measuring a macho personality constellation', *Journal of Research in Personality* 18/2 (1984), pp. 150–63.
11. Erica Scharrer, 'Tough guys: the portrayal of hypermasculinity and aggression in televised police dramas', *Journal of Broadcasting and Electronic Media* 45 (2001), p. 616.
12. *Predator 2* (Stephen Hopkins, 1990) differs markedly from the first film and from the other hypermasculine films of the decade since it features an African-American hero. The film will therefore be analysed in Chapter 4.
13. Jeffords, *Hard Bodies*, p. 24.
14. Steve Neale, 'Masculinity as spectacle: reflections on men and mainstream cinema', *Screen* 24/6 (1983), pp. 2–17.
15. Richard Dyer, 'Don't look now', *Screen* 23/3–4 (1982), p. 71.
16. Ibid.

17. Jeff Goldblum, 'Fear of the flesh, the making of *The Fly*', *La mouche: édition prestige*, DVD distributed by Fox Pathé Europa (2006).
18. Yannick Dahan, 'Le film d'action: Idéologie "Ramboesque" et violence chorégraphiée', *Positif* 443 (January 1998), pp. 70–5.
19. Sue Short, *Cyborg Cinema and Contemporary Subjectivity* (Basingstoke: Palgrave Macmillan, 2005).
20. James Chapman and Nicholas J. Cull, *Projecting Tomorrow, Science Fiction and Popular Cinema* (London: I.B.Tauris, 2013), p. 187.
21. Ibid., p. 189.
22. With the exception of *Predator 2*, which will be analysed in Chapter 4.
23. A satiric tone noted by Rita Kempley in her review for *The Washington Post* (17 July 1987) and Roger Ebert in his review for the *Chicago Sun-Times* (17 July 1987). Available at http://www.rogerebert.com/reviews/robocop-1987 (accessed 23 May 2017). Michael Miner, one of the scriptwriters, explicitly describes *RoboCop* as social satire in the 'making of' section of the MGM Video DVD extras (2002).
24. Jeffords, *Hard Bodies*, p. 24.
25. 'And there is pointed social satire, too, as the robocop takes on some of the attributes and some of the popular following of a Bernhard Goetz.' Ebert, review of *RoboCop*.
26. Patterson, *Restless Giant*, pp. 172–3.
27. Valerie Walkerdine, 'Video replay – families, films and fantasies', in Victor Burgin, James Donald and Cora Kaplan (eds), *Formations of Fantasy* (London: Methuen, 1986), p. 172, quoted by Yvonne Tasker, *Spectacular Bodies: Gender, Genre and the Action Cinema* (London: Routledge, 1993), p. 71.
28. Pierre Melandri, *Histoire des Etats-Unis depuis 1865* (Paris: Nathan, 2000), p. 246.
29. Claudia Springer, 'Muscular circuitry: the invincible armored cyborg in cinema', *Genders* 18 (Winter 1993), pp. 87–101.
30. Jeffords, *Hard Bodies*.
31. Yvonne Tasker, *Spectacular Bodies*, p. 123.
32. Laura Mulvey, 'Visual pleasure and narrative cinema', *Screen* 16/3 (Autumn 1975), pp. 6–18.
33. Pat Kirkham and Janet Thumim, *You Tarzan: Masculinity, Movies and Men* (London: Lawrence and Wishart), 1993, p. 5.
34. Neale, 'Masculinity as spectacle', p. 9.
35. From *Hamlet*, Act V, Scene 2.
36. Sean French's description of this scene from *The Terminator* underscores in an amusing way the excitement and anticipation felt by the spectator: 'The Terminator turns his attention to his wrecked eye. He grabs the scalpel to

anticipatory groans from the audience. Is he really going to? Are we going to see it? He is. We are.' Sean French, *The Terminator* (London: BFI, 1996), p. 58.
37. Linda Williams, 'Melodrama revised', in Nick Browne (ed.), *Refiguring American Film Genres. Theory and History* (Berkeley, CA: University of California Press, 1998), pp. 42–88.
38. Ibid., p. 65.
39. Paul Verhoeven, interviewed by Christine Cornea, *Science Fiction Cinema: Between Fantasy and Reality* (Edinburgh: Edinburgh University Press, 2007), p. 134.
40. Cornea, *Science Fiction Cinema*, p. 69.
41. Ibid., p. 83n.16.
42. A tradition in the United States since the nineteenth century set by the best-selling novel *Uncle Tom's Cabin* (Harriett Beecher Stowe, 1852).
43. Sally Robinson, *Marked Men: White Masculinity in Crisis* (New York: Columbia University Press, 2000), p. 6.
44. Joseph Sartelle, 'Dreams and nightmares in the Hollywood blockbuster', in Geoffrey Nowell-Smith (ed.), *The Oxford History of World Cinema* (Oxford: Oxford University Press, 1997), p. 525.
45. Elizabeth Badinter, among others, shows how endurance of pain is, in many societies including Western societies, part and parcel of the ritualistic construction of masculinity. *XY: De l'identité masculine* (Paris: Odile Jacob, 1992), pp. 114, 143.
46. Cynthia J. Fuchs, '"Death is irrelevant": cyborgs, reproduction, and the future of male hysteria', *Genders* 18 (Winter 1993), p. 116.
47. See Donna Haraway, 'A cyborg manifesto: science, technology, and socialist-feminism in the late twentieth century', in *Simians, Cyborgs and Women: The Reinvention of Nature* (London: Free Association Books, 1991), pp. 149–81.
48. LeiLani Nishime, 'The mulatto cyborg: imagining a multiracial future', *Cinema Journal* 44/2 (Winter 2005), p. 45.
49. David Roche, 'L' "horreur viscérale" de David Cronenberg ou l'horreur de l' "anti-nature"', in Anne-Marie Paquet-Deyris (ed.), 'Les cinémas de l'horreur', *CinémAction* 136 (2010), p. 147.
50. For more on David Cronenberg and body horror, see David Roche, 'David Cronenberg's having to make the word be flesh', *Post Script* 23/2 (2004), pp. 72–87.
51. Short, *Cyborg Cinema*, p. 37.
52. Fuchs, '"Death is irrelevant"', p. 117.
53. James Cameron, interviewed by David Chute, *Film Comment* 1 (January/February 1985), pp. 57–9.
54. Mosher and Sirkin, 'Measuring a macho personality constellation'.

55. J.A. Hall, 'Development and validation of the Expanded Hypermasculinity Inventory and the Ideology of Machismo Scale', unpublished master's thesis, University of Connecticut, Storrs, 1992.
56. Short, *Cyborg Cinema*, p. 26. On 'robotism', see also Mark Crispin Miller, 'The robot in the Western mind', in *Boxed In: The Culture of TV* (Evanston, IL: Northwestern University Press, 1988), pp. 285–308.
57. Janet Maslin, review of *The Terminator*, *The New York Times*, 26 October 1984. See also the review of *The Terminator* in *Variety*, 31 October 1984.
58. See Mosher and Sirkin, 'Measuring a macho personality constellation', or Dominic Parrott and Amos Zeichner, 'Effects of hypermasculinity on physical aggression against women', *Psychology of Men and Masculinity* 4/1 (2003), pp. 70–8.
59. Fabien Boully, 'Des Surhommes accablés (*Dead Zone* et *The Fly* de David Cronenberg)', *CinémAction* 112 (June 2004), p. 263.
60. 'There's a little bit of the terminator in everybody. In our private fantasy world we'd all like to be able to walk in and shoot somebody we don't like, or to kick a door instead of unlocking it; to be immune and just to have our own way every minute. The terminator is the ultimate rude person. He operates completely outside all the built-in social constraints. It's a dark, cathartic fantasy … But then when we go back to Reese and Sarah, you get the other side of it, what it would be like on the receiving end.' James Cameron, *Film Comment*, p. 59.
61. Tasker, *Spectacular Bodies*, pp. 109, 111.
62. Thomas Schatz, *Hollywood Genres: Formulas, Filmmaking and the Studio System* (New York: McGraw Hill, 1981), p. 35.

Chapter 2: Dystopia and Class War

1. Ronald L. Davis, *Celluloid Mirrors, Hollywood and American Society Since 1945* (Orlando, FL: Harcourt Brace, 1997), p. 150.
2. The main exception and starting point for this chapter is an article by Michael Ryan and Douglas Kellner, 'Technophobia/dystopia', in Sean Redmond (ed.), *Liquid Metal: The Science Fiction Film Reader* (London: Wallflower Press, 2007), pp. 48–56.
3. In the 2004 enlarged edition of *Screening Space*, Vivian Sobchack devotes the last chapter to an analysis of science fiction films released after 1977, which for her tend to 'celebrate a thoroughly domestic space and domesticated technology, embrace the alien Other, and realize a temporal reformulation of the genre's traditional "futurism"' (p. 229). The analysis is convincing when applied to the *Star Wars* trilogy, *Back to the Future*, *Tron* or *ET* but these films are oddly juxtaposed with *Blade Runner* and *The Terminator*, whose tone, mood and

message are starkly different. Vivian Sobchack, *Screening Space: The American Science Fiction Film* (New Brunswick, NJ: Rutgers University Press, 1997), pp. 223–306.
4. See for example Peter Ruppert, '*Blade Runner*: the utopian dialectics of science fiction films', *Cineaste* 17/2 (1989), pp. 8–13; Giuliana Bruno, 'Ramble City: postmodernism and *Blade Runner*', in Annette Kuhn (ed.), *Alien Zone: Cultural Theory and Contemporary Science Fiction Cinema* (London: Verso, 1990), pp. 183–94; or Scott Bukatman, *Blade Runner* (London: BFI, 1997).
5. Interestingly, many of the films quoted are either foreign or come from independent cinema.
6. Christopher Lasch, *The Culture of Narcissism: American Life in an Age of Diminishing Expectations* (New York: Norton, 1979).
7. In *The Confidence Gap: Business, Labor and Government in the Public Mind*, Lipset and Schneider state that 24 per cent of American citizens said they did not trust their leaders in 1958, which had risen to 73 per cent by 1980. Furthermore, trust in the business world fell from 70 per cent in 1968 to only 19 per cent of Americans in 1980. Seymour Martin Lipset and William Schneider, *The Confidence Gap: Business, Labor and Government in the Public Mind* (New York: The Johns Hopkins University Press, 1987).
8. Joseph A. McCartin, 'Labor', in Stephen J. Whitfield (ed.), *A Companion to 20th Century America* (Malden, MA: Blackwell, 2004), p. 263.
9. James T. Patterson, *Restless Giant: The United States from Watergate to Bush v. Gore* (Oxford: Oxford University Press, 2005), p. 166.
10. Bureau of Labor Statistics Data. Available at http://data.bls.gov/PDQ/servlet/SurveyOutputServlet?data_tool=latest_numbers&series_id=LNU04000000&years_option=all_years&periods_option=specific_periods&periods=Annual+Data (accessed 7 February 2014).
11. Patterson, *Restless Giant*, p. 167.
12. Joseph Pleck, 'The male sex role: definitions, problems, and sources of change', *Journal of Social Issues* 32 (1976), p. 157, quoted in Michael Winter and Ellen Robert, 'Male dominance, late capitalism, and the growth of instrumental reason', *Berkeley Journal of Sociology* 24–5 (1980), p. 259.
13. Exceptions include Julie F. Codell, 'Murphy's law, Robocop's body, and capitalism's work', *Jump Cut* 34/3–4 (1989), pp. 12–19; Fred Glass, 'The "new bad future": *RoboCop* and 1980s sci-fi films', *Science as Culture* 5 (1989), pp. 7–49; and David Desser, 'Race, space and class: the politics of cityscapes in science fiction films', in Annette Kuhn (ed.), *Alien Zone II* (London: Verso, 1999), pp. 80–96.
14. I am drawing on Raphaëlle Moine's argument, which seeks to reconcile ritual interpretations of genre with ideological ones. Raphaëlle Moine, *Les Genres du cinéma* (Paris: Nathan, 2002), p. 78.

15. See for example David B. Clarke (ed.), *The Cinematic City* (London and New York: Routledge, 1997).
16. Advisory Committee on Intergovernmental Relations, 'Bankruptcies, Defaults and other local government financial emergencies', March 1985, pp. 44–7. Available at http://www.library.unt.edu/gpo/acir/Reports/policy/a-99.pdf (accessed 12 February 2014).
17. 'The 841 slayings [of the first semester of 1988] are close to half of the 1981 record total.' David E. Pitt, 'Crime rates rise in New York City', *The New York Times*, 17 September 1988. See also New York Crime Rates 1960–2015. Available at http://www.disastercenter.com/crime/nycrime.htm (accessed 12 February 2014).
18. John Carpenter, 'Présentation par John Carpenter', DVD extra from *New York 1997* distributed by Studio Canal, 2003.
19. Vincent Canby, review of *Escape from New York*, *The New York Times*, 10 July 1981.
20. Ruppert, '*Blade Runner*'. See also Barbara Mennel, *Cities and Cinema* (London and New York: Routledge, 2008), pp. 145–6.
21. Vertical division of space is especially common in science fiction film, and *Blade Runner* clearly draws here on *Metropolis* (Lang, 1927). See Desser, 'Race, space and class', p. 94.
22. Michael Rogin, *Ronald Reagan, the Movie: and Other Episodes in Political Demonology* (Berkeley, CA: University of California Press, 1987).
23. Robin Wood, *Hollywood from Vietnam to Reagan ... and Beyond* (New York: Columbia University Press, 2003), p. 166.
24. For more on the similarities between *Blade Runner* and *Metropolis*, see Douglas Kellner, Flo Leibowitz and Michael Ryan, '*Blade Runner*: a diagnostic critique', *Jump Cut* 29 (1984), pp. 6–8; Desser, 'Race, space and class', pp. 94–5; and Bukatman, *Blade Runner*, pp. 73–4.
25. Rogin, *Ronald Reagan*, p. 45.
26. Canby, review of *Escape from New York*.
27. Donald Bogle, *Toms, Coons, Mulattoes, Mammies and Bucks: An Interpretive History of Blacks in American Films* (New York: Continuum, 2001), p. 13.
28. John Carpenter, DVD extra.
29. Michelle Fine, Lois Weis, Judi Addleston and Julia Marusza, '(In) secure times: constructing white working-class masculinities in the late 20th century', *Gender and Society* 11/1 (Februrary 1997), p. 55.
30. Ruppert, '*Blade Runner*', p. 11.
31. David Desser, '*Blade Runner*: science fiction and transcendence', *Literature/Film Quarterly* 13 (1985), p. 176.
32. Here I disagree with Forest Pyle, who emphasises the dichotomy between Roy's symbolic association with Christ and his 'far from Christ-like' narrative

position since he has just murdered the 'father'. Indeed, the power of symbolic images tends to outweigh narrative logic throughout *Blade Runner* and especially in this sequence. See Forest Pyle, 'Making cyborgs, making humans: of terminators and blade runners', in Jim Collins, Hilary Radner and Ava Preacher Collins (eds), *Film Theory Goes to the Movies* (London: Routledge, 1993), p. 229.
33. For a more developed analysis of Roy's death, see Marcus A. Doel and David B. Clarke, 'From Ramble City to the screening of the eye: *Blade Runner*, death and symbolic exchange', in David B. Clarke (ed.), *The Cinematic City* (London and New York: Routledge, 1997), pp. 161-3.
34. See for instance Thomas B. Byers, 'Commodity Futures', in Kuhn, *Alien Zone*, p. 44; Desser, 'Race, space and class', p. 95.
35. Kellner, Leibowitz and Ryan see the proximity between Deckard and Roy as one of the film's main liberal elements as they both 'renounce their warrior roles'. '*Blade Runner*', p. 7.
36. Yves Chevrier, for instance, criticises Deckard as a 'simplified puppet [...] less real than the society he grovels through.' '*Blade Runner* or the sociology of anticipation', *Science Fiction Studies* 11/1 (March 1984), p. 57.
37. Ruppert, '*Blade Runner*', p. 10.
38. Janet Maslin, review of *Blade Runner*, *The New York Times*, 25 June 1982.
39. The expression was all the more prescriptive as it was used at a commencement ceremony in Berkeley in 1986. Patterson, *Restless Giant*, p. 186.
40. 'Making millions with your money, investor "Ivan the Terrible" Boesky', *Time*, 1 December 1986.
41. Patterson, *Restless Giant*, p. 169.
42. According to Rebecca Morales in *Flexible Production: Restructuring the International Automobile Industry* (Cambridge: Polity Press, 1994), p. 57, more than 200,000 thousand jobs were lost between 1978 and 1980.
43. Robert F. Arnold, 'Termination or transformation? The *Terminator* films and recent changes in the US Auto industry', *Film Quarterly* 52/1 (Autumn 1998), p. 23.
44. Ibid.
45. Although it is actually Sarah, a woman, who gets the better of the machine, a point that will be discussed in the next chapter.
46. Arnold, 'Termination or transformation', p. 25.
47. Codell, 'Murphy's law', p. 17.
48. Bruce Schulman, *The Seventies: The Great Shift in American Culture, Society and Politics* (New York: Simon and Schuster, 2001), p. 249.
49. Haynes Johnson, *Sleepwalking Through History: America in the Reagan Years* (New York: Anchor Books, 1992), pp. 20-1.

50. Mark C. Carnes, 'The culture of work', in Mark C. Carnes (ed.), *The Columbia History of Post World War II America* (New York: Columbia University Press, 2007), p. 122.
51. Patterson, *Restless Giant*, p. 168.
52. Jon Davison, 'Flesh and steel: the making of *RoboCop*', DVD extra, *RoboCop*, MGM Video, 2002.
53. I am drawing on Fred Glass's analysis of Robocop as a 'cultural transitional object' easing the transition from an industrialised America into a new economic order. Glass, 'The "new bad future"'.
54. Paul Verhoeven, 'Flesh and steel: the making of *RoboCop*', DVD extra.
55. 'To have a blue-collar individual, who's been stomped on by both the good guys and the bad guys, come up and be empowered to do something, is a very fulfilling experience for an unempowered audience.' Michael Miner, ibid.
56. Phil Tippett, designer of ED 209, ibid.
57. Fred Glass, 'Totally recalling Arnold: sex and violence in the new bad future', *Film Quarterly* 44/1 (Autumn 1990), p. 4.
58. Carole Marks, 'The urban underclass', *Annual Review of Sociology* 17 (1991), pp. 445–66.
59. Myron Magnet, 'Who are the underclass?', *Fortune Magazine*, 17 May 1987, p. 139, quoted by Marks, 'The urban underclass', p. 454.
60. Ibid.
61. Ibid., p. 459. Original emphasis.
62. Glass, 'Totally recalling Arnold', p. 6.
63. 'Most of the truly "masculine" jobs, those that demand hard physical labor, are gone, replaced by jobs in the service sector, jobs that not only pay less but do not offer the "hard" real confrontation with physicality that was embedded in jobs of former years, jobs that encouraged the production of a certain type of masculinity.' Lois Weis, Amira Proweller and Craig Centrie, 'Reexamining "a moment in history": loss of privilege inside white working-class masculinity in the 1990s', in Michelle Fine, Lois Weis, Linda C. Powell and L. Mun Wong (eds), *Off White: Readings on Race, Power and Society* (New York: Routledge, 1997), p. 211.
64. Kuhn, *Alien Zone*, p. 5.
65. Steve Neale, 'Hollywood strikes back: special effects in recent American cinema', *Screen* 21/3 (1980), p. 105.
66. On metalepsis in *Total Recall*, see Daniel Tron, 'Psychoses diégétiques: *We Can Remember it for you Wholesale* et *Total Recall*', in Roger Bozzetto and Gilles Menegaldo (eds), *Les Nouvelles formes de la science-fiction*, Colloque de Cerisy, 2003, pp. 321–38.
67. Glass, 'The "new bad future"', pp. 33–4.

68. In this way, the films return to the original concerns of the books they adapt, especially Philip K. Dick's *Do Androids Dream of Electric Sheep?* and *We Can Remember it for You Wholesale*. For an interesting analysis of *Blade Runner*'s adaptation of *Do Androids Dream of Electric Sheep?*, see Peter Fitting, 'Futurecop: the neutralization of revolt in *Blade Runner*', *Science Fiction Studies* 14/3 (1987), pp. 340–54. For more on the adaptations of Philip K. Dick, see Jason P. Vest, *Future Imperfect: Philip K. Dick at the Movies* (Lincoln, NE: University of Nebraska Press, 2009).
69. Kuhn, *Alien Zone*, p. 7.
70. Davison, 'Flesh and steel'.
71. Michael Stern, 'Making culture into nature', in Kuhn, *Alien Zone*, p. 70.

Chapter 3: Sidelining Women

1. In the wake of Yvonne Tasker's *Spectacular Bodies: Gender, Genre, and the Action Cinema* (London; New York: Routledge, 1993), most books on women in science fiction and more generally the action adventure genre focus on 'tough women' and include case studies of Ripley and/or Connor: see, for instance, Sherrie Inness, *Tough Girls: Women Warriors and Wonder Women in Popular Culture* (Philadelphia, PA: University of Pennsylvania Press, 1999); Silke Andris and Ursula Frederick, *Women Willing to Fight: The Fighting Woman in Film* (Newcastle: Cambridge Scholars Publishing, 2007); and Robin Ann Reid, *Women in Science Fiction and Fantasy* (Westport, CT: Greenwood Press, 2009). Furthermore, Ximena Gallardo and C. Jason Smith, as well as Elizabeth Graham have devoted whole books to Ellen Ripley (Ximena Gallardo and C. Jason Smith, *Alien Woman: The Making of Lt Ellen Ripley* (New York: Continuum, 2004); Elizabeth Graham, *Meanings of Ripley: The Alien Quadrology and Gender* (Newcastle: Cambridge Scholars Publishing, 2010)).
2. To my knowledge, only one article surveys the history and evolution of women's roles in science fiction film: Dean Conrad, 'Femmes futures: one hundred years of female representation in sf cinema', *Science Fiction Film and Television* 4/1 (Spring 2011), pp. 79–99.
3. Tasker, *Spectacular Bodies*, p. 15.
4. Andris and Frederick, *Women Willing to Fight*, p. 2.
5. Christine Cornea, *Science Fiction Cinema: Between Fantasy and Reality* (Edinburgh: Edinburgh University Press, 2007), p. 160. Again, though her analysis of female heroes is centred on only three films, including *Terminator 2*, Cornea never really emphasises that female heroes are the exception, not the norm.

6. I counted all science fiction productions, excluding superhero films, listed in the 50 yearly top-grossing films on Box Office Mojo (http://www.boxofficemojo.com) between the year 1980 and the year 2015. There were only two female-led films in the 1980s (*Aliens* and *The Abyss*), six in the 1990s (*Terminator 2*, *Alien³*, *Species*, *Contact*, *Alien Resurrection*, *The X Files*), only one in the 2000s (*The Stepford Wives*) and eight between 2000 and 2015 (the four *Hunger Games*, two *Divergent* films, *Lucy* and *Mad Max: Fury Road*). The ratio is even smaller if one includes superhero films.
7. For more on women scientists in 1950s science fiction, see Bonnie Noonan, *Women Scientists in Fifties Science Fiction Films* (Jefferson, NC: McFarland, 2005) and Patrick B. Sharp, 'Darwin's soldiers: gender, evolution and warfare in *Them!* and *Forbidden Planet*', *Science Fiction Film and Television* 1/2 (Autumn 2008), pp. 215–30.
8. See Susan Faludi, *Backlash: The Undeclared War against American Women* (1991) (New York: Three Rivers Press, 2006).
9. Laura Mulvey, 'Visual pleasure and narrative cinema', *Screen* 16/3 (Autumn 1975), pp. 6–18.
10. Tasker, *Spectacular Bodies*, p. 16
11. Ibid.
12. See, for instance, Patrick Goldstein's review for the *Los Angeles Times*, '"The Fly": artful remake of a tacky 1958 classic', 14 August 1986, or Pam Cook's review in *Monthly Film Bulletin* 54/637 (February 1987), pp. 45–6.
13. In 'Fear of the flesh, the making of *The Fly*', *La mouche: édition prestige*, DVD distributed by Fox Pathé Europa, 2006.
14. William Beard, 'Cronenberg, Flyness and the Other-self', *Cinemas* 4/2 (Winter 1994), p. 164.
15. Cook, review of *The Fly*.
16. Peter Krämer, 'Women first: *Titanic*, action-adventure films and Hollywood's female audience', in Kevin S. Sandler and Gaylin Studlar (eds), *Titanic: Anatomy of a Blockbuster* (New Brunswick, NJ: Rutgers University Press, 1999), p. 112.
17. Gallardo and Smith, *Alien Woman*, p. 3.
18. US Bureau of the Census, 'Statistical abstract of the United States', Washington, DC, September 1994. Available at http://www2.census.gov/prod2/statcomp/documents/1994-01.pdf (accessed 12 September 2014).
19. Jennifer E. Manning and Ida A. Brudnick, 'Women in the United States Congress, 1917–2013: biographical and committee assignment information, and listings by State and Congress', Congressional Research Service Report, 7 November 2013, p. 78. Available at http://fas.org/sgp/crs/misc/RL30261.pdf (accessed 12 September 2014).

20. Women in Military Service for America Memorial Foundation. Available at http://chnm.gmu.edu/courses/rr/s01/cw/students/leeann/historyand collections/collections/photopages/phespersgulf.html (accessed 18 September 2014).
21. Raphaëlle Moine, *Les Femmes d'action au cinéma* (Paris: Armand Colin, 2010), p. 6.
22. See Sylvestre Meininger, 'Corps mortels. L'évolution du personnage de Ripley dans la trilogie *Alien*', *Cinémas* 7/1–2 (Autumn 1996), p. 32.
23. Andrew Ross, 'Cowboys, Cadillacs and cosmonauts: families, film genre, and technocultures', in Joseph A. Boone and Michael Cadden (eds), *Engendering Men: The Question of Male Feminist Criticism* (New York: Routledge, 1990), p. 101.
24. For instance by Pauline Kael in *The New Yorker* 62 (11 August 1986), Andrew Kopkind in *The Nation* 20 (September 1986) and Ari Korpivaara in *Ms.* 15/3 (September 1986).
25. Harvey Greenberg, 'Fembo: *Aliens*' intentions', *Journal of Popular Film and Television* 15/4 (Winter 1988), pp. 165–71.
26. Walter Goodman, review of *Aliens*, *The New York Times*, 18 July 1986.
27. Sean French, *The Terminator* (London: BFI, 1996), p. 51.
28. Margot Dougherty, 'A new body of work', *Entertainment Weekly*, 12 July 1991.
29. Julie Baumgold, 'Killer women: here come the hardbodies', *New York*, 29 July 1991, p. 26.
30. Mandy Johnson, 'Women as action heroes: is violence a positive direction for females?', *Glamour* (March 1994), p. 153.
31. Krämer, 'Women first', p. 112.
32. Peter Wood even goes against the idea that Ripley is a feminist hero, arguing that she is consistent with patriarchal ideas of woman and motherhood. Peter Wood, 'Redressing Ripley: disrupting the female hero', in Elizabeth Graham (ed.), *Meanings of Ripley: The Alien Quadrology and Gender* (Newcastle: Cambridge Scholars Publishing, 2010), pp. 32–59.
33. Meininger, 'Corps mortels', p. 135, my translation.
34. The alien queen is Barbara Creed's first example in and of *The Monstrous-Feminine* (London: Routledge, 1993), p. 6.
35. David Ansen, 'Conan the humanitarian', *Newsweek*, 8 July 1991.
36. According to David Ansen, a large part of the film's enormous budget was spent on Arnold Schwarzenegger ($12 million, 'because he can pack movie houses all over the world') while Linda Hamilton was paid only $1 million. Ibid. On the Terminator's parenting and warrior skills, see Marianne Kac-Vergne, 'Losing visibility? The rise and fall of hypermasculinity in science fiction films', *InMedia* 2, 2012. Available at http://inmedia.revues.org/491#toc-to1n3 (accessed 29 July 2016).

37. Thomas Doherty, 'Genre, gender and the *Aliens* trilogy', in Barry Keith Grant (ed.), *The Dread of Difference: Gender and the Horror Film* (Austin, TX: University of Texas Press, 2015), p. 196.
38. Gallardo and Smith, *Alien Woman*, p. 76.
39. For more on the negative stereotyping of feminists in the mass media, see Susan J. Douglas, *Where the Girls Are: Growing up Female with the Mass Media* (London: Penguin, 1995).
40. Naomi Wolf, *Fire With Fire: The New Female Power and How It Will Change the 21st Century* (New York: Random House, 1993); Rene Denfeld, *The New Victorians: A Young Woman's Challenge to the Old Feminist Order* (New York: Warner Books, 1995).
41. Stéphanie Genz and Benjamin A. Brabon, *Postfeminism: Cultural Texts and Theories* (Edinburgh: Edinburgh University Press, 2009), pp. 1–41; Yvonne Tasker and Diane Negra, *Interrogating Postfeminism: Gender and the Politics of Popular Culture* (London: Duke University Press, 2007), p. 2. The two books focus on a wide range of postfeminist productions, including *Tomb Raider* (Core Design, 1996–), *Sex in the City* (HBO, 1998–2004), *Charmed* (WB Television Network, 1998–2006), *Bridget Jones's Diary* (Maguire, 2001) and *Kill Bill* (Tarantino, 2003, 2004).
42. John Carpenter interviewed by Gilles Boulenger in *John Carpenter par John Carpenter* (Paris: Le Cinéphage, 2001), p. 271.
43. Grier's first part was as a lesbian in *Big Bird Cage* (Hill, 1972). Interestingly, in the DVD commentary, John Carpenter indicates that Grier was opposed to being cast as a man-hating lesbian and would have preferred being given a more open sexuality. DVD of *Ghosts of Mars* distributed by Film office éditions, Neuilly sur Seine, 2002.
44. John Carpenter interviewed by Gilles Boulenger, p. 271.
45. Paul Verhoeven, audio commentary, *Starship Troopers*, DVD distributed by Buena Vista home entertainment, 2006.
46. Susan Faludi, *The Terror Dream: Myth and Misogyny in an Insecure America* (New York: Picador, 2007).
47. Ann Braithwaite, 'Politics and/of backlash', *Journal of International Women's Studies* 5/5 (2004), p. 25.
48. Charles-Antoine Courcoux, 'D'une peur de la modernité technologique déclinée au féminin', in Laurent Guido (ed.), *Les peurs de Hollywood* (Lausanne: Editions Antipodes, 2006), p. 238 (my translation).
49. Judy Wajcman, *Technofeminism* (Cambridge: Polity Press, 2004), p. 12.
50. Ibid., p. 14.
51. Donna Haraway, *Simians, Cyborgs and Women: The Reinvention of Nature* (London: Free Association Books, 1991), p. 181.

52. Donna Haraway, in Constance Penley and Andrew Ross, 'Cyborgs at large: interview with Donna Haraway', *Social Text* 24/5 (1990), p. 23.
53. Genz and Brabon, *Postfeminism*, p. 37.
54. Without an extensive study of reception, this is a hypothesis, but the comparison between Silicon Valley and *Elysium* is often found in critical articles on the Valley's bigwigs: see, for instance, John Kennedy, 'So Google wants to cure death – an Elysium for rich folk', Silicon Republic, 19 September 2013. Available at https://www.siliconrepublic.com/innovation/so-google-wants-to-cure-death-an-elysium-for-rich-folk (accessed 30 July 2016). Another blogger quotes a speech made by Balaji Srinivasan, cofounder of a startup in genomics, who suggested that Silicon Valley secede from the United States, building on Paypal founders' visions of building Elysium-like colonies on Mars (an idea proposed by Elon Musk) or in the middle of the sea (Peter Thiel's seasteading vision). Interestingly, the blogger ends his post on 'Silicon Valley assholes' by specifically targeting Marissa Mayer, Yahoo's female CEO, included in a large portrait photo, whom he denounces solely for publishing a book of notes written by enthusiastic employees, a rather small, if vain, offence. See Dave Cohen, 'Silicon Valley – where the assholes are', 15 December 2013. Available at http://www.declineoftheempire.com/2013/12/silicon-valley-where-the-assholes-are.html (accessed 30 July 2016).
55. Also visible in *I, Robot* with an artificial intelligence named VIKI, as we shall see in Chapter 4.
56. Claudia Springer's argument still holds true for recent Hollywood films: high technologies are figured in terms of feminised technoerotic conventions, in contrast to the phallic metaphors used to depict older mechanical technologies. *Electronic Eros: Bodies and Desire in the Post-industrial Age* (London: Athlone Press, 1996), p. 111.
57. Sharp, 'Darwin's soldiers', p. 221.
58. Holly Hassel, 'The 'babe scientist' phenomenon, the illusion of inclusion in 1990s American action films', in Suzanne Ferris and Mallory Young (eds), *Chick Flicks: Contemporary Women at the Movies* (New York: Routledge, 2008), pp. 190, 196.
59. Roger Ebert, review of *Planet of the Apes*, Chicago Sun Times, 27 July 2001. Available at http://www.rogerebert.com/reviews/planet-of-the-apes-2001 (accessed 30 July 2016).
60. A critique of hegemonic masculinity reinforced by the casting of Charlton Heston, 'the embodiment of self assured 20th century man', which can be contrasted with Mark Wahlberg's far less emblematic screen persona. See Eric Greene, Planet of the Apes *as American Myth* (Jefferson, NC: McFarland, 1996), pp. 41–9.

61. See Marianne Kac-Vergne, 'The limits of hypermasculinity: intimacy in American science fiction films of the 1980s', in David Roche and Isabelle Schmitt-Pitiot (eds), *Intimacy in Cinema* (Jefferson, NC: McFarland, 2014), pp. 119–32.
62. Two recent exceptions are *Mad Max: Fury Road* (Miller, 2015) and *Star Wars: The Force Awakens* (Abrams, 2015), but the women are, in both cases, partnered up with a male (albeit less skilful) character.

Chapter 4: 'White Folks Ain't Planning for Us to be Here'

1. Adilifu Nama, *Black Space: Imagining Race in Science Fiction Film* (Austin, TX: University of Texas Press, 2008).
2. James T. Patterson, *Restless Giant: The United States from Watergate to Bush v. Gore* (Oxford: Oxford University Press, 2005), p. 241. See also William Julius Wilson, *The Declining Significance of Race* (1978) (Chicago, IL: University of Chicago Press, 2012).
3. Ed Guerrero, *Framing Blackness: The African-American Image in Film* (Philadelphia, PA: Temple University Press, 1993), p. 160.
4. Patterson, *Restless Giant*, p. 306.
5. In the mid-1990s, one half of blacks lived in neighbourhoods that were 50 per cent or more white, while the decade saw a 70 per cent increase in black-white marriages. Ibid., pp. 307, 309.
6. Sandra L. Barnes, Zandria F. Robinson and Earl Wright II (eds), 'Introduction', in *Repositioning Race: Prophetic Research in a Postracial Obama Age* (Albany, NY: State University of New York Press, 2014), p. 3.
7. Eduardo Bonilla-Silva with Trenita Brookshire Childers, 'Race matters in "post-racial" Obamerica and how to climb out of the rabbit hole', in Barnes, Robinson and Wright II, *Repositioning Race*, p. 29.
8. Ibid., p. 30.
9. In his report entitled 'The negro family: the case for national action', Assistant Secretary of Labor Daniel Patrick Moynihan explained persistent black poverty by the absence of fathers in African-American families. The report was criticised by many groups, including the NAACP and black activists like the clinical psychologist William Ryan, who argued in *Blaming the Victim* (New York: Random House, 1988) that the report diverted attention from structural factors to focus on the behaviours and culture of the poor. (Office of Planning and Research, United States Department of Labor, 'The negro family: the case for national action', March 1965. Available at http://web.stanford.edu/~mrosenfe/Moynihan%27s%20The%20Negro%20Family.pdf (accessed 29 June 2017).

10. Richard Dyer, *White* (London: Routledge, 1997), p. 1.
11. Todd Boyd, 'A small introduction to the "G" funk era: gangsta rap and black masculinity in Los Angeles', in Michael J. Dear, H. Eric Schockman and Greg Hise (eds), *Rethinking Los Angeles* (Thousand Oaks, CA: Sage Publications, 1996), p. 132.
12. Guerrero, *Framing Blackness*, p. 59; Nama, *Black Space*, p. 3.
13. Ibid., p. 71.
14. Nama further identifies the four long fangs crisscrossing the lower part of the Predator's face as 'clearly evoking *National Geographic* pictures of tribal Africans with white animal bones piercing their noses and other parts of their faces' (ibid., p. 76) while Ximena Gallardo suggests that 'its salient features (the oversized cranium covered in slime, the inner mouth filled with rows of pointed teeth, the larger outer mouth framed by elongated fangs) are distinctively reminiscent of the "Africanist" markers of blackface.' See 'Aliens, cyborgs and other invisible men: Hollywood's solutions to the black "problem" in sf cinema', *Science Fiction Film and Television* 6/2 (Summer 2013), p. 232.
15. Nama, *Black Space*, p. 88.
16. Donald Bogle, *Toms, Coons, Mulattoes, Mammies and Bucks: An Interpretive History of Blacks in American Films* (New York: Continuum, 2001), pp. 13–14.
17. While Mark Bould argues that Brother is trapped by commodities, Janani Subramanian argues that 'he learns how to use a commodified landscape beneficially. His adeptness with electronics and his ability to experience a range of black experiences through his "second sight" can be read as successful manipulations of a technological commodity culture to improve the black community.' Mark Bould, 'The false salvation of the here and now: aliens, images, and the commodification of desire in *The Brother from Another Planet*', in Diane Carson and Heidi Kenaga (eds), *Sayles Talk: New Perspectives on Independent Filmmaker John Sayles* (Detroit, MI: Wayne State University Press, 2006), pp. 79–102; Janani Subramanian, 'Alienating identification: black identity in *The Brother from Another Planet* and *I Am Legend*', *Science Fiction Film and Television* 3/1 (Spring 2010), p. 44.
18. Linda Mizejewski, 'Action bodies in futurist spaces: bodybuilder stardom as special effect', in Annette Kuhn (ed.), *Alien Zone II* (London: Verso, 1999), p. 168.
19. Guerrero, *Framing Blackness*, p. 59.
20. The album was certified platinum in July 1989 and double platinum in 1992; see Recording Industry Association of America (RIAA) website. Available at http://www.riaa.com/goldandplatinumdata.php (accessed 7 June 2015).
21. Patterson, *Restless Giant*, p. 245.
22. Richard Slotkin, *Regeneration Through Violence* (Middletown, CT: Wesleyan University Press, 1973).

23. Linda Mizejewski ('Action bodies', p. 169) offers a very interesting analysis of the 'bond' between Phoenix and Spartan that underlines the camp appeal of 'the two "naturally different" super bodies'.
24. Director's commentary, Collector's edition of *Predator 2* distributed by Pathé Europa, 2005.
25. James Nadell, '*Boyz n the Hood*: A Colonial Analysis', *Journal of Black Studies* 25/4 (March 1995), pp. 447–8.
26. 'In an opinion poll conducted by *the New York Times*/CBS in 1990, 60% of blacks in New York believe or at least admit the possibility that the easy accessibility of drugs in poor black communities is part of a government conspiracy.' Jason DeParle, 'For some blacks, social ills seem to follow white plans', *The New York Times*, 11 August 1991, quoted in Kenneth Chan, 'The construction of black male identity in black action films of the nineties', *Cinema Journal* 37/2 (Winter 1998), p. 37.
27. Nama, *Black Space*, p. 138.
28. Gretchen Bakke, 'Dead white men: an essay on the changing dynamics of race in US action cinema', *Anthropological Quarterly* 83/2 (Spring 2010), p. 404. See also my analysis of *Predator* in Chapter 1.
29. The Predator spares the female detective (Maria Conchita Alonso) when he sees that she is pregnant, even though she has a gun, thus participating in the marginalisation of female sidekicks analysed in Chapter 3.
30. Director's commentary.
31. Régis Dubois, *Images du Noir dans le cinéma américain blanc (1980–1995)* (Paris: L'Harmattan, 1997), p. 59, my translation.
32. An homage to blaxploitation, especially to the films of Jim Kelly.
33. Boyd, 'A small introduction to the "G" funk era', pp. 128, 132.
34. See the chapter on black male violence in bell hooks, *We Real Cool: Black Men and Masculinity* (New York and London: Routledge, 2004) for an insightful examination of the link between patriarchy and black male violence.
35. Nama, *Black Space*, pp. 92–3.
36. Emanuel Levy, review of *Demolition Man*, *Variety*, 8 October 1993.
37. Hal Hinson, review of *Demolition Man*, *The Washington Post*, 9 October 1993.
38. Bogle, *Toms, Coons*, p. 409.
39. Michael Rogin, *Independence Day, or How I Learned to Stop Worrying and Love the Enola Gay* (London: BFI, 1998), p. 50.
40. Michael Lerner and Cornel West, *Jews and Blacks: Let the Healing Begin* (Rutherford, NJ: G.P. Putnam and Sons, 1995).
41. Rogin, *Independence Day*, pp. 41–4.
42. Ibid., p. 51.
43. The film's imperialism was denounced by all French critics upon its release. See Laurence Alfonsi, 'La réception du film *Independence Day* en France. Un

exemple de contre-acculturation?', *Cinémas* 8/3 (1998), pp. 9–29. She quotes, for instance, the review in *Les Cahiers du cinéma* entitled 'America *is* the world' (505, September 1996, p. 50, my translation), and in *Télérama*, entitled 'Hollywood imposes the new planetary order' (2438, 2 October 1996, p. 32, my translation).

44. Christopher Sharrett, 'End of story: the collapse of myth in postmodern narrative film', in Jon Lewis (ed.), *The End of Cinema as We Know It* (New York: New York University Press, 2001), p. 326.
45. Joshua Clover, *The Matrix* (London: BFI, 2007), p. 21.
46. R.L. Rutsky, 'Being Keanu', in Lewis, *The End of Cinema as We Know It*, p. 191.
47. *Bill and Ted's Excellent Adventure*, Stephen Herek, 1989; *Bill and Ted's Bogus Journey*, Pete Hewitt, 1991.
48. Patricia Hill Collins, *Black Feminist Thought* (New York: Routledge, 2000).
49. Tani Dianca Sanchez, 'Neo-abolitionists, colorblind epistemologies and black politics: the *Matrix* trilogy', in Daniel Bernardi (ed.), *The Persistence of Whiteness: Race and Contemporary Hollywood Cinema* (London and New York: Routledge, 2008), p. 107.
50. Nama, *Black Space*, p. 144.
51. Ibid., pp. 102–24.
52. Gallardo, 'Aliens, cyborgs and other invisible men', p. 243.
53. Sanchez, 'Neo-abolitionists', p. 112.
54. Ibid., p. 120.
55. Krin Gabbard, *Black Magic: White Hollywood and African American Culture* (New Brunswick, NJ: Rutgers University Press, 2004), p. 168. Richard C. King and David J. Leonard even label Morpheus 'a modern Uncle Tom' for his unconditional support of Neo, which overlooks completely his rebellious stand against the white matrix. 'Is Neo white? Reading race, watching the trilogy', in Matthew Kapell and William G. Doty (eds), *Jacking in to the Matrix Franchise: Cultural Reception and Interpretation* (New York: Continuum, 2004), p. 39.
56. Amy Taubin, 'Playing it straight: REM meets a post-Rodney King world in *Independence Day*', *Sight and Sound* 6/8 (1996), pp. 6–8.
57. Dyer, *White*, p. 210.
58. Bakke, 'Dead white men', p. 407.
59. See Dyer's analysis of the androids in *Blade Runner* in *White*, pp. 213–15.
60. Gallardo, 'Aliens, cyborgs and other invisible men', p. 236.
61. Sean Brayton, 'The post-white imaginary in Alex Proyas's *I, Robot*', *Science Fiction Studies* 35/1 (2008), p. 75.
62. bell hooks, *Black Looks: Race and Representation* (Boston, MA: South End Press, 1992), p. 169.

63. Ibid., p. 172.
64. David Roche, *Making and Remaking Horror in the 1970s and 2000s: Why Don't They Do It Like They Used To?* (Jackson, MS: University Press of Mississippi, 2014), p. 184.
65. Roche, *Making and Remaking Horror*, p. 186.
66. Richard Matheson, *I Am Legend* (New York: Gold Medal Books, 1954).
67. Akiva Goldsman, 'Creating *I Am Legend*', *I Am Legend*, DVD distributed by Warner Bros France, 2008.
68. He can be seen in 'Creating *I Am Legend*', ibid.
69. Brayton, 'The post-white imaginary', pp. 69–70.
70. Bakke, 'Dead white men', p. 405.
71. Contrary to what Gallardo says, *I Am Legend* does indicate that the curing serum is derived from Neville's blood, when he records his failure to 'transfer [his] immunity to infected hosts', although it is far less clear than in *The Omega Man*, where the white Neville extracts his 'genuine-160-proof old Anglo-Saxon' blood onscreen. Gallardo, 'Aliens, cyborgs and other invisible men', p. 248.
72. Ibid., p. 240.
73. Nama, *Black Space*, p. 39.
74. See Richard Majors and Janet Mancini Billson, *Cool Pose: The Dilemma of Black Manhood in America* (New York: Touchstone, 1992).
75. Ibid., p. 2.
76. Here I disagree with Gallardo's analysis, which contrasts the 'incapacitated, impotent' black cyborg with 'the empowered "hard body" of the white Robocop'. As I have argued in Chapter 1 and in 'The limits of hypermasculinity', Robocop is also presented as impotent, while the film insists on his suffering and pain. Gallardo, 'Aliens, cyborgs and other invisible men', p. 240; Marianne Kac-Vergne, 'The limits of hypermasculinity: intimacy in American science fiction films of the 1980s', in David Roche and Isabelle Schmitt-Pitiot (eds), *Intimacy in Cinema* (Jefferson, NC: McFarland, 2014), pp. 119–32.
77. Brayton, 'The post-white imaginary', p. 80.
78. Kobena Mercer, *Welcome to the Jungle: New Positions in Black Cultural Studies* (New York and London: Routledge, 1994), p. 140.
79. For an overview of *I, Robot*'s reception, see Lorrie Palmer, 'Black man/white machine: Will Smith crosses over', *The Velvet Light Trap* 67 (Spring 2011), pp. 28–40.
80. Todd Gilchrist, '*I, Robot*: an interview with Will Smith', *Black Film*, July 2004. Available at http://www.blackfilm.com/20040709/features/willsmith.shtml (accessed 13 July 2015).

81. This scene is mentioned at the very beginning of his interview by Will Smith as one of the reasons that made him want to do the film. Ibid.
82. Subramanian, 'Alienating identification', p. 48.
83. Will Smith, 'Creating *I Am Legend*'. DVD extra.
84. Claire Sisco King, 'Legendary troubles: trauma, masculinity and race in *I Am Legend*', in Timothy Shary (ed.), *Millenial Masculinity: Men in Contemporary American Cinema* (Detroit, MI: Wayne State University Press, 2013), pp. 250–1.
85. Guerrero, *Framing Blackness*, p. 126.
86. Sanchez, 'Neo-abolitionists', p. 113.
87. Brayton, 'The post-white imaginary', p. 79.
88. Gilchrist, Interview with Will Smith.
89. Roche, *Making and Remaking Horror*, ch. 8.
90. Contrary to Nama's reading of the Family as Black Power radicals (*Black Space*, p. 48) and even though the Family's second-in-command is black and it welcomes African-American Lisa after she 'turns', I find that the film's imagery rather brings to mind white supremacist groups because of the members' extreme albinism and pale blue eyes, the leader's insistence on the 'marks' borne by all of its members and his rejection of all those who have not 'turned' white.
91. As mentioned in the introduction to Chapter 4, the idea of a post-racial America has always been controversial, and it has been severely undermined by the numerous high-profile cases of police killings of African Americans in 2014–15, the 2014 Ferguson riots, the rise of the 'Black Lives Matter' movement and the racially divisive rhetoric of the 2016 Donald Trump campaign. See for instance Ta Nehisi Coates, 'There is no post-racial America', *The Atlantic*, July–August 2015; Dan Balz and Scott Clement, 'On racial issues, America is divided both black and white and red and blue', *The Washington Post*, 27 December 2014; Maya Rhodan, 'Donald Trump's missed opportunity on race', *Time*, 27 September 2016.
92. Subramanian, 'Alienating identification', p. 50.
93. Bonilla-Sanchez, 'Race matters in "post-racial" Obamerica', p. 29.
94. Palmer, 'Black man/white machine', p. 34.
95. For a critique of post-racialism, see Bonilla-Sanchez, 'Race matters in "post-racial" Obamerica', Howard Winant, *The New Politics of Race* (Minneapolis, MN: University of Minnesota Press, 2004) and Milton Vickerman, *The Problem of Post-Racialism* (Basingstoke: Palgrave Macmillan, 2013).
96. Subramanian, 'Alienating identification', p. 44.
97. Sean Brayton, 'The racial politics of disaster and dystopia in *I Am Legend*', *The Velvet Light Trap* 67 (Spring 2011), p. 75.
98. Charles-Antoine Courcoux develops a very interesting analysis of Spooner's fear of technology as fear of the feminine. 'D'une peur de la modernité

technologique déclinée au féminin', in Laurent Guido (ed.), *Les peurs de Hollywood* (Lausanne: Editions Antipodes, 2006), pp. 233–6.
99. Brayton, 'The racial politics of disaster and dystopia', p. 73.
100. It is interesting to notice that none of the exterior scenes featuring Anna visiting New York, including the scene where she visits St Patrick's cathedral, which is discussed at some length in 'Creating *I Am Legend*', made it into the final cut.
101. See King, 'Legendary troubles' for a discussion of *I Am Legend*'s reworking and overcoming of the national trauma of 9/11.
102. Brayton, 'The racial politics of disaster and dystopia', p. 73.
103. See for instance Manohla Dargis's review for *The New York Times* entitled 'A father-son outing goes terribly wrong' (30 May 2013) or Scott Foundas's review for *Variety* (29 May 2013) describing it as 'a grim hodgepodge of "Avatar," "The Hunger Games" and "Life of Pi" that won't come anywhere near equaling those juggernauts with the ticketbuying public'. Many reviewers denounced the film's insistence on the overcoming of fear as a reference to Scientology's foundational text, *Dianetics* by Ron L. Hubbard, rather than as an initiation into patriarchal masculinity; see Dargis or Matt Patches, '*After Earth* is Will Smith's love letter to Scientology', *Vulture*, 31 May 2013. Available at http://www.vulture.com/2013/05/after-earth-will-smith-love-letter-to-scientology.html (accessed 20 July 2015).
104. Despite a production budget of $130 million, the film grossed only $60 million in the domestic market, ranking at 59 in the 2013 domestic grosses. See Box Office Mojo. Available at http://www.boxofficemojo.com/movies/?id=1000ae.htm (accessed 20 July 2015).
105. hooks, *We Real Cool*, p. 61.
106. Robert Staples, *Black Masculinity: The Black Male's Role in American Society* (San Francisco, CA: The Black Scholar Press, 1982), p. 2.
107. Dyer, *White*.
108. Contrary to *The Brother From Another Planet* or the Romero living dead series, where black men reject the sexist behaviours and materialistic values of their white peers in, for instance, *Night of the Living Dead* (1968), *Dawn of the Dead* (1978) and *Day of the Dead* (1985).

Chapter 5: Redefining Masculinity in Times of 'Crisis'

1. Brendan J. Malin, *American Masculinity under Clinton* (New York: Peter Lang, 2005), pp. 8–9.
2. This movement was extremely popular in the second half of the 1980s, when its weekend retreats attracted more than 50,000 participants, according to Susan

Faludi in *Backlash: The Undeclared War against American Women* (1991) (New York: Three Rivers Press, 2006), p. 319. Robert Bly's book condensing the philosophy of the movement, *Iron John: A Book about Men* (New York: Addison-Wesley Publishing, 1990), was in *The New York Times* bestseller list and inspired many others, like Robert Moore and Douglas Gillette, *King, Warrior, Magician, Lover: Rediscovering the Archetypes of the Masculine Nature* (San Francisco, CA: HarperCollins, 1990) or Sam Keen, *Fire in the Belly: On Being a Man* (New York: Bantam, 1991).

3. The Promise Keepers organised men in groups of 'brothers' and held mass rallies, the biggest of which attracted more than one million men on the Washington, DC Mall in 1997. See Susan Faludi, *Stiffed: The Betrayal of the American Man* (New York: Perennial, 1999), pp. 224–89.
4. The Promise Keepers have been repeatedly criticised by the National Organization for Women for promoting patriarchy, homophobia and misogyny. See for instance Jena Recer, 'Whose promise are they keeping?', *National NOW Times*, August 1995.
5. Nancy Cohen, *The 1990s Social History of the United States* (Santa Barbara, CA: ABC Clio, 2009), p. 143.
6. See for instance Sally Robinson, *Marked Men: White Masculinity in Crisis* (New York: Columbia University Press, 2000).
7. Barbara Berg, *Sexism in America: Alive, Well and Running our Future* (Chicago, IL: Lawrence Hills Books, 2009), p. 103. See also Kristin J. Anderson, *Modern Misogyny: Anti-Feminism in a Post-Feminist Era* (Oxford: Oxford University Press, 2015); Susan Faludi, *The Terror Dream: Myth and Misogyny in an Insecure America* (New York: Picador, 2007); Stacy Takacs, 'Jessica Lynch and the regeneration of American identity post 9/11', in Peter C. Rollins and John E. O'Connor (eds), *Why We Fought: America's Wars in Film and History* (Lexington, KY: University Press of Kentucky, 2008), pp. 489–92; Mathias Nilges, 'The aesthetics of destruction: contemporary US cinema and TV culture', in Jeff Birkenstein, Anna Froula and Karen Randell (eds), *Reframing 9/11: Film, Popular Culture and the 'War on Terror'* (New York: Continuum, 2010), pp. 23–34.
8. See Dan Hassler-Forest, 'From flying man to falling man: 9/11 discourse in *Superman Returns* and *Batman Begins*', in Véronique Bragard, Christophe Dony and Warren Rosenberg (eds), *Portraying 9/11: Essays on Representations in Comics, Literature, Film and Theatre* (Jefferson, NC: McFarland, 2011), pp. 134–46; Yann Roblou, 'Complex masculinities: the superhero in modern American movies', *Culture, Society and Masculinities* 4/1 (2012), pp. 76–91.
9. Examining the 50 top-grossing films from 1980 to 2015 on boxofficemojo. com, I found that science fiction production remained relatively stable in the 1980s and 1990s at 39 and 34 science fiction releases respectively, while it declined in the 2000s, with 27 releases from 2000 to 2010. Superhero films

on the other hand experienced a significant boom, with more than 30 productions in the first decade of the millenium, according to Richard J. Gray and Betty Kaklamanidou (*The 21st Century Superhero: Essays on Gender, Genre and Globalization in Film* (Jefferson, NC: McFarland, 2011), p. 1). I counted 27 superhero films in the 50 top-grossing productions between 2010 and 2015.

10. Steve Neale, 'Masculinity as spectacle: reflections on men and mainstream cinema', *Screen* 24/6 (1983), pp. 2–17; Richard Dyer, 'Don't look now', *Screen* 23/3-4 (1982), pp. 61–73.
11. '[H]e brings no more or less than he ever does to his role, which translates into agreeable eye candy for some and boredom for others.' Todd McCarthy, review of *The Matrix*, *Variety*, 28 March 1999.
12. Janet Maslin, review of *The Matrix*, *The New York Times*, 31 March 1999.
13. Charles Taylor, 'Something in the way he moves', *Salon*, 29 April 1999. Available at http://www.whoaisnotme.net/articles/1999_0429_som.htm (accessed 2 June 2017).
14. Laura Mulvey, 'Visual pleasure and narrative cinema', *Screen* 16/3 (Autumn 1975), p. 10.
15. Roz Kaveney, *From Alien to the Matrix: Reading Science Fiction Film* (London: I.B.Tauris, 2005), p. 97.
16. Nicola Rehling, *Extra-ordinary Men: White Heterosexual Masculinity in Contemporary Popular Cinema* (Plymouth: Lexington Books, 2009), p. 117.
17. Anne Balsamo, 'Forms of technological embodiment', in Mike Featherstone and Roger Burrows (eds), *Cyberspace/Cyberbodies/Cyberpunk* (London: Sage, 1995), p. 229.
18. Echoes of war come from the obvious references to the Rodney King riots (the fires, roadblocks and military presence in the streets in addition to an act of police brutality caught on film) as well as the casting of Vincent D'Onofrio as one of the mad policemen, whose distorted face in close-up as he tries to shoot Mace recalls a similar close-up in *Full Metal Jacket* before his character shoots his drilling instructor.
19. Steven Shaviro, '"Straight from the cerebral cortex": vision and affect in *Strange Days*', in Deborah Jermyn and Sean Redmond (eds), *The Cinema of Kathryn Bigelow, Hollywood Transgressor* (London: Wallflower Press, 2003), p. 167.
20. The constructedness of male identity is at the heart of many science fiction films of the period, including *Virtuosity* (Leonard, 1995), *The Truman Show* (Weir, 1998), or *Galaxy Quest* (Parisot, 1999).
21. Charles Bellinger, *The Genealogy of Violence* (Oxford: Oxford University Press, 2001), p. 38.
22. On extreme whiteness, see Richard Dyer, *White* (London: Routledge, 1997), pp. 207–23.

23. John P. Garry, 'Strange Days and the post-revisionist era: the possibility of redemption', Film International 7/3 (2009), p. 41.
24. Such an organising structure is lacking in Dark City, where the Stranger imprinted with Murdoch's memories resembles the others too closely to stand out as a villain, as well as in Johnny Mnemonic where too many villains appear one after another, so that the films feel muddled and labyrinthine.
25. See, for instance, Jermyn and Redmond, The Cinema of Kathryn Bigelow, p. 10, Steven Shaviro, who develops a comparison with Michael Powell's Peeping Tom (1961) in 'Straight from the cerebral cortex', pp. 167–70, or Janet Maslin's and Roger Ebert's reviews, in The New York Times, 6 October 1995 and The Chicago Sun Times, 13 October 1995, respectively.
26. Rehling, Extra-ordinary Men, p. 120.
27. Christina Lane, 'The strange days of Kathryn Bigelow and James Cameron', in Jermyn and Redmond, The Cinema of Kathryn Bigelow, p. 185.
28. Ibid., p. 186.
29. Rehling, Extra-ordinary Men, p. 127.
30. Susanne Kord and Elisabeth Krimmer, Contemporary Hollywood Masculinities: Gender, Genre and Politics (New York: Palgrave Macmillan, 2011), p. 91.
31. Strange Days changes its focus in the last third of the film, away from the voyeuristic tape of Iris's rape, which Lenny and Max discuss at length and which Mace does not watch, to centre on the tape of Jeriko's murder, which Mace watches and convinces Lenny to make public, sidelining Max in the process.
32. Rehling, Extra-ordinary Men, p. 116.
33. See Chapter 4 and Rehling, Extra-ordinary Men, p. 116.
34. Pat Mellencamp, 'The Zen of masculinity – rituals of heroism in The Matrix', in Jon Lewis (ed.), The End of Cinema as We Know It: American Film in the Nineties (New York: New York University Press, 2001), p. 83.
35. See Dyer, White.
36. James Cameron's original scriptment insists on Faith's 'ivory skin', 'creamy skin', or 'milk-white skin'. Available at http://www.jamescameron.fr/images/strange-days/strangedays-script.pdf (accessed 1 June 2017).
37. Hélène Charlery, 'Racial bodies in Kathryn Bigelow's Strange Days', in Marianne Kac-Vergne and Julie Assouly (eds), Moving to the Mainstream: Women On and Off Screen in Television and Film (London: I.B.Tauris, forthcoming).
38. Lane, 'The strange days of Kathryn Bigelow and James Cameron', p. 191. Lane argues that it was Kathryn Bigelow's input that gave much more importance to Mace, moving away from James Cameron's script.
39. Rehling, Extra-ordinary Men, p. 131.
40. Shaviro, 'Straight from the cerebral cortex', p. 167.
41. Claudia Springer, 'The pleasure of the interface', Screen 32/3 (Autumn 1991), p. 310.

42. Garry, '*Strange Days* and the post-revisionist era', p. 47.
43. Robert Kolker, *A Cinema of Loneliness* (Oxford: Oxford University Press, 2000), p. 284.
44. Shaviro, 'Straight from the cerebral cortex', p. 176.
45. Christopher Williams, 'Mastering the real: Trinity as the "real" hero of *The Matrix*', *Film Criticism* 27/3 (March 2003), p. 17.
46. Quoted in Rehling, *Extra-ordinary Men*, p. 123.
47. Such questioning can be found also in *The Lawnmower Man* (Leonard, 1992), *Starship Troopers* (Verhoeven, 1997), *Gattaca* (Niccol, 1997) and *The Truman Show* (Weir, 1998), for example.
48. See Susan Jeffords, *Hard Bodies: Masculinity in the Reagan Era* (New Brunswick, NJ: Rutgers University Press, 1994), p. 164. For a textual analysis of the film, see also Marianne Kac-Vergne, 'Losing visibility? The rise and fall of hypermasculinity in science fiction films', *InMedia* 2 (2012). Available at http://inmedia.revues.org/491#tocto1n3 (accessed 29 July 2016).
49. 'Mr Bush says Government should "crack down on deadbeat dads, the ones who can't be bothered to pay child support"'. Andrew Rosenthal, 'The 1992 campaign: political memo; President goes south, tooting his own horn', *The New York Times*, 6 March 1992.
50. 'I know not everybody is going to be in a stable, traditional family like you see in one of those 1950s sitcoms, but we'd be better off if more people were.' Bill Clinton, remarks to the National Baptist Convention, New Orleans, 9 September 1994.
51. Guy Corneau, *Absent Fathers, Lost Sons: the Search for a Masculine Identity* (Boston, MA: Shambhala Publications, 1991); David Blankenhorn, *Fatherless America: Confronting our Most Urgent Social Problem* (New York: Basic Books, 1995); Lynne Segal, *Slow Motion: Changing Masculinities, Changing Men* (New Brunswick, NJ: Rutgers University Press, 1990); Faludi, *Stiffed*.
52. Nilges, 'The aesthetics of destruction', p. 26.
53. Claire Sisco King, 'Legendary troubles: trauma, masculinity and race in *I Am Legend*', in Timothy Shary (ed.), *Millenial Masculinity: Men in Contemporary American Cinema* (Detroit, MI: Wayne State University Press, 2013), p. 252.
54. Hannah Hamad, *Postfeminism and Paternity in Contemporary US Film* (New York and London: Routledge, 2014), p. 55.
55. Faludi, *The Terror Dream*.
56. Hamad, *Postfeminism and Paternity*, p. 54. Emphasis mine.
57. Gary Arms and Thomas Riley, 'The "big-little" film and philosophy: two takes on Spielbergian innocence', in Dean A. Kowalski (ed.), *Steven Spielberg and Philosophy: We're Gonna Need a Bigger Book* (Lexington, KY: The University Press of Kentucky, 2008), p. 13.

58. Nigel Morris, *The Cinema of Steven Spielberg: Empire of Light* (London and New York: Wallflower Press, 2007), p. 157.
59. Hannah Hamad, 'Extreme parenting: recuperating fatherhood in Steven Spielberg's *War of the Worlds* (2005)', in Hilary Radner and Rebecca Stringer (eds), *Feminism at the Movies: Understanding Gender in Contemporary Popular Cinema* (London: Routledge, 2011), p. 241.
60. The film departs considerably from McCarthy's original novel in this respect, since the mother is hardly present in the novel and the flashbacks where she appears are unglamorous, even acid, contrasting with the film's colourful and blissful first flashbacks.
61. Stella Bruzzi, *Bringing up Daddy: Fatherhood and Politics in Postwar Hollywood* (London: BFI, 2006), p. 134.
62. Hamad, *Postfeminism and Paternity*, p. 17.
63. Hamad, 'Extreme parenting', p. 250.
64. Ibid.
65. Juliana Schiesari, *The Gendering of Melancholia: Feminism, Psychoanalysis, and the Symbolics of Loss in Renaissance Literature* (Ithaca, NY: Cornell University Press, 1992), p. 13.
66. Nilges, 'The aesthetics of destruction', p. 32.
67. Morris, *The Cinema of Steven Spielberg*, p. 159.
68. Ray's impoverishment and estrangement from his children as a result of his divorce, as well as his wife's remarriage with a wealthier man, echo the claims of the fathers' rights movement, which are belied by statistics showing that more than half of divorced fathers in the US do not pay child support and often drop out of their children's lives while women tend to become poorer after a divorce. See Michael Kimmel, *Misframing Men: The Politics of Contemporary Masculinities* (New Brunswick, NJ: Rutgers University Press, 2010), p. 26.
69. Morris, *The Cinema of Steven Spielberg*, p. 173.
70. Arms and Riley, 'The "big-little" film and philosophy', p. 21.
71. Ibid.
72. Andrew Gordon, *Empire of Dreams: The Science Fiction and Fantasy Films of Steven Spielberg* (London: Rowman & Littlefield, 2008), p. 663.
73. Morris, *The Cinema of Steven Spielberg*, p. 163.
74. Unlike for instance in *2012* (Emmerich, 2009), where the new husband dies and the hero reconciles with his former wife.
75. Tanner Mirrlees, 'Hollywood's uncritical dystopias', *Cineaction* 95 (2015), p. 13. The author criticises the scene, somewhat unfairly in my opinion, as 'maudlin'.
76. Susan Faludi, 'Man in a can', in *Stiffed*, pp. 451–529.
77. Latham Hunter, 'Fathers, sons and business in the Hollywood "office movie"', in Elwood Watson and Marc E. Shaw (eds), *Performing American Masculinities* (Bloomington, IN: Indiana University Press, 2011), p. 77.

78. Margaret D. Stetz, '"Orienting" to new "worlds", Hollywood fathers and daughters "adapt" in 1964 and 2004', *Literature/Film Quarterly* 35/1 (2007), p. 68. This trend continues to this day, notably with the *Taken* franchise.
79. Hamad, *Postfeminism and Paternity*; Nilges, 'The aesthetics of destruction'.
80. Benjamin Brabon, 'The spectral phallus: re-membering the postfeminist man', in Benjamin Brabon and Stéphanie Genz (eds), *Postfeminist Gothic – Critical Interventions in Contemporary Culture* (London: Palgrave Macmillan, 2007), p. 57.
81. In the list drawn up by Hamad of apocalyptic films featuring fathers and children, there are only three films with black heroes: *Beasts of the Southern Wild*, *I Am Legend* and *After Earth*; Hamad, *Postfeminism and Paternity*, p. 55. In the other titles I found, the heroes are always white: e.g. *Arctic Blast* (2010), *Goodbye World* (2013), *World War Z* (2013).

Afterword: The Gender Politics of Science Fiction Blockbusters

1. See Lorena O'Neil, 'Men's rights activists call for boycott of "Mad Max: Fury Road", citing feminist agenda', CNN Entertainment, 15 May 2015. Available at http://edition.cnn.com/2015/05/15/entertainment/mad-max-fury-road-boycott-mens-rights-thr-feat/ (accessed 2 June 2017); Caroline Framke, 'How the all-female reboot of *Ghostbusters* became a lightning rod of controversy', Vox, 15 July 2016. Available at http://www.vox.com/2016/6/30/12027882/ghostbusters-reboot-all-female-backlash-sexism-sony (accessed 2 June 2017); Carly Lane, 'Why some people are upset over the new *Rogue One: A Star Wars Story* Trailer', *teenVogue*, 7 April 2016. Available at http://www.teenvogue.com/story/rogue-one-star-wars-trailer-backlash (accessed 2 June 2017).
2. Donald Trump, 'Now they're making *Ghostbusters* with only women, what's going on?', 20 July 2016. Available at https://www.youtube.com/watch?v=dhVtgojbmKU (accessed 2 June 2017).
3. See Amanda Marcotte, 'Make America male again: 2016 was a great year for feminist pop culture – and the punishment was Donald Trump', *Salon*, 21 December 2016. Available at http://www.salon.com/2016/12/21/make-america-male-again-2016-was-a-great-year-for-feminist-pop-culture-and-the-punishment-was-donald-trump/ (accessed 2 June 2017).

Bibliography

Alfonsi, Laurence, 'La réception du film *Independence Day* en France. Un exemple de contre-acculturation?', *Cinémas* 8/3 (1998), pp. 9–29.

Andris, Silkes and Ursula Frederick, *Women Willing to Fight: The Fighting Woman in Film* (Newcastle: Cambridge Scholars Publishing, 2007).

Arms, Gary and Thomas Riley, 'The "big-little" film and philosophy: two takes on Spielbergian innocence', in Dean A. Kowalski (ed.), *Steven Spielberg and Philosophy: We're Gonna Need a Bigger Book* (Lexington, KY: The University Press of Kentucky, 2008), pp. 7–37.

Arnold, Robert F., 'Termination or transformation? The *Terminator* films and recent changes in the US Auto industry', *Film Quarterly* 52/1 (Autumn 1998), pp. 20–30.

Badinter, Elizabeth, *XY: De l'identité masculine* (Paris: Odile Jacob, 1992).

Baker, Brian, *Contemporary Masculinities in Fiction, Film and Television* (New York and London: Bloomsbury, 2015).

Bakke, Gretchen, 'Dead white men: an essay on the changing dynamics of race in US action cinema', *Anthropological Quarterly* 83/2 (Spring 2010), pp. 400–28.

Balsamo, Anne, 'Forms of technological embodiment', in Mike Featherstone and Roger Burrows (eds), *Cyberspace/Cyberbodies/Cyberpunk* (London: Sage, 1995), pp. 215–37.

Barnes, Sandra L., Zandria F. Robinson and Earl Wright II (eds), *Repositioning Race: Prophetic Research in a Postracial Obama Age* (Albany, NY: State University of New York Press, 2014).

Beard, William, 'Cronenberg, Flyness and the Other-self', *Cinemas* 4/2 (Winter 1994), pp. 153–73.

Bellinger, Charles, *The Genealogy of Violence* (Oxford: Oxford University Press, 2001).

Bly, Robert, *Iron John: A Book about Men* (New York: Addison-Wesley Publishing, 1990).

Bogle, Donald, *Toms, Coons, Mulattoes, Mammies and Bucks: An Interpretive History of Blacks in American Films* (New York: Continuum, 2001).

Bonilla-Silva, Eduardo with Trenita Brookshire Childers, 'Race matters in "postracial" Obamerica and how to climb out of the rabbit hole', in Sandra L. Barnes, Zandria F. Robinson and Earl Wright II (eds), *Repositioning Race: Prophetic*

Research in a Postracial Obama Age (Albany, NY: State University of New York Press, 2014), pp. 23–48.

Bould, Mark, 'The false salvation of the here and now: aliens, images, and the commodification of desire in *The Brother from Another Planet*', in Diane Carson and Heidi Kenaga (eds), *Sayles Talk: New Perspectives on Independent Filmmaker John Sayles* (Detroit, MI: Wayne State University Press, 2006), pp. 79–102.

Boulenger, Gilles, *John Carpenter par John Carpenter* (Paris: Le Cinéphage, 2001).

Boully, Fabien, 'Des Surhommes accablés (*Dead Zone* et *The Fly* de David Cronenberg)', *CinémAction* 112 (June 2004), pp. 259–65.

Boyd, Todd, 'A small introduction to the "G" funk era: gangsta rap and black masculinity in Los Angeles', in Michael J. Dear, H. Eric Schockman and Greg Hise (eds), *Rethinking Los Angeles* (Thousand Oaks, CA: Sage Publications, 1996), pp. 127–46.

Brabon, Benjamin, 'The spectral phallus: re-membering the postfeminist man', in Benjamin Brabon and Stéphanie Genz (eds), *Postfeminist Gothic – Critical Interventions in Contemporary Culture* (London: Palgrave Macmillan, 2007), pp. 56–67.

Braithwaite, Ann, 'Politics and/of backlash', *Journal of International Women's Studies* 5/5 (2004), pp. 18–33.

Brayton, Sean, 'The post-white imaginary in Alex Proyas's *I, Robot*', *Science Fiction Studies* 35/1 (2008), pp. 72–87.

——, 'The racial politics of disaster and dystopia in *I Am Legend*', *The Velvet Light Trap* 67 (Spring 2011), pp. 66–76.

Bruno, Giuliana, 'Ramble City: postmodernism and *Blade Runner*', in Annette Kuhn (ed.), *Alien Zone: Cultural Theory and Contemporary Science Fiction Cinema* (London: Verso, 1990), pp. 183–94.

Bruzzi, Stella, *Bringing up Daddy: Fatherhood and Politics in Postwar Hollywood* (London: BFI, 2006).

Buchbinder, David, *Performance Anxieties: Re-Producing Masculinity* (Crows Nest, NSW: Allen and Unwin, 1998).

Bukatman, Scott, *Blade Runner* (London: BFI, 1997).

Byers, Thomas B., 'Commodity futures', in Annette Kuhn (ed.), *Alien Zone: Cultural Theory and Contemporary Science-Fiction Cinema* (London: Verso, 1990), pp. 39–52.

Cameron, James, interviewed by David Chute, *Film Comment* 1 (January/February 1985), pp. 57–9.

Carnes, Mark C. (ed.), *The Columbia History of Post World War II America* (New York: Columbia University Press, 2007).

Carrasco Carrasco, Rocio, *New Heroes on Screen: Prototypes of Masculinity in Contemporary Science Fiction Cinema* (Huelva: Universidad de Huelva, 2007).

Bibliography

Carrigan, Tim, Bob Connell and John Lee, 'Toward a new sociology of masculinity', *Theory and Society* 14/5 (September 1985), pp. 551-604.

Chambliss, Julian C., William Svitavsky and Thomas Donaldson (eds), *Ages of Heroes, Eras of Men: Superheroes and the American Experience* (Newcastle upon Tyne: Cambridge Scholars Publishing, 2013).

Chan, Kenneth, 'The construction of black male identity in black action films of the nineties', *Cinema Journal* 37/2 (Winter 1998), pp. 35-48.

Chapman, James and Nicholas J. Cull, *Projecting Tomorrow, Science Fiction and Popular Cinema* (London: I.B.Tauris, 2013).

Charlery, Hélène, 'Racial bodies in Kathryn Bigelow's *Strange Days*', in Marianne Kac-Vergne and Julie Assouly (eds), *Moving to the Mainstream: Women On and Off Screen in Television and Film* (London: I.B.Tauris, forthcoming).

Chevrier, Yves, '*Blade Runner* or the sociology of anticipation', *Science Fiction Studies* 11/1 (March 1984), pp. 50-60.

Clarke, David B. (ed.), *The Cinematic City* (London and New York: Routledge, 1997).

Clover, Joshua, *The Matrix* (London: BFI, 2007).

Codell, Julie F., 'Murphy's law, Robocop's body, and capitalism's work', *Jump Cut* 34/3-4 (1989), pp. 12-19.

Cohen, Nancy, *The 1990s Social History of the United States* (Santa Barbara, CA: ABC Clio, 2009).

Collins, Patricia Hill, *Black Feminist Thought* (New York: Routledge, 2000).

Connell, R.W. and James W. Messerschmidt, 'Hegemonic masculinity: rethinking the concept', *Gender and Society* 19/6 (2005), pp. 829-59.

Conrad, Dean, 'Femmes futures: one hundred years of female representation in sf cinema', *Science Fiction Film and Television* 4/1 (Spring 2011), pp. 79-99.

Cornea, Christine, *Science Fiction Cinema: Between Fantasy and Reality* (Edinburgh: Edinburgh University Press, 2007).

Courcoux, Charles-Antoine, 'D'une peur de la modernité technologique déclinée au féminin', in Laurent Guido (ed.), *Les peurs de Hollywood* (Lausanne: Editions Antipodes, 2006), pp. 229-48.

Creed, Barbara, *The Monstrous-Feminine* (London: Routledge, 1993).

Dahan, Yannick, 'Le film d'action: Idéologie "Ramboesque" et violence chorégraphiée', *Positif* 443 (January 1998), pp. 70-5.

Dallek, Robert, *Ronald Reagan, The Politics of Symbolism* (Cambridge, MA: Harvard University Press, 1999).

Davis, Ronald L., *Celluloid Mirrors, Hollywood and American Society Since 1945* (Orlando, FL: Harcourt Brace, 1997).

Demetriou, Demetrakis Z., 'Connell's concept of hegemonic masculinity: a critique', *Theory and Society* 30/3 (2001), pp. 337-61.

Desser, David, '*Blade Runner*: science fiction and transcendence', *Literature/Film Quarterly* 13 (1985), pp. 172-9.

Bibliography

——, 'Race, space and class: the politics of cityscapes in science fiction films', in Annette Kuhn (ed.), *Alien Zone II* (London: Verso, 1999), pp. 80–96.

Doel, Marcus A. and David B. Clarke, 'From Ramble City to the screening of the eye: *Blade Runner*, death and symbolic exchange', in David B. Clarke (ed.), *The Cinematic City* (London and New York: Routledge, 1997), pp. 140–67.

Doherty, Thomas, 'Genre, gender and the Aliens trilogy', in Barry Keith Grant (ed.), *The Dread of Difference: Gender And the Horror Film* (Austin, TX: University of Texas Press, 2015), pp. 209–27.

Douglas, Susan J., *Where the Girls Are: Growing up Female with the Mass Media* (London: Penguin, 1995).

Dubois, Régis, *Images du Noir dans le cinéma américain blanc (1980–1995)* (Paris: L'Harmattan, 1997).

Dyer, Richard, 'Don't look now', *Screen* 23/3–4 (1982), pp. 61–73.

——, *White* (London: Routledge, 1997).

Faludi, Susan, *Backlash: The Undeclared War against American Women* (1991) (New York: Three Rivers Press, 2006).

——, *Stiffed: The Betrayal of the American Man* (New York: Perennial, 1999).

——, *The Terror Dream: Myth and Misogyny in an Insecure America* (New York: Picador, 2007).

Fine, Michelle, Lois Weis, Judi Addleston and Julia Marusza, '(In) secure times: constructing white working-class masculinities in the late 20th century', *Gender and Society* 11/1 (February 1997), pp. 52–68.

Fitting, Peter, 'Futurecop: the neutralization of revolt in *Blade Runner*', *Science Fiction Studies* 14/3 (1987), pp. 340–54.

French, Sean, *The Terminator* (London: BFI, 1996).

Fuchs, Cynthia J., '"Death is irrelevant": cyborgs, reproduction, and the future of male hysteria', *Genders* 18 (Winter 1993), pp. 113–33.

Gabbard, Krin, *Black Magic: White Hollywood and African American Culture* (New Brunswick, NJ: Rutgers University Press, 2004).

Gallardo, Ximena, 'Aliens, cyborgs and other invisible men: Hollywood's solutions to the black "problem" in sf cinema', *Science Fiction Film and Television* 6/2 (Summer 2013), pp. 219–51.

Gallardo, Ximena and C. Jason Smith, *Alien Woman: The Making of Lt Ellen Ripley* (New York: Continuum, 2004).

Garry, John P., '*Strange Days* and the post-revisionist era: the possibility of redemption', *Film International* 7/3 (2009), pp. 36–49.

Genz, Stéphanie and Benjamin A. Brabon, *Postfeminism: Cultural Texts and Theories* (Edinburgh: Edinburgh University Press, 2009).

Gilchrist, Todd, '*I, Robot*: an interview with Will Smith', *Black Film*, July 2004. Available at http://www.blackfilm.com/20040709/features/willsmith.shtml (accessed 13 July 2015).

Bibliography

Glass, Fred, 'The "new bad future": *RoboCop* and 1980s sci-fi films', *Science as Culture* 5 (1989), pp. 7–49.

——, 'Totally recalling Arnold: sex and violence in the new bad future', *Film Quarterly* 44/1 (Autumn 1990), pp. 2–13.

Goldberg, Jonathan. 'Recalling totalities: the mirrored stages of Arnold Schwarzenegger', *Differences: A Journal of Feminist Cultural Studies* 4/1 (1992), pp. 171–204.

Gordon, Andrew, *Empire of Dreams: The Science Fiction and Fantasy Films of Steven Spielberg* (London: Rowman & Littlefield, 2008).

Graham, Elizabeth, *Meanings of Ripley: The Alien Quadrology and Gender* (Newcastle: Cambridge Scholars Publishing, 2010).

Gray, Richard J. and Betty Kaklamanidou, *The 21st Century Superhero: Essays on Gender, Genre and Globalization in Film* (Jefferson, NC: McFarland, 2011).

Greenberg, Harvey, 'Fembo: *Aliens*' intentions', *Journal of Popular Film and Television* 15/4 (Winter 1988), pp. 165–71.

Greene, Eric, *Planet of the Apes as American Myth* (Jefferson, NC: McFarland, 1996).

Guerrero, Ed, *Framing Blackness: The African-American Image in Film* (Philadelphia, PA: Temple University Press, 1993).

Hall, J.A., 'Development and validation of the Expanded Hypermasculinity Inventory and the Ideology of Machismo Scale', unpublished master's thesis, University of Connecticut, Storrs, 1992.

Hamad, Hannah, 'Extreme parenting: recuperating fatherhood in Steven Spielberg's *War of the Worlds* (2005)', in Hilary Radner and Rebecca Stringer (eds), *Feminism at the Movies: Understanding Gender in Contemporary Popular Cinema* (London: Routledge, 2011), pp. 241–54.

——, *Postfeminism and Paternity in Contemporary US Film* (New York and London: Routledge, 2014).

Haraway, Donna, *Simians, Cyborgs and Women: The Reinvention of Nature* (London: Free Association Books, 1991).

Hassel, Holly, 'The 'babe scientist' phenomenon, the illusion of inclusion in 1990s American action films', in Suzanne Ferris and Mallory Young (eds), *Chick Flicks: Contemporary Women at the Movies* (New York: Routledge, 2008), pp. 190–203.

Hassler-Forest, Dan, 'From flying man to falling man: 9/11 discourse in *Superman Returns* and *Batman Begins*', in Véronique Bragard, Christophe Dony and Warren Rosenberg (eds), *Portraying 9/11: Essays on Representations in Comics, Literature, Film and Theatre* (Jefferson, NC: McFarland, 2011), pp. 134–46.

hooks, bell, *Black Looks: Race and Representation* (Boston, MA: South End Press, 1992).

——, *We Real Cool: Black Men and Masculinity* (New York and London: Routledge, 2004).

Bibliography

Hunter, Latham, 'Fathers, sons and business in the Hollywood "office movie"', in Elwood Watson and Marc E. Shaw (eds), *Performing American Masculinities* (Bloomington, IN: Indiana University Press, 2011), pp. 76–102.

Inness, Sherrie, *Tough Girls: Women Warriors and Wonder Women in Popular Culture* (Philadelphia, PA: University of Pennsylvania Press, 1999).

Jameson, Fredric, *Postmodernism or the Cultural Logic of Late Capitalism* (Durham, NC: Duke University Press, 1991).

Jeffords, Susan, *Hard Bodies: Masculinity in the Reagan Era* (New Brunswick, NJ: Rutgers University Press, 1994).

Jermyn, Deborah and Sean Redmond (eds), *The Cinema of Kathryn Bigelow, Hollywood Transgressor* (London: Wallflower Press, 2003).

Johnson, Haynes, *Sleepwalking Through History: America in the Reagan Years* (New York: Anchor Books, 1992).

Kac-Vergne, Marianne, 'Losing visibility? The rise and fall of hypermasculinity in science fiction films', *InMedia* 2, 2012. Available at http://inmedia.revues.org/491#toctoln3 (accessed 29 July 2016).

———, 'The limits of hypermasculinity: intimacy in American science fiction films of the 1980s', in David Roche and Isabelle Schmitt-Pitiot (eds), *Intimacy in Cinema* (Jefferson, NC: McFarland, 2014), pp. 119–32.

Kaveney, Roz, *From Alien to the Matrix: Reading Science Fiction Film* (London: I.B.Tauris, 2005).

Kimmel, Michael, *Manhood in America: A Cultural History* (New York: Free Press, 1996).

———, *The History of Men: Essays on the History of American and British Masculinities* (Albany, NY: State University of New York Press, 2005).

———, *Misframing Men: The Politics of Contemporary Masculinities* (New Brunswick, NJ: Rutgers University Press, 2010).

King, Claire Sisco, 'Legendary troubles: trauma, masculinity and race in *I Am Legend*', in Timothy Shary (ed.), *Millenial Masculinity: Men in Contemporary American Cinema* (Detroit, MI: Wayne State University Press, 2013), pp. 243–64.

King, Geoff and Tanya Krzywinska, *Science Fiction Cinema, From Outerspace to Cyberspace* (London: Wallflower, 2000).

King, Richard C. and David J. Leonard, 'Is Neo white? Reading race, watching the trilogy', in Matthew Kapell and William G. Doty (eds), *Jacking in to the Matrix Franchise: Cultural Reception and Interpretation* (New York: Continuum, 2004), pp. 32–47.

Kirkham, Pat and Janet Thumim, *You Tarzan: Masculinity, Movies and Men* (London: Lawrence and Wishart), 1993.

Kolker, Robert, *A Cinema of Loneliness* (Oxford: Oxford University Press, 2000).

Bibliography

Kord, Susanne and Elisabeth Krimmer, *Contemporary Hollywood Masculinities: Gender, Genre and Politics* (New York: Palgrave Macmillan, 2011).

Krämer, Peter, 'Women first: *Titanic*, action-adventure films and Hollywood's female audience', in Kevin S. Sandler and Gaylin Studlar (eds), *Titanic: Anatomy of a Blockbuster* (New Brunswick, NJ: Rutgers University Press, 1999), pp. 108-31.

Kuhn, Annette, (ed.), *Alien Zone: Cultural Theory and Contemporary Science-Fiction Cinema* (London: Verso, 1990).

———, (ed.) *Alien Zone II* (London: Verso, 1999).

Lane, Christina, 'The strange days of Kathryn Bigelow and James Cameron', in Deborah Jermyn and Sean Redmond (eds), *The Cinema of Kathryn Bigelow, Hollywood Transgressor* (London: Wallflower Press, 2003), pp. 178-98.

Lasch, Christopher, *The Culture of Narcissism: American Life in an Age of Diminishing Expectations* (New York: Norton, 1979).

Lerner, Michael and Cornel West, *Jews and Blacks: Let the Healing Begin* (Rutherford, NJ: G.P. Putnam and Sons, 1995).

Levy, Donald P., 'Hypermasculinity', in Michael Flood, Judith Kegan Gardiner, Bob Pease and Keith Pringle (eds), *International Encyclopedia of Men and Masculinity* (London: Routledge, 2007), pp. 325-6.

Majors, Richard and Janet Mancini Billson, *Cool Pose: The Dilemma of Black Manhood in America* (New York: Touchstone, 1992).

Malin, Brendan J., *American Masculinity under Clinton* (New York: Peter Lang, 2005).

Marks, Carole, 'The urban underclass', *Annual Review of Sociology* 17 (1991), pp. 445-66.

McCartin, Joseph A., 'Labor', in Stephen J. Whitfield (ed.), *A Companion to 20th Century America* (Malden, MA: Blackwell, 2004), pp. 247-65.

Meininger, Sylvestre, 'Corps mortels. L'évolution du personnage de Ripley dans la trilogie *Alien*', *Cinémas* 7/1-2 (Autumn 1996), pp. 121-50.

Mellencamp, Pat, 'The Zen of masculinity – rituals of heroism in *The Matrix*', in Jon Lewis (ed.), *The End of Cinema as We Know It: American Film in the Nineties* (New York: New York University Press, 2001), pp. 83-94.

Mennel, Barbara, *Cities and Cinema* (London and New York: Routledge, 2008).

Mercer, Kobena, *Welcome to the Jungle: New Positions in Black Cultural Studies* (New York and London: Routledge, 1994).

Miller, Mark Crispin, *Boxed In: The Culture of TV* (Evanston, IL: Northwestern University Press, 1988).

Mirrlees, Tanner, 'Hollywood's uncritical dystopias', *Cineaction* 95 (2015), pp. 4-15.

Mizejewski, Linda, 'Action bodies in futurist spaces: bodybuilder stardom as special effect', in Annette Kuhn (ed.), *Alien Zone II* (London: Verso, 1999), pp. 152-72.

Moine, Raphaëlle, *Les Genres du cinéma* (Paris: Nathan, 2002).

Bibliography

———, *Les Femmes d'action au cinéma* (Paris: Armand Colin, 2010).
Morales, Rebecca, *Flexible Production: Restructuring the International Automobile Industry* (Cambridge: Polity Press, 1994).
Morris, Nigel, *The Cinema of Steven Spielberg: Empire of Light* (London and New York: Wallflower Press, 2007).
Mosher, Donald and Mark Sirkin, 'Measuring a macho personality constellation', *Journal of Research in Personality* 18/2 (1984), pp. 150–63.
Mulvey, Laura, 'Visual pleasure and narrative cinema', *Screen* 16/3 (Autumn 1975), pp. 6–18.
Nadell, James, '*Boyz n the Hood*: A Colonial Analysis', *Journal of Black Studies* 25/4 (March 1995), pp. 447–63.
Nama, Adilifu, *Black Space: Imagining Race in Science Fiction Film* (Austin, TX: University of Texas Press, 2008).
Neale, Steve, 'Hollywood strikes back: special effects in recent American cinema', *Screen* 21/3 (1980), pp. 101–5.
———, 'Masculinity as spectacle: reflections on men and mainstream cinema', *Screen* 24/6 (1983), pp. 2–17.
Nilges, Mathias, 'The aesthetics of destruction: contemporary US cinema and TV culture', in Jeff Birkenstein, Anna Froula and Karen Randell (eds), *Reframing 9/11: Film, Popular Culture and the 'War on Terror'* (New York: Continuum, 2010), pp. 23–34.
Nishime, LeiLani, 'The mulatto cyborg: imagining a multiracial future', *Cinema Journal* 44/2 (Winter 2005), pp. 34–49.
Noonan, Bonnie, *Women Scientists in Fifties Science Fiction Films* (Jefferson, NC: McFarland, 2005).
Orman, John, *Comparing Presidential Behavior: Carter, Reagan and the Macho Presidential Style* (New York: Greenwood Press, 1987).
Palmer, Lorrie, 'Black man/white machine: Will Smith crosses over', *The Velvet Light Trap* 67 (Spring 2011), pp. 28–40.
Parrott, Dominic and Amos Zeichner, 'Effects of hypermasculinity on physical aggression against women', *Psychology of Men and Masculinity* 4/1 (2003), pp. 70–8.
Patterson, James T., *Restless Giant: The United States from Watergate to Bush v. Gore* (Oxford: Oxford University Press, 2005).
Penley, Constance and Andrew Ross, 'Cyborgs at large: interview with Donna Haraway', *Social Text* 24/5 (1990), pp. 8–23.
Pleck, Joseph, 'The male sex role: definitions, problems, and sources of change', *Journal of Social Issues* 32 (1976), pp. 155–64.
Pyle, Forest, 'Making cyborgs, making humans: of terminators and blade runners', in Jim Collins, Hilary Radner and Ava Preacher Collins (eds), *Film Theory Goes to the Movies* (London: Routledge, 1993), pp. 227–41.

Bibliography

Rehling, Nicola, *Extra-ordinary Men: White Heterosexual Masculinity in Contemporary Popular Cinema* (Plymouth: Lexington Books, 2009).

Reid, Robin Ann, *Women in Science Fiction and Fantasy* (Westport, CT: Greenwood Press, 2009).

Robinson, Sally, *Marked Men: White Masculinity in Crisis* (New York: Columbia University Press, 2000).

Roblou, Yann, 'Complex masculinities: the superhero in modern American movies', *Culture, Society and Masculinities* 4/1 (2012), pp. 76–91.

Roche, David, 'David Cronenberg's having to make the word be flesh', *Post Script* 23/2 (2004), pp. 72–87.

——, 'L' "horreur viscérale" de David Cronenberg ou l'horreur de l' "anti-nature"', in Anne-Marie Paquet-Deyris (ed.), 'Les cinémas de l'horreur', *CinémAction* 136 (2010), pp. 141–9.

——, *Making and Remaking Horror in the 1970s and 2000s: Why Don't They Do It Like They Used To?* (Jackson, MS: University Press of Mississippi, 2014).

Rogin, Michael, *Ronald Reagan, the Movie: and Other Episodes in Political Demonology* (Berkeley, CA: University of California Press, 1987).

——, *Independence Day, or How I Learned to Stop Worrying and Love the Enola Gay* (London: BFI, 1998).

Ross, Andrew, 'Cowboys, Cadillacs and cosmonauts: families, film genre, and technocultures', in Joseph A. Boone and Michael Cadden (eds), *Engendering Men: The Question of Male Feminist Criticism* (New York: Routledge, 1990), pp. 87–101.

Ruppert, Peter, '*Blade Runner*: the utopian dialectics of science fiction films', *Cineaste* 17/2 (1989), pp. 8–13.

Rutsky, R.L., 'Being Keanu', in Jon Lewis (ed.), *The End of Cinema as We Know It* (New York: New York University Press, 2001), pp. 185–94.

Ryan, Michael and Douglas Kellner, 'Technophobia/dystopia', in Sean Redmond (ed.), *Liquid Metal: The Science Fiction Film Reader* (London: Wallflower Press, 2007), pp. 48–56.

Sanchez, Tani Dianca, 'Neo-abolitionists, colorblind epistemologies and black politics: the *Matrix* trilogy', in Daniel Bernardi (ed.), *The Persistence of Whiteness: Race and Contemporary Hollywood Cinema* (London and New York: Routledge, 2008), pp. 102–24.

Sartelle, Joseph, 'Dreams and nightmares in the Hollywood blockbuster', in Geoffrey Nowell-Smith (ed.), *The Oxford History of World Cinema* (Oxford: Oxford University Press, 1997), pp. 516–26.

Scharrer, Erica, 'Tough guys: the portrayal of hypermasculinity and aggression in televised police dramas', *Journal of Broadcasting and Electronic Media* 45 (2001), pp. 615–34.

Schatz, Thomas, *Hollywood Genres: Formulas, Filmmaking and the Studio System* (New York: McGraw Hill, 1981).

Bibliography

Schiesari, Juliana, *The Gendering of Melancholia: Feminism, Psychoanalysis, and the Symbolics of Loss in Renaissance Literature* (Ithaca, NY: Cornell University Press, 1992).

Schulman, Bruce, *The Seventies: The Great Shift in American Culture, Society and Politics* (New York: Simon and Schuster, 2001).

Segal, Lynne, *Slow Motion: Changing Masculinities, Changing Men* (New Brunswick, NJ: Rutgers University Press, 1990).

Sexton, Patricia, *The Feminized Male* (New York: Random House, 1969).

Sharp, Patrick B., 'Darwin's soldiers: gender, evolution and warfare in *Them!* and *Forbidden Planet*', *Science Fiction Film and Television* 1/2 (Autumn 2008), pp. 215–30.

Sharrett, Christopher, 'End of story: the collapse of myth in postmodern narrative film', in Jon Lewis (ed.), *The End of Cinema as We Know It* (New York: New York University Press, 2001), pp. 319–31.

Shaviro, Steven, '"Straight from the cerebral cortex": vision and affect in *Strange Days*', in Deborah Jermyn and Sean Redmond (eds), *The Cinema of Kathryn Bigelow, Hollywood Transgressor* (London: Wallflower Press, 2003), pp. 159–77.

Short, Sue, *Cyborg Cinema and Contemporary Subjectivity* (Basingstoke: Palgrave Macmillan, 2005).

Slotkin, Richard, *Regeneration Through Violence* (Middletown, CT: Wesleyan University Press, 1973).

Sobchack, Vivian, *Screening Space: The American Science Fiction Film* (New Brunswick, NJ: Rutgers University Press, 1997).

Springer, Claudia, 'The pleasure of the interface', *Screen* 32/3 (Autumn 1991), pp. 303–23.

———, 'Muscular circuitry: the invincible armored cyborg in cinema', *Genders* 18 (Winter 1993), pp. 87–101.

———, *Electronic Eros: Bodies and Desire in the Post-industrial Age* (London: Athlone Press, 1996).

Staples, Robert, *Black Masculinity: The Black Male's Role in American Society* (San Francisco, CA: The Black Scholar Press, 1982).

Stern, Michael, 'Making culture into nature', in Annette Kuhn (ed.), *Alien Zone: Cultural Theory and Contemporary Science-Fiction Cinema* (London: Verso, 1990), pp. 66–72.

Stetz, Margaret D., '"Orienting" to new "worlds", Hollywood fathers and daughters "adapt" in 1964 and 2004', *Literature/Film Quarterly* 35/1 (2007), pp. 358–68.

Strinati, Dominic, *An Introduction to Theories of Popular Culture* (London: Routledge, 2004).

Subramanian, Janani, 'Alienating identification: black identity in *The Brother from Another Planet* and *I Am Legend*', *Science Fiction Film and Television* 3/1 (Spring 2010), pp. 37–55.

Bibliography

Suvin, Darko, *Metamorphoses of Science Fiction: On the Poetics and History of a Literary Genre* (New Haven, CT: Yale University Press, 1979).

Takacs, Stacy, 'Jessica Lynch and the regeneration of American identity post 9/11', in Peter C. Rollins and John E. O'Connor (eds), *Why We Fought: America's Wars in Film and History* (Lexington, KY: University Press of Kentucky, 2008), pp. 489–92.

Tasker, Yvonne, *Spectacular Bodies: Gender, Genre and the Action Cinema* (London: Routledge, 1993).

Tasker, Yvonne and Diane Negra, *Interrogating Postfeminism: Gender and the Politics of Popular Culture* (Durham and London: Duke University Press, 2007).

Taubin, Amy, 'Playing it straight: REM meets a post-Rodney King world in *Independence Day*', *Sight and Sound* 6/8 (1996), pp. 6–8.

Taylor, Charles, 'Something in the way he moves', *Salon*, 29 April 1999. Available at http://www.whoaisnotme.net/articles/1999_0429_som.htm (accessed 2 June 2017).

Telotte, J.P., *Science Fiction Film* (Cambridge University Press, 2001).

Tron, Daniel, 'Psychoses diégétiques: *We Can Remember it for you Wholesale* et *Total Recall*', in Roger Bozzetto and Gilles Menegaldo (eds), *Les nouvelles formes de la science-fiction*, Colloque de Cerisy, 2003, pp. 321–38.

Vest, Jason P., *Future Imperfect: Philip K. Dick at the Movies* (Lincoln, NE: University of Nebraska Press, 2009).

Vickerman, Milton, *The Problem of Post-Racialism* (Basingstoke: Palgrave Macmillan, 2013).

Wajcman, Judy, *Technofeminism* (Cambridge: Polity Press, 2004).

Walkerdine, Valerie, 'Video replay – families, films and fantasies', in Victor Burgin, James Donald and Cora Kaplan (eds), *Formations of Fantasy* (London: Methuen, 1986), pp. 167–99.

Weis, Lois, Amira Proweller and Craig Centrie, 'Reexamining "a moment in history": loss of privilege inside white working-class masculinity in the 1990s', in Michelle Fine, Lois Weis, Linda C. Powell and L. Mun Wong (eds), *Off White: Readings on Race, Power and Society* (New York: Routledge, 1997), pp. 210–26.

Williams, Christopher, 'Mastering the real: Trinity as the "real" hero of *The Matrix*', *Film Criticism* 27/3 (March 2003), pp. 2–17.

Williams, Linda, 'Melodrama revised', in Nick Browne (ed.), *Refiguring American Film Genres: Theory and History* (Berkeley, CA: University of California Press, 1998), pp. 42–88.

Wilson, William Julius, *The Declining Significance of Race* (1978) (Chicago, IL: University of Chicago Press, 2012).

Winant, Howard, *The New Politics of Race* (Minneapolis, MN: University of Minnesota Press, 2004).

Bibliography

Winter, Michael and Ellen Robert, 'Male dominance, late capitalism, and the growth of instrumental reason', *Berkeley Journal of Sociology* 24–5 (1980), pp. 249–80.

Wolf, Naomi, *Fire With Fire: The New Female Power and How It Will Change the 21st Century* (New York: Random House, 1993).

Wood, Peter, 'Redressing Ripley: disrupting the female hero', in Elizabeth Graham (ed.), *Meanings of Ripley: The Alien Quadrology and Gender* (Newcastle: Cambridge Scholars Publishing, 2010), pp. 32–59.

Wood, Robin, *Hollywood from Vietnam to Reagan … and Beyond* (New York: Columbia University Press, 2003).

Filmography

The primary corpus includes the actors mentioned in the book, the studio distributor and the US lifetime box office results (rounded down to the nearest million for easier reading). Sources: www.imdb.com; www.boxofficemojo.com.

Primary corpus

After Earth, directed by M. Night Shyamalan, with Will Smith (Cypher Raige), Jaden Smith (Kitai Raige), Zoe Kravitz (Senshi Raige). Columbia Pictures, 2013. $60 million.

Aliens, directed by James Cameron, with Sigourney Weaver (Ripley), Carrie Henn (Newt), Michael Biehn (Corporal Hicks), Paul Reiser (Burke), Lance Henriksen (Bishop). Twentieth Century Fox, 1986. $85 million.

Blade Runner, directed by Ridley Scott, with Harrison Ford (Deckard), Rutger Hauer (Roy), Joe Turkel (Tyrell), William Sanderson (Sebastian), Daryl Hannah (Pris), Sean Young (Rachael). Warner Bros, 1982. $27 million.

Dark City, directed by Alex Proyas, with Rufus Sewell (John Murdoch), William Hurt (Inspector Frank Bumstead), Kiefer Sutherland (Dr Schreber), Jennifer Connelly (Emma Murdoch), Mr Book (Ian Richardson). New Line Cinema, 1998. $5 million.

The Day the Earth Stood Still, directed by Scott Derrickson, with Keanu Reeves (Klaatu), Jennifer Connelly (Dr Helen Benson), Kathy Bates (Secretary of Defense Jackson), Jaden Smith (Jacob Benson), John Cleese (Professor Barnhardt). Twentieth Century Fox, 2008. $79 million.

Demolition Man, directed by Marco Brambilla, with Sylvester Stallone (John Spartan), Wesley Snipes (Simon Phoenix), Sandra Bullock (Lenina Huxley), Nigel Hawthorne (Dr Raymond Cocteau), Denis Leary (Edgar Friendly). Warner Bros, 1993. $58 million.

Elysium, directed by Neill Blomkamp, with Matt Damon (Max), Jodie Foster (Secretary of Defense Delacourt), Sharlto Copley (Kruger), Alice Braga (Frey). Sony Pictures Entertainment, 2013. $93 million.

Escape from New York, directed by John Carpenter, with Kurt Russell (Snake), Isaac Hayes (the Duke), Donald Pleasance (the President). Embassy Pictures, 1981. $52 million.

Filmography

The Fly, directed by David Cronenberg, with Jeff Goldblum (Seth Brundle), Geena Davis (Veronica), John Getz (Stathis). Twentieth Century Fox, 1986. $37 million.

Ghosts of Mars, directed by John Carpenter, with Natasha Henstridge (Lt Melanie Ballard), Ice Cube (Desolation Williams), Jason Statham (Sgt Jericho Butler), Pam Grier (Commander Helena Braddock), Joanna Cassidy (Whitlock), Richard Cetrone (Big Daddy Mars). Screen Gems, 2001. $8 million.

I Am Legend, directed by Francis Lawrence, with Will Smith (Dr Neville), Alice Braga (Anna), Salli Richardson (Zoe Neville), Willow Smith (Marley Neville), Emma Thompson (Dr Krippin). Warner Bros, 2007. $256 million.

I, Robot, directed by Alex Proyas, with Will Smith (Detective Spooner), Bridget Moynahan (Dr Susan Calvin), Alan Tudyk (Sonny), James Crowell (Dr Lanning), Bruce Greenwood (Lawrence Robertson), Adrian Ricard (Granny). Twentieth Century Fox, 2004. $144 million.

Independence Day, directed by Roland Emmerich, with Will Smith (Captain Steve Hiller), Bill Pullman (President Whitmore), Jeff Goldblum (David Levinson), Mary McDonnell (First Lady Whitmore), Judd Hirsch (Julius Levinson), Randy Quaid (Russell Casse), Margaret Colin (Constance Soprano), Vivica A. Fox (Jasmine Dubrow). Twentieth Century Fox, 1996. $306 million.

Interstellar, directed by Christopher Nolan, with Mathew McConaughey (Cooper), Jessica Chastain (adult Murph), Mackenzie Foy (young Murph), Anne Hathaway (Dr Brand), Michael Caine (Professor Brand), Matt Damon (Dr Mann). Paramount, 2014. $187 million.

Johnny Mnemonic, directed by Robert Longo, with Keanu Reeves (Johnny Mnemonic), Dina Meyer (Jane), Ice-T (J-Bone), Dolph Lundgren (Street Preacher), Udo Kier (Ralphi). TriStar Pictures, 1995. $19 million.

The Matrix, directed by Lilly and Lana Wachowski (as the Wachowski brothers), with Keanu Reeves (Neo/ Mr Anderson), Carrie-Ann Moss (Trinity), Laurence Fishburne (Morpheus), Hugo Weaving (Agent Smith), Gloria Foster (the Oracle), Joe Pantoliano (Cypher), Marcus Chong (Tank), Julian Arahanga (Apoc), Belinda McClory (Switch), Anthony Ray Parker (Dozer). Warner Bros, 1999. $171 million.

The Matrix Reloaded, directed by Lilly and Lana Wachowski (as the Wachowski brothers), with Keanu Reeves (Neo/ Mr Anderson), Carrie-Ann Moss (Trinity), Laurence Fishburne (Morpheus), Hugo Weaving (Agent Smith), Gloria Foster (the Oracle), Niobe (Jada Pinkett Smith), Commander Lock (Harry Lennix), the Merovingian (Lambert Wilson). Warner Bros, Village Roadshow Pictures, 2003. $281 million.

The Matrix Revolutions, directed by Lilly and Lana Wachowski (as the Wachowski brothers), with Keanu Reeves (Neo/ Mr Anderson), Carrie-Ann Moss (Trinity), Laurence Fishburne (Morpheus), Hugo Weaving (Agent Smith), Mary Alice (the Oracle), Niobe (Jada Pinkett Smith), Commander Lock (Harry Lennix), Link (Harold Perrineau). Warner Bros, 2003. $139 million.

Filmography

Planet of the Apes, directed by Tim Burton, with Mark Wahlberg (Captain Leo Davidson), Helena Bonham Carter (Ari), Tim Roth (Thade), Estella Warren (Daena), Paul Giamatti (Limbo). Twentieth Century Fox, 2001. $180 million.

Predator, directed by John McTiernan, with Arnold Schwarzenegger (Dutch), Carl Weathers (Dillon), Bill Duke (Mac), Sonny Landham (Billy), Kevin Peter Hall (the Predator). Twentieth Century Fox, 1987. $59 million.

Predator 2, directed by Stephen Hopkins, with Danny Glover (Lieutenant Harrigan), Kevin Peter Hall (the Predator), Gary Busey (Agent Keyes), Maria Conchita Alonso (Leona). Twentieth Century Fox, 1990. $30 million.

The Road, directed by John Hillcoat, with Viggo Mortensen (the father), Kodi Smit-McPhee (the son), Charlize Theron (the mother), Michael Kenneth Williams (the thief). Dimension Films, 2009. $8 million.

RoboCop, directed by Paul Verhoeven, with Peter Weller (Murphy/Robocop), Nancy Allen (Ann Lewis), Ronny Cox (Dick Jones), Miguel Ferrer (Bob Morton). Orion Pictures, 1987. $53 million.

RoboCop 2, directed by Irvin Kershner, with Peter Weller (Robocop), Nancy Allen (Ann Lewis), Belinda Bauer (Dr Juliette Faxx). Orion Pictures, 1990. $45 million.

RoboCop 3, directed by Fred Dekker, with Robert John Burke (Robocop), Nancy Allen (Ann Lewis), Remy Ryan (Nikko), Mako (Kanemitsu). Orion Pictures, 1993. $10 million.

Starship Troopers, directed by Paul Verhoeven, with Casper Van Dien (Johnny Rico), Dina Meyer (Dizzy Flores), Denise Richards (Lt Carmen Ibanez), Michael Ironside (Rasczak). TriStar Pictures, 1997. $54 million.

Strange Days, directed by Kathryn Bigelow, with Ralph Fiennes (Lenny), Angela Bassett (Mace), Tom Sizemore (Max), Juliette Lewis (Faith), Michael Wincott (Philo Grant), Vincent D'Onofrio (Officer Steckler), Glenn Plummer (Jeriko One). Twentieth Century Fox, 1995. $7 million.

The Terminator, directed by James Cameron, with Arnold Schwarzenegger (the Terminator), Michael Biehn (Kyle Reese), Linda Hamilton (Sarah Connor). Orion Pictures, 1984. $38 million.

Terminator 2: Judgment Day, directed by James Cameron, with Arnold Schwarzenegger (the Terminator), Linda Hamilton (Sarah Connor), Edward Furlong (John Connor), Robert Patrick (T1000), Joe Morton (Miles Dyson). TriStar Pictures, 1991. $204 million.

Terminator 3, directed by Jonathan Mostow, with Arnold Schwarzenegger (the Terminator), Nick Stahl (John Connor), Claire Danes (Kate Brewster), Kristanna Loken (the Terminatrix). C-2 Pictures, 2003. $150 million.

Terminator Genisys, directed by Alan Taylor, with Arnold Schwarzenegger (Pops the Terminator), Jason Clarke (John Connor), Emilia Clarke (Sarah Connor), Jai Courtney (Kyle Reese). Paramount, 2015. $89 million.

Filmography

Total Recall, directed by Paul Verhoeven, with Arnold Schwarzenegger (Douglas Quaid/Hauser), Rachel Ticotin (Melina), Sharon Stone (Lori), Ronny Cox (Cohaagen). TriStar Pictures, 1990. $119 million.

Universal Soldier, directed by Roland Emmerich, with Jean-Claude Van Damme (GR44), Dolph Lundgren (GR13), Ally Walker (Veronica Roberts). TriStar Pictures, 1992. $36 million.

War of the Worlds, directed by Steven Spielberg, with Tom Cruise (Ray Ferrier), Dakota Fanning (Rachel), Justin Chatwin (Robbie), Miranda Otto (Mary Ann), Tim Robbins (Harlan Ogilvy), Ann Robinson (Grandmother), Gene Barry (Grandfather). Paramount and DreamWorks, 2005. $234 million.

Secondary corpus

2001: A Space Odyssey, Stanley Kubrick, MGM, 1968.
AI, Steven Spielberg, Warner Bros/Dreamworks, 2001.
Alien, Ridley Scott, Twentieth Century Fox, 1979.
Alien³, David Fincher, Twentieth Century Fox, 1992.
Alien Resurrection, Jean-Pierre Jeunet, Twentieth Century Fox, 1997.
Alien vs Predator, Paul W.S. Anderson, Twentieth Century Fox, 2004.
Arrival, Denis Villeneuve, Paramount Pictures, 2016.
Attack of the Crab Monsters, Roger Corman, Allied Artists, 1957.
Avatar, James Cameron, Twentieth Century Fox, 2009.
Back to the Future trilogy, Robert Zemeckis, Universal Pictures, 1985, 1989, 1990.
The Brother from Another Planet, John Sayles, Cinecom, 1984.
Creature from the Black Lagoon, Jack Arnold, Universal International, 1954.
The Day After Tomorrow, Roland Emmerich, 20th Century Fox, 2004.
The Day the Earth Stood Still, Robert Wise, Twentieth Century Fox, 1951.
The Empire Strikes Back, Irvin Kershner, Twentieth Century Fox, 1980.
ET the Extra-Terrestrial, Steven Spielberg, Universal Pictures, 1982.
The Fly, Kurt Neumann, Twentieth Century Fox, 1958.
Forbidden Planet, Fred M. Wilcox, MGM, 1956.
Gattaca, Andrew Niccol, Columbia Pictures, 1997.
Ghostbusters, Paul Feig, Columbia Pictures, 2016.
Her, Spike Jonze, Warner Bros, 2013.
Inception, Christopher Nolan, Warner Bros, 2010.
Independence Day: Resurgence, Roland Emmerich, Twentieth Century Fox, 2016.
Invasion of the Body Snatchers, Philip Kaufman, United Artists, 1978.
Logan's Run, Michael Anderson, MGM, 1976.
Mad Max: Fury Road, George Miller, Warner Bros, 2015.
Metropolis, Fritz Lang, Parufamet, 1927.

Filmography

Minority Report, Steven Spielberg, Dreamworks/Twentieth Century Fox, 2002.
The Omega Man, Boris Sagal, Warner Bros, 1971.
Outland, Peter Hyams, Warner Bros, 1981.
Planet of the Apes, Franklin J. Schaffner, Twentieth Century Fox, 1968.
Return of the Jedi, Richard Marquand, Twentieth Century Fox, 1983.
RoboCop, José Padilha, MGM, 2014.
Rogue One: A Star Wars Story, Gareth Edwards, Walt Disney, 2016.
Rollerball, Norman Jewison, United Artists, 1975.
The Running Man, Paul Michael Glaser, TriStar Pictures, 1987.
Self/less, Tarsem Singh, Focus Features, 2015.
Signs, M. Night Shyamalan, Touchstone, 2002.
Silent Running, Douglas Trumbull, Universal Pictures, 1972.
Soylent Green, Richard Fleischer, MGM, 1973.
Them!, Gordon Douglas, Warner Bros, 1954.
They Live, John Carpenter, Universal Pictures, 1988.
THX 1138, George Lucas, Warner Bros, 1971.
Total Recall, Len Wiseman, Columbia Pictures, 2012.
The War of the Worlds, Byron Haskin, Paramount Pictures, 1953.
The World, the Flesh and the Devil, Ranald MacDougall, MGM, 1959.

Index

Page numbers in **bold** refer to figures.

2001: A Space Odyssey (1968), 84
9/11 (attacks), 108, 152, 158, 175, 176, 182, 189, 191, 218n.101

action heroine, 83–5, 94–102, 108, 114, 118, 169
ageing, 68, 180, 187–8
After Earth (2013), 123, 143, 146, 147, 149, 150, 151, 153, 176, 195
A.I. (2001), 155
Alien (1979), 6, 44, 83, 94, 95, 99, 129, 207n.1
Alien³ (1992), 100, 207n.1, 208n.6
Aliens (1986), 6, 83, 84, 94–100, 102, 105, 129, 169, 207 n.1, 208n.6
Alien Resurrection (1997), 100, 102, 207n.1, 208n.6
Alien vs Predator (2004), 118
alienation, 44, 69–70, 72–3, 78–80, 124
Allen, Nancy, 26, 85–6
Arms, Gary, and Thomas Riley, 183, 184
Arnold, Robert F., 58, 60
Arrival (2016), 155
Avatar (2009), 194

Bassett, Angela, 163, 169
Biehn, Michael, 13
Black Buck, 49, 52, 125, 132–3

black masculinity *see* masculinity, black
blacks, demonisation of, 21–2, 49–52, 74–5, 121, 123–7
Blade Runner (1982), 1, 43, 46–8, 53–7, 63, 67, 68, 76, 77, 105, 197n.3, 202n.3, 204n.21, 204n.24, 205n.32, 215n.59
blaxploitation, 49, 104, 106, 147, 214n.32
blockbusters, 4, 12, 108, 117, 193–5
body (female), 93–4, 96–9, 106–7, 109, 169–72, 181
body (male), 2, 17, 18, 21, 23–5, 27–9, 31–2, 34–9, 42, 50, 51, 61, 69, 158, 162, 179, 183, 194, 216n.76
    black body, 20, 125–7, 131, 136, 148, 154
    hypermasculine body, 11–16, 18–19, 22–4, 90–2, 117–18
Bonilla-Silva, Eduardo, 122, 152, 217n.95
Brabon, Benjamin, 103, 191
Brayton, Sean, 145, 146, 148, 151, 152
Brother from Another Planet, The (1984), 121, 126, 150, 213n.17, 218n.108
Bruzzi, Stella, 179
Buchbinder, David, 4
Bukatman, Scott, 1, 203n.4, 204n.24
Bush, George H., 121, 175

241

Index

Cameron, James, 11, 39, 42, 97, 174
Canby, Vincent, 47, 49, 57
Chapman, James, and Nicholas J. Cull, 21
Charley, Hélène, 171
Clarke, Emilia, 180
Cleese, John, 114
Clinton, Bill, 157, 175, 191
Codell, Julie F., 160, 203n.13
cognitive estrangement, 2, 5, 124
Connell, R.W., and Messerschmidt, James W., 2–6
Connelly, Jennifer, 113
cool (pose), 3, 147, 149
Cornea, Christine, 84, 197n.5
Courcoux, Charles-Antoine, 109, 218n.98
Cox, Ronny, 64, 66
Creature from the Black Lagoon (1954), 89
Cronenberg, David, 16, 35, 88, 93
Cruise, Tom, 177
cyborg, 3, 18, 19, 29, 35, 37, 57, 58, 61, 62, 79–80, 110–11, 146, 148, 159, 186, 216n.76

Damon, Matt, 112, 180
Dark City (1998), 158, 159, 161, 163–5, 174, 194, 221n.24
Davis, Geena, 16, 85, 88, 93
Dawn of the Planet of the Apes (2014), 118
Day after Tomorrow, The (2004), 176, 191
Day the Earth Stood Still, The (1951), 114, 134
Day the Earth Stood Still, The (2008), 109, 113–15
Demetriou, Demetrakis, 3

Demolition Man (1993), 123, 124, 126–30, 132–4
Duke, Bill, 20
Dyer, Richard, 5, 14, 144, 154, 160, 215n.59, 221 n.22
dystopia, 6, 43–7, 56–9, 80–1, 121, 194

Ebert, Roger, 22, 115, 200n.23, 221n.25
Elysium (2013), 109–12, 118, 194, 211n.54
Escape from New York (1981), 43, 46–53, 56–7, 121
ET the Extra-Terrestrial (1982), 43, 203n.3

Faludi, Susan, 9, 108, 176, 187, 219n.2, n.3, n.7
Farrakhan, Louis, 135, 153, 157
fatherhood, 149, 158, 175–83, 191
femininity, feminine, 3–4, 10, 86–8, 98–103, 111, 154, 160–1, 167, 169–71, 189, 191, 218n.98
feminisation, feminised, 3, 10, 14, 86, 111–12, 159, 166, 170–1, 173, 174, 191, 211n.56
feminism, 2, 9, 83, 98, 101, 110, 118, 157, 209n.32, 210n.39
  postfeminism, 85, 103, 106–8, 111–13, 118, 176, 181, 191, 210n.41
  Second Wave feminism, 84, 94, 102–4, 106–8
Fiennes, Ralph, 161
Fishburne, Laurence, 139, 192
Fly, The (1958), 16, 88
Fly, The (1986), 11, 13–16, 18, 23, 24, 36–42, 84, 85, 88–9, 93–4, 136
Forbidden Planet (1956), 58, 89, 208n.7
Ford, Harrison, 48, 57

242

Index

French, Sean, 97, 201n.36
Fuchs, Cynthia, 34, 35, 38

Gallardo, Ximena, 94, 102, 142, 147, 148, 207n.1, 213n.14, 216n.71, n.76
Garry, John P., 165, 173
Gattaca (1997), 155, 222n.47
gaze, 6, 24, 29, 86, 90–1, 94, 117, 148, 159, 161, 167–8, 171, 173
genre (science fiction), 1–2, 4, 5, 6, 11, 42, 43, 45, 78–9, 81, 83, 84, 93, 94, 118, 127, 143, 147, 195, 197n.4, 202n.3, 207n.1
Genz, Stéphanie, 103
Ghostbusters (2016), 195
Ghosts of Mars (2001), 6, 85, 103–8, 118
Glass, Fred, 73, 76, 79, 206n.53
Glover, Danny, 123, 128, 131–2
Goldblum, Jeff, 13–15, 88, 135, 136
Grier, Pam, 105–6, 210n.43
Guerrero, Ed, 122, 125, 127, 150

Hall, Kevin Peter, 124, 131
Hamad, Hannah, 176–7, 181, 182, 191, 197n.5, 224n.81
Hamilton, Linda, 83, 97, 100, 210n.36
Haraway, Donna, 35, 111
Hauer, Rutger, 54
Hayes, Isaac, 49
hegemonic masculinity *see* masculinity, hegemonic
Henstridge, Natasha, 85
Her (2013), 155
Heston, Charlton, 16, 115, 146, 153, 211n.60
heterosexuality, heterosexual, 3, 5, 10, 91, 106, 173

hooks, bell, 145, 153, 214n.34
horror, 36, 39, 93, 118, 127, 145, 201n.50

I Am Legend (2007), 123, 143–52, 154, 176, 195
I, Robot (2004), 19, 113, 114, 117, 123, 143–52, 154, 211n.55
impotence, 91–3, 117, 118, 162, 216n.76
Inception (2010), 155
Independence Day (1995), 123, 134–9, 143, 215n.43
Independence Day: Resurgence (2016), 195
Interstellar (2014), 155, 158, 176, 178, 180–1, 184, 187–90, 192
Invasion of the Body Snatchers (1978), 44, 85

Jameson, Fredric, 2
Jeffords, Susan, 10, 23, 42, 175
Johnny Mnemonic (1995), 158–65, 169–74, 221n.24

Kael, Pauline, 42, 209n.24
Kaveney, Roz, 161
Kellner, Douglas, 202n.2, 204n.24, 205n.35
Kimmel, Michael, 5, 223n.68
King, Claire Sisco, 149, 176, 218n.101
King, Geoff, 1
Kirkham, Pat, and Janet Thumim, 25
Kord, Susanne, and Elisabeth Krimmer, 168
Kuhn, Annette, 77, 79

Lane, Christina, 168, 172, 221n.38
Lasch, Christopher, 44

Index

Logan's Run (1976), 84, 124, 147, 154
Loken, Kristanna, 109
Lundgren, Dolph, 17, 89

Mad Max: Fury Road (2015), 195, 208n.6, 212n.62
masculinity,
  black, 3, 7, 20, 21, 50, 60, 74, 124, 131–2, 136, 143, 147–55, 192, 194, 195, 214n.34, 218n.108, 224n.81
  challenge to hegemonic, 149, 159, 161, 163–4, 168–9, 173–4, 176, 186, 189, 190–4
  hegemonic, 2–7, 9–12, 14, 32, 37, 41–2, 115–17, 119, 124, 149, 152–4, 158, 181, 184, 195, 211n.60
  middle-class, 3, 124, 135, 136, 139, 147, 154, 195
  white, 3, 5, 7, 9–11, 19–23, 32, 41, 48–52, 68, 75–6, 80, 162, 164, 168–9, 171–2, 174, 224n.81
  working-class, 3, 6, 44–5, 51, 58, 67, 70, 76, 79–81, 181–3
Maslin, Janet, 57, 160, 221n.25
Matrix, The (1999), 123, 134, 139–43, 145, 147, 150, 154, 158–62, 164–5, 168–74, 192, 197n.5
Matrix Reloaded, The (2003), 142, 154, 168
Matrix: Revolutions, The (2003), 142, 154, 168
McConaughey, Mathew, 178
Mellencamp, Pat, 170
melodrama, melodramatic, 30–2, 175, 180–2
Metropolis (1927), 48, 84, 204n.21, n.24
Meyer, Dina, 85, 103, 107, 169

middle-class *see* masculinity, middle-class
Minority Report (2002), 155
Moine, Raphaëlle, 95, 204n.14
Morris, Nigel, 177, 183, 186
Mosher, Donald (and Mark Sirkin), 11, 39–40
Moss, Carrie-Ann, 169, 192
motherhood, mothers, 33, 38, 86, 91–2, 99–103, 105, 110, 115, 153, 177–8, 181–2, 185, 186, 190, 209n.32, 223n.60
Moynahan, Bridget, 113, 148
Mulvey, Laura, 24, 90, 161, 167
muscles, 6, 13, 14, 24, 97, 114, 160, 162

Nama, Adilifu, 121, 125, 130, 133, 134, 147, 213n.14, 217n.90
Neale, Steve, 12, 25, 78, 160
Nilges, Mathias, 176, 182, 191, 219n.7
Nishime, Leilani, 35

Obama, Barack, 122, 151
Omega Man, The (1971), 85, 145, 149–51, 153, 216n.71
Outland (1981), 43, 46

Patterson, James, 67
Planet of the Apes (1968), 16, 84, 115–16
Planet of the Apes (2001), 113, 115–17
Pleasance, Donald, 49, 50
post-apocalyptic, 158, 178, 182, 186, 188, 190–2, 197n.5
postfeminism *see* feminism, postfeminism
Predator (1987), 11, 13, 19–22, 121

Index

Predator 2 (1990), 123–32, 134, 154, 213n.14, 214n.29
Promise Keepers, the, 157, 175, 219n.3
Pryor, Richard, 21, 124, 147

Rambo, 22, 96–7
Reagan, Ronald, 9–10, 18, 21, 22, 44–6, 57, 60, 63–4, 66, 80, 142, 199n.5, n.7
Reeves, Keanu, 114, 139, 159–61, 162
Rehling, Nicola, 162, 167, 168, 173, 197n.5
Richards, Denise, 85, 103, 107
riots, race, 122, 123, 127–8, 132, 134, 141, 217n.91, 220n.18
Rise of the Planet of the Apes (2011), 118
Road, The (2009), 158, 176–8, 180–4, 186–90, 192, 194
Robinson, Sally, 32, 198n.18
RoboCop (1987), 11, 13, 18, 21, 26–8, 30–8, 42, 43, 46–7, 59–65, 67, 69–71, 76, 78–9, 84–5, 86, 89–90, 92, 93, 94, 103, 111, 121, 193, 200n.23
RoboCop (2014), 118, 194
RoboCop 2 (1990), 11, 21–3, 29, 33, 34, 36, 37, 86
RoboCop 3 (1993), 11, 17, 30, 86
Roche, David, 35, 145, 151, 201n.50
Rogin, Michael, 48, 135, 136
Rogue One: A Star Wars Story (2016), 195
Rollerball (1975), 44
Running Man, The (1987), 43
Ruppert, Peter, 53, 203n.4
Russell, Kurt, 50

Sanchez, Tani Dianca, 141–3, 150
Schatz, Thomas, 42

Schwarzenegger, Arnold, 9, 12–13, 14, **15**, 19, 25, 39, 66, 71, 73, 76, 80, 123, 131, 159, 178, 179, 187, 209n.36
Self/less (2015), 194
Sewell, Rufus, 159
Short, Sue, 18, 37
Signs (2002), 176, 191
Silent Running (1972), 84
Sizemore, Tom, 165
Smith, Jada Pinkett, 142
Smith, Jaden, 149, 153
Smith, Will, 7, 19, 113, 117, 123, 135–6, 143–4, 146–55, 173, 194–5, 217n.81
Smith, Willow, 149
Snipes, Wesley, 123, 124, 134
Sobchack, Vivian, 197n.4, 202n.3
Soylent Green (1973), 44, 84
special effects, 45, 78–81
Springer, Claudia, 23, 42, 173, 211n.56
Stallone, Sylvester, 123, 126, 133, 134
Star Wars: The Force Awakens (2015), 212n.62
Star Wars trilogy (1977, 1980, 1983), 4, 5, 58, 85
Starship Troopers (1997), 85, 103, 107–8, 222n.47
Stetz, Margaret D., 189
Strange Days (1995), 134, 147, 150, 158, 161–74, 194
superhero (films), 5, 41, 158, 191, 194, 208n.6, 220n.9
Suvin, Darko, 5

Tasker, Yvonne, 23, 42, 83, 91, 103, 207n.1
Taylor, Charles, 160
technophobia, 6, 59, 77, 79, 81

Index

Telotte, J.P., 1
Terminator, The (1984), 11, 12, 14–16, 18–19, 21, 22, 23, 25–6, 29, 36–42, 43, 59–60, 62, 77, 79–80, 83, 97, 121, 179, 190, 201n.36
Terminator 2 (1991), 6, 11, 13, 83, 97–103, 105, 131, 169, 174, 179, 188, 190, 193, 208n.5, n.6, 210n.36
Terminator 3 (2003), 83, 109–12, 118
Terminator Genisys (2015), 155, 158, 176, 178–81, 184, 187–92
Them! (1954), 43, 84
They Live (1988), 43
THX 1138 (1971), 85
Total Recall (1990), 11, 12, **13**, 22–3, 25, 37, 43, 46, 63, 66–7, 71–8, 121, 159, 194, 207n.66
Total Recall (2012), 194
Trump, Donald, 63, 195, 217n.91

Universal Soldier (1992), 11, 17, 23–4, 85, 87–9, 91–4, 159, 193

Van Damme, Jean-Claude, 14, 17, 87, 92
Verhoeven, Paul, 11, 30, 43, 60, 63, 64, 70, 85, 107
victim, victimisation, 6, 12, 27, 30, 32, 33, 42, 44, 103, 109, 149

Vietnam War, 10, 87, 95, 96
virtual reality, 158, 164, 169, 172, 173, 191, 197n.5
Virtuosity (1995), 134, 145, 147, 220n.20
vulnerability
  male, 6, 12, 23–6, 28, 30–1, 42, 91, 92, 117, 148–9, 159, 161, 193–4
  female, 109, 171, 189

Wahlberg, Mark, 115, 212n.60
Walker, Ally, 85, 87
War of the Worlds (2005), 158, 176–8, 180–1, 183–5, 187–90, 192, 194
War of the Worlds, The (1953), 44, 134, 177
Weathers, Carl, 13, 14, 20
Weaver, Sigourney, 83, 100
Weller, Peter, 18–19
whiteness, 20, 138–51, 154–5, 165, 195
  critique of white society, 121–5, 127–34, 192, 217n.90
Williams, Christopher, 174
Williams, Linda, 30–2
Wonder, Stevie, 148
working-class *see* masculinity, working-class
World, the Flesh and the Devil, The (1959), 121, 146, 148–50, 153

www.ingramcontent.com/pod-product-compliance
Lightning Source LLC
Chambersburg PA
CBHW072140290426
44111CB00012B/1931